CORBA
Design Patterns

CORBA
DESIGN PATTERNS

THOMAS J. MOWBRAY, PH.D.

RAPHAEL C. MALVEAU

WILEY COMPUTER PUBLISHING

John Wiley & Sons, Inc.

New York ➤ Chichester ➤ Weinheim ➤ Toronto ➤ Singapore ➤ Brisbane

Publisher: Katherine Schowalter
Editor: Robert M. Elliott
Managing Editor: Robert S. Aronds
Electronic Products, Associate Editor: Michael Green
Text Design & Composition: North Market Street Graphics, Selena R. Chronister

This text is printed on acid-free paper.

Library of Congress Cataloging-in-Publication Data:
   Mowbray, Thomas J.
      Corba design patterns / Thomas J. Mowbray, Raphael Malveau.
            p.   cm.
      Includes bibliographical references.
      ISBN 0-471-15882-8 (pbk. : alk. paper)
      1. Object-oriented programming (Computer science)   2. Computer
   architecture.   I. Malveau, Raphael.   II. Title.
   QA76.64.M68   1997
   005.1—dc20   96-44734
                                                          CIP

Printed in the United States of America
10 9 8 7 6 5 4 3 2 1

This book is dedicated to
Kate Mowbray, CPA

and

Carrie Malveau

Without struggle there is no progress.
——FREDERICK DOUGLASS

Contents

Preface

The long-term goal of design patterns research is to construct an architectural handbook for software engineering, similar in form and purpose to other types of engineering handbooks (electronics, civil engineering, and so forth). A handbook of this sort would provide useful solutions to commonplace software problems. This is our attempt at such a book.

Through our involvement in the Object Management Group and Object World we have delivered tutorials and mentored the construction of distributed systems worldwide. We have seen a common need for practical explanations on how to solve software challenges. People don't want esoteric theories; they want practical guidance on how to design and build systems.

We have found that understanding software architecture is the key to developing many important software solutions. Therefore, in this book we cover software architecture comprehensively and systematically, integrating this coverage with programming solutions.

Our work spans many different scales of software engineering—we have developed software from small prototypes through multiapplication systems. We have defined and managed the implementation of enterprisewide solutions as well as global architectures and standards. These various scales exhibit dramatic differences in design forces. In contrast, some principles apply at multiple scales. Much of the published design patterns focus on small scales or do not consider scale.

Lack of understanding of design forces at various scales can lead to many common software problems and mistakes. We present a mature approach to scalability, showing that the impact of scale is critical to software decisions.

A synopsis of the book is contained in the "Executive Summary." Our intention is that advanced readers begin with Chapter 3, which contains key definitions used throughout the book.

T.J.M.
R.M.
McLean, Virginia, U.S.A.

Acknowledgments

We wish to thank our friends and supporters, without whom this book would have never been written. In particular:

Richard Barnwell, Tom Beadle, Lydia Bennett, Peter Bower, Tim Brinson, Bernadette Clemente, Lou Castro, Mark Chen, David Curtis, David Dikel, Joe DiLiberto, John Eaton, Bob Elliott, Lawrence Eng, Charlie Green, Jack Hassall, Thomas Herron, Bill Hoffman, Dr. Barry Horowitz, Michael Stal, Barbara Kitchenham, Bill Brown, Peter Krupp, Dr. Pat Mallett, Henry Rothkopf, Chuck Lockard, Mark Ryland, Dan Harkey, Bob Orfali, Jeri Edwards, David Berkowitz, Frank Mara, Huet Landry, Maj. J.P. LeBlanc, William Cox, Cory Casanave, John Slitz, Michael Guttman, Jason Matthews, Mark Roy, Alan Ewald, Kendall White, Professor Juggy Jaganathan, Andrew Watson, Jvergen Boldt, Ron Burns, Noah Spivak, Leslie Gellman, Julie Gravallese, Professor Mary Shaw, Dr. Mark Maybury, Thad Scheer, Theresa Smith, Don Joder, Professor Ralph Johnson, David Kane, Melony Katz, Paul Klinker, Ken Kolence, Dr. Fred Kuhl, Dr. Cliff Kottman, Eric Leach, Diane Mularz, Didi Murnane, Marie Lenzi, Dave Lutz, Skip McCormick, Kate Mowbray CPA, John Polger, Janis Putman, Ellen Reavis, Bill Ruh, Professor Doug Schmidt, Dr. Jon Siegel, Dr. Richard Soley, Chris Stone, Scott Surer, Shel Sutton, Dr. Bhavani Thuraisingham, John Tisaranni, Peter Waegemann, John Weiler, Doug Vandermade, and Ron Zahavi.

Executive Summary

This is an architectural handbook for designing and developing distributed software systems. The book shows readers how they can exploit available technologies to build more adaptable systems faster and with better software reuse and software interoperability. In order to make the handbook as useful as possible, we have used widely supported technologies in our examples, such as CORBA's Interface Definition Language (IDL) and Java.

THE SOFTWARE CRISIS

Software development entails very high risk. About one-third of software projects are canceled; only about one-sixth of software projects are successful. The balance of the projects are two to three times over schedule and over budget. Delivered systems often fail to provide all desired features and are difficult and expensive to change. As a result, software technology fails to keep up with changing business needs. Object-orientation and client-server solutions have not changed these expected outcomes; neither have methodologies and tools.

Software challenges are increasing.

➤ Due to the Internet, personal computers, and local area networks, distributed computing is a necessity. Systems must also be heterogeneous (consisting of many types of computers and software packages). Heterogeneous distributed computing is complex, fault-prone, and expensive to develop, test, and maintain.

➤ User expectations are increasing due to the ready availability of fast consumer hardware, increasingly capable consumer software, and the Internet.

➤ Commercial technology presents challenges and opportunities. It may provide many off-the-shelf capabilities. New products have their own costs and risks, including bugs, training, support, and upgrade. Dependency upon vendors yields mixed results. Computer technologies are rapidly changing, creating obsolesence and maintenance costs.

The sophistication of software professionals has not evolved with the escalating risks, technology changes, and new challenges. Stable infrastructure, software architectures, and sophisticated guidance are key elements needed to resolve these problems.

CORBA

The Common Object Request Broker Architecture (CORBA) is a standard for distributed computing that has gained widespread acceptance and commercial product support. CORBA simplifies heterogeneous distributed computing. CORBA has many advantages over previous infrastructure technologies, such as location transparency, activation transparency, language independence, and platform neutrality. CORBA is object-oriented, enabling many potential benefits such as reuse.

CORBA's Interface Definition Language (IDL) is an international standard that has become the universal notation for software interfaces. CORBA, and in particular CORBA's IDL, is the de facto infrastructure for legacy systems, commercial software, and object technology.

Adoption of CORBA is a positive step, *but it is not enough* to resolve the most critical software challenges. If software development proceeds to use the same architectures and practices that led to today's software crisis, the results will be the same: high-risk development, failed projects, and inadequate and inflexible systems. Better guidance is needed to build better systems.

OBJECT-ORIENTED ARCHITECTURE

Software architecture is becoming increasingly acknowledged as essential to software system success by the Software Engineering Institute, Grady Booch, and others (Booch 1995; Shaw 1993). But in our experience, very few practitioners know much about software architecture, regardless of education, credentials, and experience.

This book offers a practical definition of software architecture and explains the key concepts and practices that create outstanding architectures. We include details of architecture design as well as architecture implementation, with new and preexisting software modules and components.

DESIGN PATTERNS

Design patterns are the most effective form of software guidance available. They offer a concise, efficient way to convey expert software concepts, particularly architectural concepts. Design patterns also provide a terminology that can help practitioners become more effective and sophisticated in developing systems.

This book uses design patterns as the primary form of instruction. It provides a complete design pattern catalog—a full array of expert solutions for designing and building distributed object-oriented systems.

THE IMPORTANCE OF SCALE

A sense of scale is missing from most software design patterns. We believe that many serious software mistakes are made because the impact of scale is poorly understood and applied.

In this book, we present a conceptual framework that identifies and defines the scales of software architecture (Figure E.1). We show how these scales can have a critical impact on software design decisions. Our pattern catalog contains the key design patterns that expert architects and developers use at each of these levels. We also show how to avoid costly software mistakes using these principles. The patterns in the catalog are linked together with related patterns to form a design pattern language that serves as an architecture handbook for software problem solving.

ORGANIZATION OF THE BOOK

The book comprises an introduction (Part I) and a design pattern catalog (Part II through Part V). For advanced readers, we recommend starting with Chapter 3, which provides an overview of the pattern language as well as key definitions.

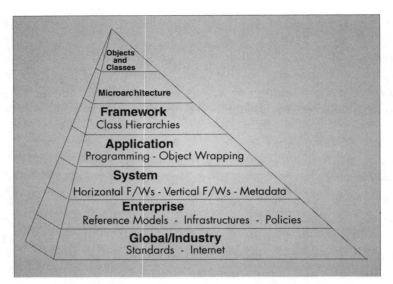

Figure E.1 An understanding of the contextual forces at different scales is essential to successful software architecture, development, and maintenance.

In Part I we introduce the topics of CORBA, object-oriented architecture, and the design pattern catalog. Chapter 1 is an overview of the whole book, including introductions to CORBA and design patterns. Chapter 2 is a tutorial introduction to object-oriented software architecture. Chapter 3 introduces the design pattern catalog, the scales of software design, and the primal forces motivating decisions at each scale.

Part II through Part V contain all of the design patterns. The patterns are standalone, in that they can be used without a detailed understanding of other patterns. The patterns are also linked together to form a design pattern language so that subsidiary problems can be quickly identified and resolved using related patterns.

Part II (Chapters 4–6) covers application design patterns that define solutions for important programming problems at the subsystem level and below. Source code examples are provided for these patterns, where relevant. Part III (Chapters 7–10) focuses on system design patterns that include the essential design solutions for adaptable software architectures. Part IV (Chapter 11) provides enterprise design patterns that solve multisystem software challenges across a distributed enterprise. Part V (Chapters 12–13) concentrates on global design patterns that include an explanation of standards (how to use and exploit them), and of Internet design patterns, including those for the Web, Orblets, and Java.

CORBA
DESIGN PATTERNS

TERM LIST

Most Applicable Scale

Solution Type

Solution Name

Intent

Diagram

References

Applicability at This Scale

Solution Summary

Key Benefits and Consequences

Variations of This Solution

Rescaling This Solution at Other Levels

Related Solutions

Example

Background

Resources

PART ONE

CORBA and Design Patterns

In Part I, we introduce background material that is essential for the understanding of CORBA design patterns. Chapters 1 and 2 provide CORBA and IDL background that is intended for readers that are new to distributed objects. Distributed computing requires many important concepts that are useful at all levels of object-oriented software development.

Advanced readers may choose to begin with Chapter 3, which introduces our reference model for the design pattern catalog, the *scalability model*. Reference models are numerous in computer science and technology. The Object Management Architecture (OMA) is the reference model for CORBA-based standards. The OMA reference model is explained in Chapter 1 and defined in Soley (1996). The OMA reference model focuses on commercial technology from a technology suppliers' viewpoint.

Technology suppliers have a perspective that is distinct from technology consumers. Different knowledge is required to produce a commercial product than that required to build an application system. An understanding of commercial technology is essential but insufficient to build successful application systems. An excellent explanation of commercial technologies is contained in Orfali (1996).

This book is written from the perspective of the technology consumer, who must integrate several commercial technologies, along with custom software, in order to create application systems and enterprise computing environments. The reference model introduced in Chapter 3 provides a framework for application problem-solving. It is a framework that captures the scales of software problem-solving that are as large as the problems themselves.

The reference model also captures common definitions. Most design patterns are written to be standalone; each pattern has a unique problem and motivational forces. This requires a unique learning curve for each pattern. The reference model defines those common forces that affect most patterns to some extent, and hence most software decision-making. Through the reference model, we define the common context of these patterns. The reference model saves a great deal of redefinition, and makes a large pattern language understandable with much less effort.

CHAPTER ONE

Introduction

For most design problems there are effective solutions. Often it takes looking at the problem differently, and doing things in ways they may have never been done before. Design patterns provide an alternative perspective to problem solving that transfers a great of deal of previous design expertise in a form that is easily transferable to solutions. In this guide, we intend to share this knowledge to show how a few key principles, forces, and patterns can lead to a powerful new way of thinking about systems and lead to much more effective architectures and successful development of systems.

Our approach shows that there is a range of design options corresponding to each solution. A design pattern is the overall concept behind many alternative design solutions. There is always some tradeoff or leeway in how the problem is solved, which allows us to choose a *design point* that balances the contextual forces, benefits, and consequences in a way that is most appropriate for the design situation (Figure 1.1).

In this guide, we assume CORBA IDL as a basis for interface definition. This is a safe assumption, given that CORBA IDL is a consensus specification from the Object Management Group (OMG), the world's largest software consortium, and is becoming an ISO standard. IDL is language- and platform-independent. A single IDL specification supports multilanguage mappings. In addition to its use in standards, IDL notation also happens to be an ideal way to define architectural boundaries in software systems. We can also rely upon a wide range of existing standard interfaces (such as the CORBAservices) for examples of the application of design patterns. These standard interfaces correspond to commercially available technologies that can be used to leverage development.

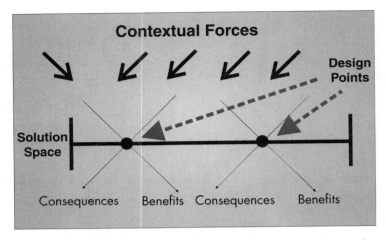

Figure 1.1 Design points are design choices that resolve problems within a particular context.

DESIGN PATTERNS

What exactly is a design pattern? A design pattern is an effective solution to an important design problem. It is reusable in that it is applicable to a range of design problems in a wide variety of different circumstances. Patterns are design and implementation solutions expressed in terms of a fixed outline, often called a template. Each element of the template answers an important question about the pattern that aids understanding. The template used here comprises the following sections:

1. Most Applicable Scale
2. Solution Type
3. Solution Name
4. Intent
5. Diagram
6. References
7. Applicability at This Scale
8. Solution Summary
9. Key Benefits and Consequences
10. Variations of This Solution
11. Rescaling This Solution at Other Levels
12. Related Solutions

This list, described in detail in Chapter 3, is the basis for description of the complete design patterns. We also have a number of tips and minipatterns that provide interesting perspectives, in addition to the main patterns.

The essence of all design patterns is the problem-solution pair. All other parts of the template add useful details and rationale to the description of the pattern (Figure 1.2).

The problem statement in a pattern concisely states the core design issue to be resolved. The solution resolves the problem. The context explains under what circumstances a problem is applicable to a particular situation. In addition, the context highlights the motivating factors which must be addressed in a useful solution to the problem. These motivating factors are frequently called *forces*.

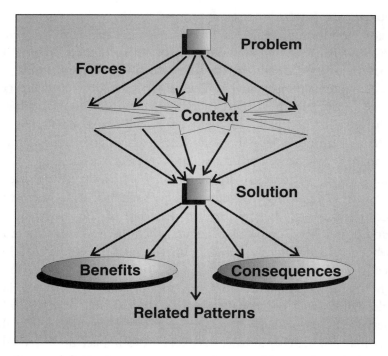

Figure 1.2 Design patterns comprise a problem and a solution that resolves contextual forces in ways that lead to benefits, consequences, and other patterns.

The purpose of the solution is to resolve the forces. Each solution resolves forces in a way that leads to benefits and consequences. In this guide, we often refer to particular CORBA standards as the basis for a design solution.

There are many different design pattern templates in popular use. Our template provides practical benefits for two key reader audiences: the expert and the inexperienced (and hopefully for everybody else in between). For both groups of readers, we have sorted the template sections in terms of importance and efficient transfer of knowledge. For the inexperienced reader, the solution summary is presented without a confusing discussion of options. These options are discussed in follow-up sections dealing with solution variations and rescaling.

Patterns are common-sense solutions; experts will already be familiar with most patterns based on experience. Our template is structured to match the reader's experience with the pattern presented. The template provides a common set of terminology and a rationale for each pattern that is useful in justifying its use to other developers, managemers, and customers. The variations, rescaling, and examples provide additional information on how other experts have applied each pattern.

One common form of guidance for designers is a standards reference model. IEEE POSIX (IEEE 1994) contains one of these models (Figure 1.4). The model has an associated standards profile, which is an organized list of recommended computer system standards. The list is broken down into categories that correspond to different portability or interoperability needs. Within each category there are a few acceptable alternative standards. Each standard is rated with respect to its readiness. Several standards reference models also indicate how each standard is assessed by other standards reference models.

At first glance, a standards reference model would seem to be the ideal handbook for open systems implementation. Many such models were created on this basis because they were believed to be a key part of the answer to interoperability and portability. The problem occurs when the developer attempts to discover what to do differently based upon the model's guidance. The tactical guidance is not obvious; there are about 300 standards in a typical reference model. Many formal standards are poorly supported by the commercial market. Often, they only focus on a small subset of the available products, which may not otherwise be particularly attractive selections. Upon detailed analysis, one discovers that the actual guidance has very little impact upon technical decisions. To take the reference model guidance seriously would require extensive cost of development to support large numbers of complex standards. The standards that can be used do not guarantee interoperability or portability, due to

A Sample Minipattern

When a pattern is used as an example or an interesting side discussion, we will frequently use an abbreviated template, called a minipattern.

Solution Name: Model-View-Controller (MVC)

Intent: How to support reuse across multiple user interfaces and business processes.

Solution Summary: Partition the application objects in three categories: the model role, the view role, and the controller role. A view object provides a user interface display of a model object. A controller object provides for user- or business-process-driven manipulation of an object. A model object has neither user interface nor business process capabilities. Because it is devoid of these roles, it is reusable across multiple views and processes.

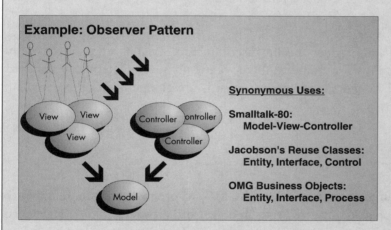

Figure 1.3 The sample pattern is a common solution that has been reinvented in many contexts.

Background: This sample pattern is well known from several sources. Perhaps the first well-known use of this pattern is as the Smalltalk-80 Model-View-Controller framework. This pattern was also described as the Observer pattern in Gamma (1994). In addition, this pattern is frequently described in Ivar Jacobson's (Jacobson 1992; Jacobson & Lindstrom 1991) work as the entity, interface, and control objects, an important lesson learned in software reuse at Ericson. Finally, this partitioning of roles is the basis for the Business Object architecture of the OMG, where they refer to entity, interface, and process objects.

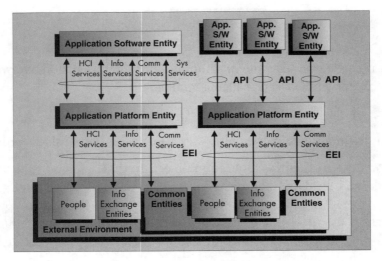

Figure 1.4 The POSIX standards reference model.

their generality and product-specific discriminators. Even if the standards delivered interoperability or portability, there are usually several alternative standards for each model category, and these standards are competing in the compliant implementations.

CORBA

CORBA is a commercial standard from OMG, whose mission is to define interfaces for interoperable software using an object-oriented technology. Their specification, CORBA, is an industry consensus standard that defines a higher-level infrastructure for distributed computing. In general, object orientation enables the development of reusable, modular software, and is moving technology towards plug-and-play software components. OMG's efforts are extending these benefits across distributed heterogeneous systems.

Figure 1.5 is an overview of the OMG's object management architecture (OMA), the industry standard reference model for object technology. The OMA Guide identifies four categories of software interfaces for standardization: the CORBA Object Request Broker (ORB), the CORBAservices, the CORBAfacilities, and the CORBAdomains. The central component of the architecture is the ORB, through which all objects communicate. The ORB functions as a communication infrastructure, transparently relaying object requests across distributed heterogeneous computing environments. CORBA-services are fundamental, enabling interfaces that are globally applicable for leveraging application development. Sample CORBAservices include object lifecycle, event notification, and distributed transactions. All other standard object interfaces are either CORBAdomains or CORBAfacilities. CORBA-domains comprise vertical market areas, such as financial services and health-care. Application interfaces comprise all the remaining software interfaces such as proprietary commercial interfaces and legacy interfaces. The number of CORBAdomains is potentially large, and represents areas for future growth of OMG standards activities. CORBAfacilities include those interfaces shared by multiple CORBAdomains. CORBAfacilities are higher-level horizontal interface standards focused on application interoperability, and are horizontally applicable across domains. Examples of CORBAfacilities include compound documents, system management, and data interchange.

There are two diagrams used to describe the OMG reference model, to reflect the two distinct levels of detail involved in fully understanding the architecture. The first diagram (Figure 1.5), the Marketing Reference Model, defines the model from the end-user or management perspective. In this diagram, the terms are used abstractly without technical detail to describe some general categories of standards. In the second diagram (Figure 1.6), a distinc-

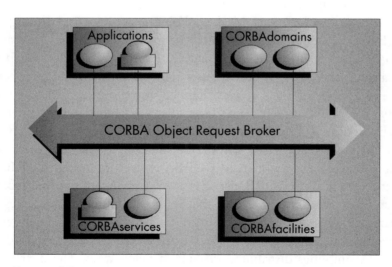

Figure 1.5 CORBA object management architecture: Marketing Reference Model.

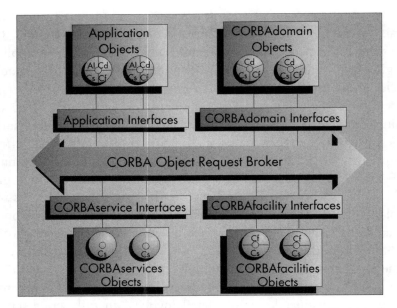

Figure 1.6 CORBA object management architecture: Technical Reference Model.

tion is made between objects and interfaces, and the reuse of interface standards between categories is addressed.

In the Technical Reference Model, all objects communicate through CORBA through interface definitions. Three of the interface categories are standardized CORBAservices, CORBAfacilities, and CORBAdomains. The fourth category, Application Interfaces, may contain user-defined, nonstandard interfaces, which may be extensions of the standards defined in other categories or custom, proprietary, or product-specific interfaces. Each category reuses interfaces and builds upon other categories in a logical way. CORBAservices objects use primitive, fundamental interfaces without reliance on other categories. CORBA-facilities objects reuse and extend CORBAservices interfaces. CORBAdomains reuse and extend both CORBAservices and CORBAfacilities interfaces. Finally, application objects have interfaces that reuse all standards categories and may add custom extensions. The Technical Reference Model explains how interface frameworks are constructed from the set of layered CORBA standards.

CORBA simplifies distributed systems in many ways. The distributed environment is defined using an object-oriented paradigm that hides all differences between programming languages, operating systems, and process locations. The

> Key reasons why CORBA is an important technology for your future:
>
> ➤ CORBA IDL: Universal notation for software interfaces.
> ➤ CORBA infrastructure: The ORB simplifies distributed computing.
> ➤ CORBA-based standard specifications: Leverage development through design reuse, commercially supplied software services, interoperability, and code reuse.

object-oriented approach allows diverse types of applications to interoperate at the same level, hiding implementation details and supporting reuse. CORBA defines a very useful notation for defining software interfaces called the Interface Definition Language (OMG IDL). CORBAservices defined in OMG IDL have a dual role: vendor-provided services and application-provided services. Developers are encouraged to reuse and extend the standard interfaces.

CORBA IDL is the standard notation for defining software interfaces. This notation can be used with CORBA products or independently. CORBA IDL is now a widely used notation by standards writers at ISO, European Computer Manufacturers Association (ECMA), OMG, X/Open, and many other standards bodies. As such, CORBA IDL is a widely accepted and very stable notation. There are standard language bindings for C, C++, Smalltalk, and Ada95. In addition, CORBA IDL is useful for defining software boundaries in end-user systems. It provides a clear separation of interfaces from implementation details. Isolation of software modules is essential to enable adaptability in software architectures and implementations.

The syntax of CORBA IDL is used to specify the attributes and operation signatures of object interfaces. With an IDL compiler for specific bindings, the interface descriptions can be compiled into language specific stubs, skeletons, and definition files. Client programs to the IDL-defined objects are developed using the object definition and stub files, which provide communication through the ORB to the object implementation. An implementation developer modifies the skeleton files by filling out the methods with application code needed to service a client's request. The client invokes the object using the stub routine, a generated local function call, which transparently communicates with the ORB (Figure 1.7). The ORB has the responsibilty of locating an implementation that can service the request, and provide whatever support is necessary for the invocation, including data marshalling to encode and decode the

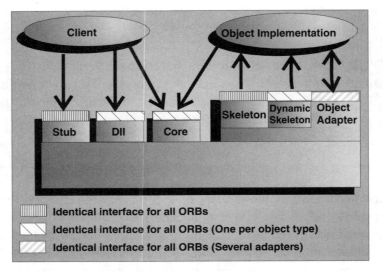

Figure 1.7 CORBA interfaces involved in method resolution between a client and a distributed object implementation.

operation's parameters into communication formats suitable for transmission. When the object implementation completes the request, the ORB sends the results back to the client, including exception information if any errors were encountered. Exceptions are CORBA error messages and can be generated by either the object implementation or by the ORB itself.

According to OMG's mission statement, CORBA was invented to provide a new networking infrastructure intended to solve software interoperability problems. It replaces legacy remote procedure call (RPC) infrastructures and precursory technologies by providing an object-oriented network interface that greatly simplifies distributed computing. CORBA ORBs are available from more than a dozen vendors (Bennett 96). CORBA-based standards are also valuable to understand and reuse. These standards are described in IDL and include a wide range of preexisting reusable designs.

Scale and Design Patterns

One of the key goals of design patterns research is the construction of an architectural handbook that provides solutions to key design problems in accessible form. Christopher Alexander realized this vision in his bricks-and-mortar architectural handbook (1977). One of the most endearing aspects of Alexander's work is the use of multiple scales of design. Each level of scale has solutions and forces that are unique. Alexander's book is structured as a *cosmic zoom* starting with patterns for large-scale communities and proceeding through successive levels of scale to finer-grained solutions.

We have noted that most existing design patterns work does not address the issue of scale. In our experience scale has a very great impact on the forces which are relevant to a particular problem. Many of the particularly pernicious software mistakes are made because developers are resolving forces inappropriately for the scale of a particular design. We do not believe it is possible to have a comprehensive software architecture handbook that does not have a strong notion of how scale impacts the contextual forces. Although no expert can claim to have enough breadth of experience to solve all information systems problems, we work frequently at each of the scales addressed in this guide, including application, system, enterprise, and global. We see strong relationships between the levels, but also key differences that are critical to success. We often see solutions that are commonly applied at some larger scale (such as the use of metadata) ignored at smaller scale. Even more commonly, we see small-scale solutions (such as fine-grained domain objects) applied inappropriately at larger scales.

Patterns for IDL Reuse

Fundamental to this work is the concept of design reuse and extension. IDL design reuse is essential for making use of generic industry standards and technologies, such as the CORBAservices. In this guide we describe a pattern for a *profile,* which is a reuse of a more generic design for specialized purposes. This reuse includes specializations of a standard that provide interoperability guarantees which go beyond the generic specification of a particular standard.

A strong software architecture requires three key design elements: horizontal interfaces, vertical interfaces, and metadata (Figure 1.8). Many of the world's software architectures today are based almost exclusively on vertical interfaces, which are unique to a particular implementation or application. Exclusive use of vertical interfaces leads to the familiar stovepipe system architectures, in which pervasive implementation-specific interconnections cause brittle interdependencies. Vertical interfaces are also very difficult to reuse and to integrate with other systems for interoperability.

To many developers, horizontal interfaces and metadata are undiscovered concepts. These play an important role in system-level architecture, where

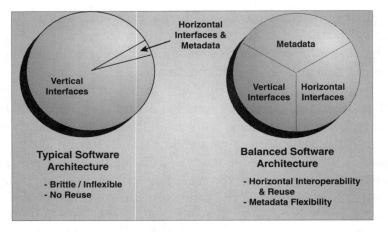

Figure 1.8 The balance of the three key design elements is critical to architectural flexibility, interoperability, and reuse.

change and complexity are the primary forces to resolve. (In our terminology these are *primal forces*.) To derive horizontal interfaces, one must have well-developed abstraction skills and be willing to try new practices (such as architecture mining) in order to design robust horizontal interfaces that isolate software modules. We explore these concepts much further in Chapter 7.

Patterns for Legacy Integration

Due to the scale and complexity of mission-critical systems, it is often too risky to develop a new system from scratch that can entirely replace the old. This is called the *cold turkey* approach (Brodie & Stonebraker 1995). Chances are high that the project will be very costly and the system will be likely to fail during initial switchover, with consequences harmful to the business.

More effective approaches involve creation of adaptable target architectures that support gradual migration and system evolution. These *chicken little* approaches involve sophisticated solutions and appropriate use of technologies. The architectural qualities of the target system must support gradual evolution and migration. These qualities are not achieved solely through the acquisition of technologies, but through the overall architecture, which incorporates products, legacy, and new software. This guide includes the foundational pattern-based solutions that reduce the risk of software development and migration.

Global Patterns for the Internet

Some important Internet technologies are applicable at both the global and enterprise levels. The use of enterprisewide *intranets* is a commonplace and growing practice at many organizations. Intranets are an example of applying global-scale solutions at smaller enterprises with significant benefits.

An understanding of readily available Internet technologies is crucial to resolving key enterprise issues. In this guide, we describe Internet solutions based on the World Wide Web, intranets, Java, and other technologies. We also describe how these technologies relate to each other and CORBA technologies, and how this set of technologies is developing.

No Silver Bullet

There are many methodologies and software products that claim to provide a single solution (or *silver bullet*) for resolving software challenges. A fundamental principle of this guide is that there is no silver bullet. Further, we believe that software success relies upon the application of many common-sense solutions (software, processes, and technologies). Patterns and solutions must be applied in a way that balances the forces at the appropriate scale and context.

CHAPTER TWO

Object-Oriented Architecture

We view the history of software engineering as a series of recurring trends and technologies that are often based on incorrect assumptions. As the problems with these new technologies become widely known, the market adopts newer yet unproven approaches.

This cycle of innovation and failure continually repeats. In our view, software professionals will remain stuck in this cycle until they develop an independent architectural viewpoint that will allow them to make decisions based on actual software benefits, not technological trends. In our pattern catalog (Chapters 4–13), we present the key architectural insights needed to develop this independent viewpoint.

SOFTWARE ENGINEERING TRENDS

Two of the most important software engineering trends are object-orientation (OO) and structured programming. One could consider structured programming to be the precursor of object-orientation. Although object-orientation has been available for more than a decade, there are still many organizations using structured programming.

A key concept of structured programming is that design is separate from coding (Figure 2.1). Requirements analysis and design are the dominant processes in the development of a structured programming system. The rationale for this separation is the assumption that most software errors are made during software design. This implies that design should be emphasized and extended so that

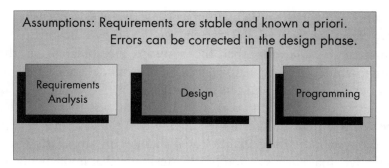

Figure 2.1 The structured programming paradigm: Assumes stable requirements and that careful design could eliminate most system errors.

most errors can be eliminated before coding. The fatal assumption of structured programming is that requirements are well known in advance and remain stable. If requirements are well known and stable, then we can make all of our design decisions before development—all design can occur top-down, followed by rapid development of the whole system. With this approach, design notations proceed from abstract representations to codelike levels of detail.

However, experience contradicts these assumptions about the stability of system requirements. First of all, in most environments, requirements are not constant, but rather change all the time in response to business needs. It is found that about 30% of development cost is due to changing requirements, and about 70% of operations and maintenance cost is due to system extensions, that is, new or modified requirements (Horowitz 1993). Overall, software changes due to changing requirements constitute more than 50% of the total cost of software systems development. Therefore, it can be seen that adaptability should be a key element of good software architecture.

No matter how carefully the requirements may have been stated prior to implementation, new user needs are also often discovered as the user gains experience with the interface. This problem has led to the invention of a new trend: *spiral development* (for example, Rapid Structured Prototyping [Connell 1987]). In spiral development approaches, prototyping and design proceed incrementally with frequent user involvement to mitigate risks. Formal, scalable processes considered this notion as the central theme for risk-driven development, by giving the end user frequent interaction with the prototype and the development team.

Perhaps structured programming's most significant flaw is the separation of the process model from the data model (i.e., separation of the program from all the variables and persistent data). In practice, software systems were very brittle whenever software changed, because changes could have unanticipated system-wide impacts on the data that the software manipulated. In the object-orientation trend, the process model and the data model are merged, in order to minimize and localize the impacts of change.

The merger of process and data models has had less-than-perfect success in practice. With current OO technologies, it is still the case that changes in one part of the system can have unanticipated changes in other parts. Part of this is due to the fact that encapsulation is imperfect, and that implementation dependencies are still frequently exposed through OO programming language interfaces. Technology, such as CORBA IDL, can help to resolve this issue by providing improved separation between clients and implementations. But the more serious issue is that interface design can expose implementation dependencies in many ways, and that these impacts are not well understood by most methodologists, architects, and developers.

Object-Orientation versus Object Technology

At this point, we should clarify the distinction between object-orientation and object technology. Object technology includes the infrastructure and tools for building systems (as opposed to designing systems). Examples of object technology include CORBA Object Request Brokers, C++ compilers, and debugging tools. Object-orientation comprises the concepts, methodologies, and notations involved in designing a software system. One could characterize object-orientation as the theory and object technology as the *infrastructure* (roads, sewers, etc.).

We believe that object technology has much to offer, and that object-orientation has had mixed results. Both areas have progressed a great deal since the inception of objects, but in different ways. Object technology has provided increasingly greater capabilities for development, and a converging market with standards such as CORBA and OpenDoc.

Object-orientation has gone through many fashions and changes; the industry has discovered ineffective approaches through hard experience. In fact, it is pointed out by the Hillside Group that the most successful system succeeded in spite of object-oriented methodology, not because of it (Coplien 1994). In this guide we intend to bring you successful problem solutions (as design patterns) that will have lasting effectiveness and impact beyond current methodology trends.

Object-orientation is a concept that has existed since the invention of Simula-67 in 1967. One of the key conceptual innovations in object-orientation was Semantic Database Modeling. In this approach, the information schema was not just a model of domain objects; conceptually, it became the domain objects. Hence the popular notion in first-generation object-orientation (i.e., the dominant practice of) that objects are things that one can touch has been a key perspective of first-generation object-orientation, that is, the dominant practice of object-orientation prior to design patterns.

A fundamental assumption of object-orientation is that the domain objects are the most stable entities in the system environment. In other words, a design of a system based directly upon domain objects will be the most resistant to change. Another rationale is that the direct modeling of domain objects in software reduces the semantic gap between software technology models and domain business models.

Object-orientation has three fundamental elements: object-oriented analysis, object-oriented design, and implementation. Object-oriented analysis is a requirement definition process. Its role is to analyze the problem domain to build a model of the real-world problem using objects. In object-oriented design, the analysis models are refined and detailed to create additional specifications that supplement the analysis models with implementation detail. Finally, implementation involves the coding of the designs in an object-oriented (or other) programming language.

These elements have the same roles as their counterparts in structured programming: Object-oriented analysis compares to requirements analysis, object-oriented design to software design, and implementation to programming.

BOUNDARIES AND ARCHITECTURE

One of the key shortcomings of object-oriented models is their lack of discrimination between interfaces and implementations. In object-oriented analysis and design there are few distinctions in the notation between design and implementation. In fact, most of the information in object-oriented analysis and design (OOAD) models is related to the characteristics of the object implementation, not to its interfaces.

Surprisingly little interface detail is included in OOAD models. This becomes evident when one attempts to convert OOAD models to CORBA IDL. CORBA IDL is a pure interface notation, devoid of any notations for implementation

Object-Oriented Methodologies

In Figure 2.2, the time phasing of analysis, design, and implementation are staggered because the experts have different opinions on how much of each is beneficial. For example, in the Shlaer-Mellor approach, object-oriented analysis dominates the process; design is intended to be minimal or produced through automatic code generation (Shlaer 88). The problem with this approach is that the automatic code generation technology has never been sufficiently robust for production software development, and it is unlikely to become sufficiently robust in the foreseeable future.

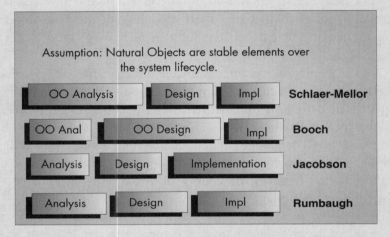

Figure 2.2 The object-oriented paradigm: Object-oriented analysis and design assume stable real-world objects, but there are disagreements on the roles of analysis and design, as well as methodologies and notations.

The Booch approach has historically been design-centered, which is similar to the role of design in structured programming (Booch 94). Because it shares assumptions similar to those of structured programming, it may share the same basic shortcomings.

Jacobson publicly minimizes the importance of analysis and design, favoring implementation (Jacobson 92). Jacobson also points out that a software engineering process needs to be much more comprehensive than those currently presented in the methodology literature in order to be effective.

(*Continued*)

Rumbaugh sees value in all elements of analysis and design and would maintain multiple models (Rumbaugh 91). Fowler claims that it is too difficult to maintain any more than one model in addition to the code, and that an obsolete model is useless (Fowler 1995).

It is clear that the experts disagree on the proper approach. This is a key reason why we believe that the most effective path to software success is in learning enough to base your decisions on your own judgement and the real benefits of design decisions, instead of making decisions based solely on dogma.

Things have not gone well for first-generation object-orientation. It has been widely acknowledged that *naive object modeling,* as it is called, is an ineffective way to design software. If object-orientation is practiced with knowledge of and focus on its real benefits, it can be very effective. However, object-orientation can be misused and does not guarantee or provide any inherent benefits. The object-oriented-ness of a design bears little or no relationship to its goodness. It is becoming increasingly clear that there needs to be something more sophisticated than "objects are things you can touch," in order to design effective OO systems. In this guide, we wish to go beyond the past fashions in object-orientation and extend the benefits of the guidance toward some sustainable software gains, that is, architectural gains.

description. When OOAD models are converted to IDL, the result is an incomplete, partial specification. The behavioral models have no interface translation; only the static models contain some interface detail. The only details that translate are the classes, public attributes, and method names. In OOAD models, there is minimal parameter or data type information. However, this information constitutes the bulk of IDL interface descriptions.

The implication is that interfaces are treated as coding details to be fleshed out at the programming level. As we describe below, this implication can have serious consequences when the interfaces are used across systems enterprises. For example, if the goal is software reuse, the interfaces have enterprisewide impact because they are intended for use in multiple systems.

Follow-on paradigms to object-orientation need to take into account the essential distinction between interfaces and implementation. Separation of implementations is the basis for isolation of changes between parts of software systems. Implementation separation through software interfaces is also the basis for any architectural boundaries that need to be enforced in a software system.

A key aspect of OO architecture is software boundaries. Weak or missing software boundaries are a fundamental cause of many software challenges:

➤ Why software systems are brittle and resist changes
➤ Why software systems cannot interoperate
➤ Why software is difficult to reuse

With an understanding of why boundaries are important, how to design good boundaries, and how to communicate this design information, we can improve systems.

Figure 2.3 introduces the elements of the architecture paradigm. This paradigm replaces previous notions of structured programming and naive object-orientation. In the formulation of this model, we needed to shelve the term *design* (as a noun) because of its linkage to previous paradigms and the lack of consensus on its meaning and role. The term *architecture* is also used differently by many experts, so we give it a unique role and definition:

> *OO Architecture defines how the software modules are put together. Architecture should resolves two key issues: 1) system discovery, by eliminating the guesswork involved in the software developer's understanding how the system works, and 2) software boundaries, by clarifying and comprehensively defining intermodule interfaces.*

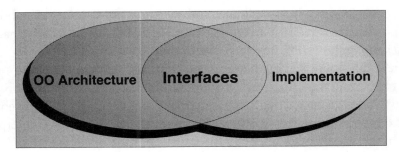

Figure 2.3 The OO architecture paradigm: OO architecture provides the stable element of the lifecycle through implementation changes. Interfaces are separate from implementations, providing isolation of changes and a compilable linkage between architecture and implementation.

In our definition, architecture is a useful abstraction of complex software. The role of architecture is to communicate useful design information to developers so that they can confidently and productively make changes and corrections to the software, without breaking the architecture or extending it in a way that will limit its future lifecycle. In this definition, architecture is independent of scale. At every scale of a software system, there is both implementation and architecture. The implementation is the realization of some finer-grained component modules; the architecture is the abstraction defining the intermodule interfaces that helps developers and maintainers understand how the modules are put together.

Other researchers have constrained their definition of software architecture to a specific scale, what we call the *system level*. While this simplified world model is very useful for helping people to understand the need for architecture, we have found it to be an oversimplification of the pervasive need for architecture. Architectural benefits are needed at many different scales, including application, system, and enterprise. Individual applications need an internal architecture to support their integration, reuse, and evolution. Systems comprising several applications need architecture to support management of complexity and change. The need is often greatest at this scale because few practitioners understand system-level forces and how to resolve them effectively. There are also enterprise architectures that have different driving forces due to their increased scales. At all levels, a need exists for an architectural abstraction defining how software is put together independent of the software implementation.

The OO Architecture Paradigm

Above, we have seen the structured programming and the object-oriented paradigms, including their fundamental assumptions. The OO architecture paradigm is the third major paradigm, and is synergistic with other paradigms; it also unifies design patterns with other trends. The fundamental assumption of the architecture paradigm is that software problems are due to poor definition and technology transfer of software boundaries.

In the OO architecture paradigm, there are three elements (Figure 2.3): the OO architecture, the interfaces, and the implementation. The OO architecture is a simplified description of the software, that is, an abstraction. Its purpose is to aid understanding. The OO architecture identifies how the software is designed to facilitate management of change, complexity, and other forces. The architecture plays its role by defining various boundaries: categories of objects, parti-

Why Is OO Architecture Needed?

Within a typical enterprise, there are many applications that have been developed without considering how the applications will interoperate. This applies to both custom and commercial applications. For example, some commercial off-the-shelf (COTS) applications provide an all-encompassing set of functionality to the user while he is working within the application (a so-called *all-in-one* application). The application source code is seldom available from the vendor, and even so, it would be undesirable to modify it, due to support costs. In most applications, data is stored in a unique, proprietary format with limited conversion capabilities. Even the more advanced applications within an organization, huge custom applications incorporating hundreds of classes and developed using state-of-the-art graphical user interface (GUI) builders and automatic code generators, only provide interoperability between applications using the same tools and framework classes. The goal of interoperability is further compromised by the existence of long-lived legacy applications that provide some degree of custom capability within an organization. Often, these legacy applications have no application program interface (API) for use by other applications and communicate using low-level communication mechanisms, such as files, Dynamic Data Exchange (DDE), or an operating system–specific protocol. Within a distributed computing environment, this problem is compounded by the interconnectiveness of the environment where the number of applications, data formats, and communication mechanisms is so numerous that no single application can be prepared to handle all of the various mechanisms interacting within the environment.

The situation illustrated in Figure 2.4 is typical of many large software environments. There are several groups of applications developed with different technology and if they interoperate at all it is through mechanisms only available in a small subset of applications within an organization. Some systems are legacy systems and have been part of the corporate infrastructure for some time. They perform their tasks well and there is little incentive to completely reengineer and redevelop these applications. They are usually not object-oriented and do not need to be in order to accomplish their tasks. Other systems are COTS packages and contain proprietary APIs with no access to the source code used to develop the application. Often, they use RPCs, or whatever was the popular communication technique at the time of their development. Other COTS packages may use higher-level communication mechanisms like Tooltalk or the Open Software Foundation Distributed Computing Environment

(*Continued*)

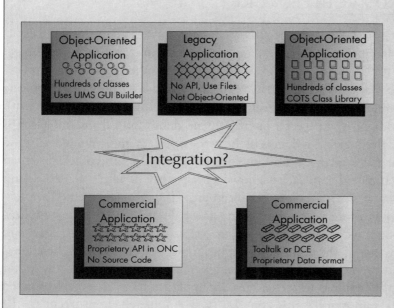

Figure 2.4 How to integrate complex software?

(OSF DCE), but intermediate data formats are proprietary and are not sharable with other applications. Even if applications are object-oriented, they are developed using different tools, class libraries, and frameworks, and provide limited, if any, means of communicating with applications not sharing an identical set of components. Many of the applications are developed using hundreds, even thousands, of classes, so migrating to a common set of components would be a tremendous undertaking. Many system architects have abandoned hope of a general-purpose method of integrating software systems and have settled for limited point-to-point integration, devoid of an overall architecture to guide system evolution. One of the goals of CORBA and design patterns is to provide a better solution to the recurring problem of software integration and interoperability.

tions, interactions, and so forth. The interfaces are the detailed definition of the architectural boundaries. At the system and enterprise levels, interfaces should be specified in CORBA IDL. At smaller scales, interfaces might use CORBA IDL or be language-dependent, as appropriate for their scale of reuse and impact. The third element in the paradigm, implementation, is the software modules encapsulated by the interfaces that provide functionality and performance.

DISTRIBUTION AND ARCHITECTURE

The advantage CORBA provides in software integration is an encapsulation capability for software applications and a communications infrastructure: the Object Request Broker (ORB). The ORB allows clients to access the applications through the object encapsulation (Figure 2.5). The encapsulation layer provides an object-oriented appearance to client applications who need only be concerned with invoking methods on the object's interface. The definition of this interface is completely separated from the details of how the object is implemented. It is the responsibility of the implementor of the object to map from the object-oriented interface to the backend applications, however they may be implemented. Using this approach, any manner of application can provide an object-oriented appearance to client applications without requiring a rewrite of the underlying applications. Some amount of code is required to map from the interface to the backend application; however, if the underlying application is object-oriented, the code is fairly trivial and even for blackboxed legacy applications it is nearly always far less than the code required to reengineer the application for an object-oriented paradigm. More importantly, this complexity is completely transparent to the client application, which can always access the functionality of the underlying system in a uniform manner, even when the backend application is replaced with another system supporting the same interface.

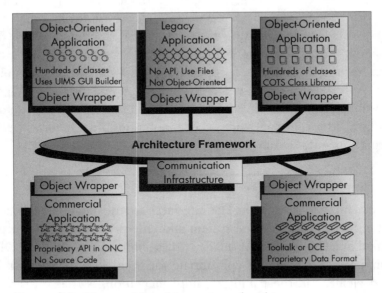

Figure 2.5 The need for object-oriented architecture.

The interfaces to the attributes and methods of the object are defined in IDL and compiled into infrastructure components called client stubs and server skeletons. The client stubs are used to invoke requests and the server skeletons are used by the developer to implement the object method. When integrating legacy software, the software developer is responsible for performing the mapping from the server to the functionality of the underlying application. This is called an *object wrapper*. IDL is not involved in how the methods are implemented and places no restrictions on how data is transferred to and from the skeleton to the underlying application. Therefore, a developer can interact with the underlying application using native APIs and file formats as long as the wrapping code converts the results back into a suitable IDL type to pass back to the client application. The client only has to be concerned with interacting with the interface and knows nothing about the conversions and transfers taking place within the object implementation.

The ORB is responsible for transparently handling differences among platforms and languages so neither the client nor the server has to be concerned with the specific operating environment details of other applications. While CORBA is a useful vehicle for integrating existing software and developing adaptable software, an understanding of the concepts of object-oriented architecture is essential in order to take advantage of the benefits CORBA has to offer. Additionally, the pattern language presented in later chapters will provide design guidance in developing successful CORBA-based systems with an object-oriented architecture robust enough to handle the complexities of distributed system development and evolution.

What Is Object-Oriented Architecture?

Object-oriented architecture comprises the set of rules, guidelines, interfaces, and conventions used to define how applications communicate and interoperate with one another. When designing an object-oriented architecture, the focus is on defining the infrastructure and interfaces between software components, not on building the components themselves. The overall goal is to provide a maintainable, scalable, reliable environment where applications can interoperate and be responsive to the needs of users throughout the evolution of the system. In order to accomplish such a rigorous and worthwhile goal, an architect's chief concern is defining a robust set of abstractions that manage complexity, change, and other forces. In addition, the architect is concerned with the issues of software partitioning, the flow of control within a software system, the flow of

The System that Jack Built (A Fictional Composite)

One organization had a knowledgeable architect for their system whose task was to implement a CORBA-based architecture. He reviewed the CORBA manuals and learned how to write compilable IDL. When he had to develop a real system and use CORBA to distribute specific key components, he examined the hundreds of interfaces in their existing system and rather than develop a few pages of meaningful, well-abstracted IDL, he wrote a small program that would convert C++ header files into IDL directly. Each operation available in each API in the system was given an IDL equivalent. When developers had to implement portions of the interface, they were initially quite pleased as all they had to do within a skeleton was call the equivalent function they were already accustomed to invoking. However, the system was very brittle and unevolvable. When new components were added, there was no existing set of IDL to describe the functionality of a new implementation of any sort. Each new program required a new set of IDL definitions to describe it. Furthermore, if the new component had to interoperate with existing components, then each component had to be programmed to communicate directly with the application's implementation. If a new implementation was unavailable, then each of the other implementations had to be modified to accommodate the change (Figure 2.6a).

Later in the system's lifecycle, the architect's replacement was responsible for re-engineering the system to provide a more flexible system that took advantage of the

(Continued)

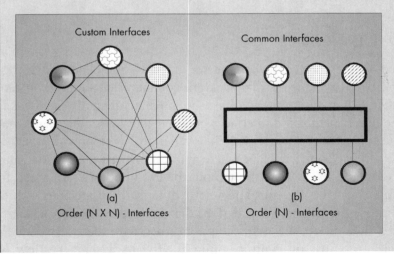

(a)	(b)
Order (N X N) - Interfaces	Order (N) - Interfaces

Figure 2.6 Stovepipes versus well-architectured systems.

underlying CORBA architectural flexibility. His first task was to develop meaningful abstractions to describe the components of the system. Rather than express the complete API in IDL, only the key areas of functionality of interest to other parts of the system were defined. Altogether, the entire description was reduced to only a few pages of IDL. The developers responsible for implementing the IDL griped a little bit at first because they needed to write a wrapper to map from the IDL request to the backend system. However, since clients were no longer tightly coupled to an implementation-specific API set, it was possible to wrapper additional legacy implementations with the same interfaces. New clients could be added easily because the interface was easy to understand and inexpensive to integrate. Horizontal and vertical services were defined in order to avoid the "N by N" integration of the previous architecture (Figure 2.6b). The system became far more adaptable and maintainable than the previous system, interprocess communication was less complex, and since the software boundaries were better defined, performance increased as the need to invoke objects across the network decreased.

information, timing and throughput relationships, interface layering and protocol standards, hardware/software allocation, and error handling.

Object Partitioning

The purpose of object-oriented analysis is to develop a logical separation of the components of a system. The object-oriented analysis produces a model of the objects in the domain and how they interoperate. The analysis involves partitioning the functionality and state of the system into meaningful groups of related objects. These groups become the basis for creating an object-oriented model by abstracting from data, operations, and structures in the domain into an encapsulated object representation. However, a domain model alone is not sufficient to build a quality software system. A system architect must augment the development process by transforming the domain model into an OO architectural model. For example, the model contains design constructs for managing system objects. The architecture provides flexibility in the event of new requirements driving modifications to the system. While the purpose of a domain model is to accurately reflect the behavior of a real-world system, an architectural model is concerned with creating a evolvable model that provides logical groupings of software components, a description of the components themselves, and a specification as to how they interact.

By explicitly defining how other applications may access its information, the interfaces ensure that the applications adhere to the black-box architectural restrictions of the software architecture. It is important to note that the quality of the abstraction dictates the reusability of a software component. Specifically, a software component that is going to be reused throughout a system or several systems must be designed from the beginning to be reusable, otherwise effort will be spent at a later date, reengineering the component to enable reuse.

The control flow and data flow in an object-oriented system can be specified in the definition of the classes and objects. The interface of the objects determine which messages can exist in the system and how data is transferred among the objects. The flow of control is an essential consideration of the object-oriented architecture as it can prevent common problems in the final system, such as bottlenecks and lack of system extensibility. Some knowledge of the expected usage patterns of the system must be factored into the architectural design. This can be accomplished by identifying potential hot spots of activity and providing the flexibility for implementation and run-time flexibility. The flow of data may affect the accessibility of information and the relationship between the software components. Identifying whether various buffer size requirements are truly static, or if they could potentially exceed an allocated region as the system expands, has a dramatic effect on the architectural choices that are made to determine the available underlying data structures. Few systems that were developed for an 8-bit system work well in current 32- and 64-bit environments without extensive modifications and system extensions.

Particularly in real-time systems, but also in systems requiring interactivity and regular responses, timing and throughput relationships must be considered in the design. In a distributed system, throughput can often be improved by designing an architecture that increases the amount of parallelism within the system. Examples of such a procedure include the partial processing pattern in Chapter 5. An often overlooked area of software architecture is the hardware and software allocation within a software system. Having an idea of the

> Always provide a module name for a set of IDL interfaces. In a distributed system, managing name spaces is everybody's business!

intended scalability of an environment may dictate many of the design choices. Key considerations include the allocation of computationally intensive applications and the bandwidth necessity to handle the interprocess communications. Many architectures provide a means of balancing service calls across many servers (load balancing) to maximize the throughput. Similarly, other means of system optimization may be supported by the software architecture.

Error Handling in a Distributed Environment

Error handling is an important part of software design and development that is frequently overlooked until coding. Object-oriented architectures address error handling as part of a complete description of interfaces. When applications are unavailable, fail to provide a desired service, or undergo one of the many other possible undesirable system maladies, there needs to be a way to ensure the integrity of the system through reclaiming resources from inactive clients and services, and notifying clients and other interested parties of the application or system failure. It is essential that error handling be part of an object-oriented architecture, as applications cannot be relied upon to provide adequate information about their state in the event of an application failure.

Moving toward Service-Based Architectures

In a distributed system, the lack of a single address space and the need for independent, reusable services are addressed by having a service-based architecture (Figure 2.7). A service-based architecture refers to the policy of only accessing distributed objects through their interface, without having knowledge about the implementation details that support a particular interface. The benefit of a service-based architecture is that the services are completely decoupled from the clients that access them. By being decoupled, services can be shared by multiple clients, which allows a service to be used and reused within the distributed environment. Over time, as a system develops, a large number of reusable components are available for clients and other services to use, minimizing the amount of new code needed for an application. Additionally, services can be replaced by new ones supporting the same interfaces without disturbing the operation of client applications. If the same functionality is provided to the client applications, their operation remains unchanged regardless of the changes occurring in the implementation of the services. This provides a tremendous benefit in terms of ability to migrate to new products, applications, and technologies.

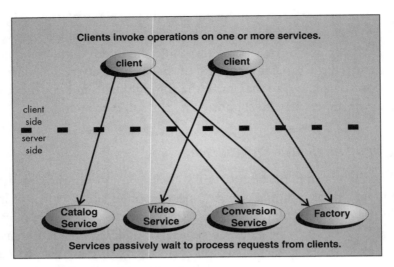

Figure 2.7 Service-based architecture.

In the CORBA model, there are currently four category of services. The lowest-level services are the CORBAservices, which provide the basic object-level functionality to client applications. Services at this level include the Naming, Lifecycle, Persistent, Transaction, Concurrency, Relationship, and the Externalization services, with more expected in the upcoming year. The CORBAservices are standardized by the OMG in order to facilitate the development of applications and higher-level services across CORBA implementations. The next level is the CORBAfacilities, which provide the set of framework-level services across a distributed environment. Many of the CORBAfacilities are likely to rely upon one or more of the CORBAservices in their implementations.

Recycling Types Provides Long-Term Interoperability

Reuse types in other modules whenever possible. In particular, there are many useful types in the CORBA module. Use the scoping operation to refer to the module even if the vendor does not provide the complete IDL source code. For example, CORBA::TypeCode and CORBA::Principal are defined implicitly by some IDL compilers (not by an IDL file). Regardless, their definitions are available for reuse through the scoped name.

The horizontal CORBAfacilities include IDL definitions in the areas of User Interface, Information Management, System Management, and Task Management. The CORBAdomains include vertical services that are standardized within a particular domain. The CORBAdomains represent technology areas that support various specialized market segments, such as imagery, health care, or financial services. The intent of the CORBAdomains is to consolidate the interface definitions within a specific industry so that clients will be able to choose among a variety of implementations with minimal application changes. Finally, there is the application level, which includes all of the applications developed using custom IDL. The application services are used to develop systems within an organization and are expected to benefit from reusing services that are standardized by the OMG.

TYPE MANAGEMENT

A key issue in the implementation of distributed OO systems is the management of types. In a small OO application, the developer has knowledge of and access to all the defined types at compile time. In larger distributed applications with multiple type systems, the developers are unlikely to have complete knowledge of and access to all type information. As a result, new data types and object types can be encountered dynamically. How these dynamically encountered types are managed and accessed is the *type management* issue.

In developing an object-oriented application, one approach is to design a custom set of classes and components and use them to construct a program. All of the classes and components are known throughout the system, and, depending on the object hierarchy used, there may even be methods available to query an object about its type. The capabilities of the types in the program are known and the developer can take advantage of this knowledge to maximize the use of the functionality within the program's objects. Furthermore, once an object's type has been identified, the allowable operations are also known and the developer can interact with the object appropriately. Having knowledge of all the available types at compile time enables rather straightforward programming without the overhead and complexity of dynamic discovery routines or the dynamic decomposition of types. This is not the case in a dynamic, distributed, CORBA environment.

The management of types in a distributed environment is more challenging. In a typical distributed system there are multiple application programs, each of which has its own unique type system. Some of the applications may not be capable of supporting an OO typing environment, for example, legacy software that is not object-oriented. Mandating a single-type system for all applications is unrealistic, and often impossible, in most distributed systems (Figure 2.8). As a result, some method of managing objects and their types across applications is necessary. In the case of CORBA, IDL may be used to define types within a limited environment. These types can be used as intermediate types, which are mapped to the specific application types in the generated server skeletons. Results from applications can then be mapped back to the IDL types and passed back to the client application. This basic method of object wrapping is sufficient for a low level of integration with a self-contained system; however, more flexible mechanisms are needed to solve the larger interoperability issues. For example, in a distributed system, it is quite possible that a type is received from another application that is unfamiliar to the receiving application. Some method of discovering enough information about a type in order to manipulate the type is required, or at least a means to detect an unknown type so that an appropriate error may be generated.

How Does CORBA Manage Types in a Distributed System?

When there is the possibility of a client receiving unknown types, there must be mechanisms in place for dealing with them. CORBA provides type management

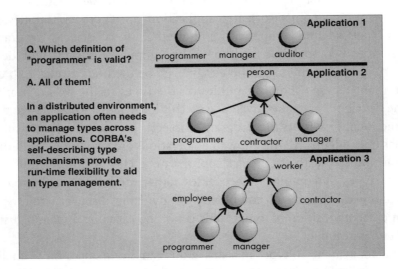

Figure 2.8 Type management differences in application development versus distributed system development.

facilities by requiring all types to have a TypeCode. A TypeCode is an opaque reference used to describe CORBA types. The TypeCode contains a description of the contents and organization of a user-defined type and can be accessed using the standard CORBA interfaces. With an accompanying TypeCode, a user-defined type can only be manipulated if the client application knows the definition of the type and how to manipulate it. However, if user-defined data is transferred with a TypeCode, a client may use the TypeCode to obtain type information. For example, the TypeCode can be used to retrieve characteristics of the type in order to parse the type and extract meaningful data from it. To facilitate the passing of TypeCodes, CORBA provides a type called *any*, which is a structure containing fields for both a TypeCode and its associated value (in the C mapping shown following). The CORBA any structure can be used in an interface definition to pass along any CORBA standard or user-defined data type and should be part of any interface definition that requires extreme flexibility in the data types being transferred. Conversely, a client or service that accepts a CORBA should take advantage of the CORBA TypeCode and use the CORBA functions to dynamically handle unknown data types where appropriate.

```
/*C*/
typedef struct CORBA_any{
     CORBA_TypeCode_type;
     void*          _value;
     }CORBA_any;
```

How are CORBA types self-describing? The CORBA standard defines several metadata interfaces that allow access to the description of user-defined data types stored in the TypeCode. With the operations CORBA provides, any Type-Code can be decomposed into its constituent (OMG 1995a). It is always possible to obtain a complete description of a user-defined type, given its TypeCode, which is sufficient for parsing through a user-defined type. The TypeCode mechanism provided by CORBA allows for a great degree of flexibility; however, it is not a complete solution. While it allows all data types to be examined and relevant data to be extracted from a type using the TypeCode interface, not

In general, the CORBA type any supports arbitrary data types. In practice, some ORBs only support basic types and structures for CORBA type any. Implementors claim that is because the CORBA standard only defines these cases.

Handling Formatted Data

Another important characteristic of data representation is the data format. For example, data formats may be file formats or internalized formats. A useful technique for handling these formats is called the formatted data representation.

A FormattedDataRep is a generic structure used to represent any data type that has a format associated with it. Files can mapped to sequences of octets. However, if the file is formatted, consider using a Formatted-DataRep instead.

```
struct FormattedDataRep {
      string format;
      any data;
};
```

Examples:

```
fdr._format="miles"
fdr.data._type=TC_long;
fdr.data._value=250;

fdr._format="Pascal"
fdr.data._type=TC_string;
fdr.data._value="BEGIN int a,b,c;a:=6;b:=4;c:=a*b'intln(c);END.";

fdr._format="jpeg";
fdr.data._type=TC_sequence_octet;
fdr.data._value=<octet sequence>;

fdr._format= "coordinates";
fdr.data._type=TC_sequence_float;
fdr.data._value=<float sequence>;
```

all of the types received at run-time can be accessed and created in all language bindings. Particularly, the C and C++ language bindings are unable to create a structure of a newly discovered user-defined data type at run-time.

When a client discovers a new interface, either through querying the interface repository or obtaining information from a trader, it is fairly straightforward to determine the signature of the interface's operation and use the DII calls to invoke a method on an object's interface. However, while the method may be invoked, there is no way to determine whether the method will produce the desired effect for a client. Merely knowing the syntax of an operation is not sufficient to determine what the operation actually does. Rather, some semantic information is needed in order to determine what an operation actually means. CORBA does not provide a way to automatically store and retrieve semantic information about an object and its interfaces. However, CORBA does allow the design of an architecture for a system in which semantic information is kept and utilized about the objects in a domain. Currently, many CORBA systems are restricted to a single enterprise, or a set of systems within an enterprise. If all of the objects in a system are well known throughout the system, then semantic information is less important. However, as larger systems are built and more systems begin to interoperate, semantic information will be necessary to discover and use new services across several enterprises. In order to prepare for future system evolution, some level of metadata to facilitate dynamic service discovery and usage needs to be part of a distributed system architecture. The purpose of metadata is to provide for growth at the enterprise level; however, its specification and usage are most effective at the system level, where application coordination and negotiation is a key concern.

ARCHITECTURE QUALITY

A good object-oriented architecture does not stop at providing the basic controls of a system environment. Rather, it also deals with several other key areas of concern, including reducing costs, managing performance, providing flexibility in component implementation, minimizing independence between modules, and providing for vendor and product independence to enable technological migration of software components. Furthermore, such architectures are seldom, if ever, born overnight. Rather, good architectures take a great deal of time and a significant amount of prototyping experience to mature.

Measuring System Quality: "When Will I Start Saving Money Using CORBA?"

An important measure of the quality of a solution is the total cost of a system. A quality system is one that saves an organization money, either through conservation of resources or through the value of its products. A system that properly manages complexity and adaptability should minimize the resources required to maintain and extend itself over its lifetime. In system development, it is important to provide enough flexibility at the higher levels to allow decisions about performance to be made at the application level. Most systems have a variety of applications with widely divergent performance levels. Performance is often a costly feature and organizations cannot always make a business case for maximizing the performance of every system component. Good architecture must balance performance with lifecycle cost concerns.

One of the important lessons of software engineering is that sacrificing on software quality by reducing the cost of the initial implementation of a system will almost certainly increase the long-term costs of an operational system. Investing large amounts of money in the development of a system is no guarantee that money will be saved in the long term. Rather than the amount of the investment, it is investing intelligently that will reduce the overall cost of the system.

Why Is It Important to Have Stable Interfaces?

A key quality of good architecture is the stability of its interfaces. It is important to clarify what is meant by stable interfaces. It would not be proper to advocate that all interfaces should be carved in stone and never extended. To do so would make new component functionality inaccessible to clients. Rather, what we advocate is to discriminate between more stable and less stable interface information, and use this knowledge in the architecture (Figure 2.9).

For example, we could have an architectural partition between two sets of software components, one tied to stable, mature interfaces that are guaranteed for the long haul, and the other to a more dynamic class of components that may be subject to more rapid changes. By making two distinctly different archi-

Partitioning Strategy	Stable/Revisable Specifications	Changeable/Specialized Specifications
Data/Interface "Partitioning"	IDL Interfaces	Data and Metadata
Interface "Specialization"	Horizontal Interfaces	Vertical Interfaces

Figure 2.9 Good architecture involves defining both stable and changeable interfaces.

tectural partitions available to developers, they have the option of developing only to stable interfaces, or to more dynamic interfaces. The stable interfaces would support lower-risk development for reusable code, whereas the dynamic components may change and require periodic updating to take advantage of new functionality.

For many applications that rely upon obtaining the maximal functionality for an application, periodic updating may be just a cost of doing business. Many commercial desktop applications fall in this category, and many desktop users have grown accustomed to periodic migration to new software versions. Other, more customized, mission-critical applications have retained the same functionality over a long period of time. For these applications, stability is a primary concern. Sometimes this is because new extensions and development are too costly or entail too great a risk.

CORBA AND OO ARCHITECTURE

The CORBA specification is composed of the IDL language and the ORB core interfaces, each of which has a distinctly different contribution to the development of good software architecture. The IDL provides an implementation-independent language for specifying interfaces. This is invaluable in partitioning software into components, as it does so without constraining the language of the component's implementation. However, as the IDL specification can be compiled into one of a number of specific languages and implemented, it provides a useful transition between component interface design and the actual coding of the component.

OMG's IDL is an essential tool in supporting software partitioning, and can be effective in designing interfaces to control the flow of data within a system. By layering interfaces, data models can be supported that provide a clear separation of services. Just as important is that these benefits are provided without compromising the ability of a system to deal directly with other system concerns. Other architectural concerns such as hardware and software allocation, timing and throughput relationships, and other implementation issues can still be dealt with outside of the design of the system interfaces. In fact, it is desirable to deal with them separately from the development of the software components themselves, as these issues are prone to change and require frequent tuning, so separating them from the more stable component interfaces serves to preserve the integrity of the system. While, admittedly, IDL isn't the only way to partition a system into useful components, its relative simplicity and sizable support from both industry and standards organizations position it as an attractive alternative.

IDL, while language-independent, may be compiled into application skeletons into one of many application languages that have an IDL binding defined for them. This allows the IDL to be a part of both the architectural specification and the implementation code (Figure 2.10). This link, while missing from many development environments, is guaranteed by OMG IDL. An application with IDL-specified interfaces is implemented using an approved binding, may use an ORB to communicate with, and will be accessible from all other languages and platforms reachable by the ORB.

However, IDL alone is an insufficient specification of software boundaries. While the interface specification defines the compile-time characteristics of software boundaries, IDL does not define the semantics of the boundaries, their allocation, or how the boundaries are used dynamically. Where the boundaries are and how they are crossed is an additional level of specification apart from the IDL.

Once a system has a set of software components with an IDL interface, then the possibility exists to distribute the software components to other implementations. CORBA and IDL support location transparency, where a distributed component is indistinguishable in its invocation from a local component. This decoupling isolates a system from changes in the implementation of the software components and enables a system to defer the physical allocation of components until run-time. If additional information is available about the optimal

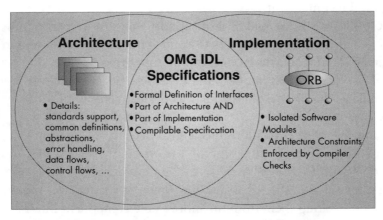

Figure 2.10 OMG IDL links architecture and implementation.

location of a component's interface, then it is possible that the system may be able to take advantage of it in the process of activating the component's implementation. One of the most common methods of benefiting from an IDL-defined software component is to use an object request broker (ORB) to manage the transparent mapping of a client request to a possibly distributed software component.

Object Request Broker (ORB)

An ORB supports the implementation of a flexible architecture by allowing the dynamic binding of a component's client invocation to the actual implementation at run-time. An ORB receives a request through either the client stubs or the DII and marshals the data to a platform and language-independent format. Next, it locates a service that supports the requested interface, or starts one up if one is not currently available. Then, the request is mapped to the implementation with the ORB providing any needed conversions to invoke the server skeleton. This process is reversed after the invocation in order to pass the any results back to the client.

The ORB supports client-side transparency, which allows the developer to make changes to the application implementation without affecting the clients using the implementations/services. Adding to the emphasis on transparency is the automatic server activation that brings up services on demand. The client does not know whether the service is running when the request is made or if it is activated and made available on the fly.

CORBA is an enabler of better architectures, but it does not guarantee better systems. Without a knowledge of good object-oriented architecture and the discipline to apply it, the advantages of using CORBA and IDL can be lost. For example, rather than developing well-thought-out IDL software components, it is possible to directly convert the APIs of existing applications directly into IDL. For example, with a little creative mapping, an undisciplined developer may convert the legacy API directly into IDL and thus have a custom IDL for a legacy database. The problem is that the design of the IDL is specifically tied to one implementation. While implementations based on these IDL definitions will operate just fine, a system based on such IDL would be a stovepipe system, requiring extensive modifications on both the client and server side when the underlying database is upgraded or the system is extended. The existing IDL would not be reusable for a new database and would need to be rewritten to support system extensions. The system would be incapable of easily adapting to

Optimizing IDL for Extensibility

Problem: To have an efficient set of IDL definitions to minimize the amount of changes needed to satisfy new system requirements.

Solutions

1) Define user exceptions for all error conditions an application can return. Do not use system exceptions for applications exceptions even if it is a perfect fit with your application code. For example, rather than using the NO_MEMORY exception, define your own APP_NO_MEMORY exception and use it instead if your application runs out of memory. Otherwise, at some point you will have no means to differentiate whether an error occurred in your application code or came from the ORB itself.

2) Use strings and longs when more flexibility is needed rather than enumerations. If new enumeration values are needed later, they can be added without having to recompile the IDL definitions.

3) CORBA type anys are more flexible than union types. Again, if the union definition changes, it will require recompilation of IDL definitions and application code. If, however, it is defined as a CORBA type any, enough flexibility exists to potentially avoid changing the IDL.

4) Objects are more flexible than structures. Use of new structures requires Type-Codes, which many CORBA environments have difficulty handling properly. Object references are easier to handle. The handling of structures is language-mapping-dependent. Also, while an object reference is easy to create in all languages at run-time, not all languages have the capability to create structures at run-time.

5) Sequences are more flexible and preferable to arrays in many cases. Both sequences and arrays represent contiguous data storage. If the type is passed dynamically, it is usually easier to access the sequence metadata than array metadata through TypeCode facilities. Sequences provide flexibility in dynamic storage optimization compared to arrays.

6) When creating a new IDL data type, it is often useful to also define a sequence for the type. This enables conveying multiple values of the type. For example, if you create:

```
struct foobar {
      long memory_address;
      long process_id;
      string hostname;
};
```

(*Continued*)

It is useful to define the following type:

```
sequence <foobar> foobarSeq;
```

In practice, if you define a new datatype in IDL, you'll frequently have to modify the IDL at a future date in order to add a sequence type for the new datatype. Additionally, this avoids the need to use sequences of the CORBA any data type when manipulating lists of known element types.

new products and technologies, and could only evolve at great expense to an organization. The development of new applications would be curtailed due to the time and expense of constantly migrating existing applications. Rather than "distribute" the mistakes made in nondistributed application development into distributed systems, an organization should take advantage of object technology to define IDL interfaces that decouple software components from their underlying implementations.

CHAPTER THREE

Overview of the Design Pattern Language

This chapter presents an overview of the patterns contained in Parts II through VI. Our pattern language augments other work in patterns research in several useful ways. A comparison of pattern approaches is presented later in this chapter. The following is a presentation of the definitions and concepts for the pattern language contained in this book.

Each pattern is a standalone solution to an important software-related problem. The essense of each pattern is a well-defined problem and a concrete solution. The problem statement is summarized as the *intent,* the specific issue addressed by the pattern. We define each pattern with a clear statement of intent and a concrete solution, and then add additional information to complete the pattern *template.*

The pattern template is a structured outline that is used to define all of the patterns consistently. The template is organized with respect to the priority of the information presented. Individual sections of the template are also organized to present the information in priority order. The initial template sections are mandatory, prioritized, and written for brevity and clarity. Sections toward the end of the template include more elaborate, detailed descriptions, examples, and background information.

The patterns are collected into a pattern catalog. A pattern catalog is a logically organized set of patterns. The patterns are also interrelated to form a pattern language (Figure 3.1). Patterns may be used independently, or in tandem, to achieve solutions.[1] In the pattern language, the related patterns identify either

---

[1] We discuss the issue of *generative* pattern languages in "Design Pattern Template," later in this chapter.

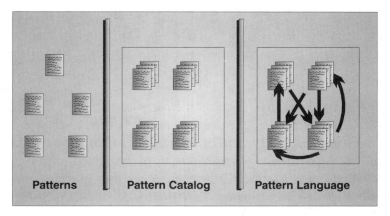

Patterns   **Pattern Catalog**   **Pattern Language**

Figure 3.1 A pattern language is an organized set of related solutions that can be used individually or in concert.

synergistic or subsidiary solutions to the problems resolved by each pattern (Figure 3.2). A synergistic solution is a pattern that can be used to augment another pattern-based solution. A subsidiary solution is a pattern that resolves finer-grained issues resulting from the application of a pattern at a given scale.

The patterns are organized into an overall architectural model, called the Scalability Model. The model is organized with respect to the scope of the software solutions. Examples of architectural scales include: application-level, system-

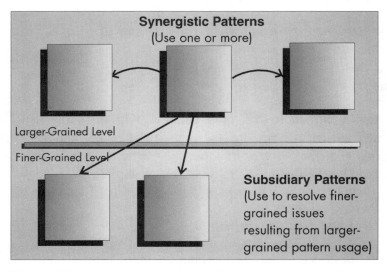

Figure 3.2 A synergistic solution leads to larger-grained solutions incorporating one or more finer-grained solutions.

level, enterprise-level, and global-level. Each pattern is logically placed in this model at the scale where it is most applicable. The form and usage of the solution at other scales is also described where appropriate. The Scalability Model provides a clear separation of issues. The purpose of the pattern language is to provide a road map for developing enterprise-system, and application-level object-oriented architectures. Each of the patterns within the language provides a solution for one of the key problems identified at each level.

This language uses design patterns to provide a CORBA-based solution that successfully resolves the issues and allows the development of a flexible object-oriented software architecture. The examples discussed in the patterns provide guidance in applying and using the CORBAservices and CORBAfacilities in the OMG's Object Management Architecture (OMA).

Three key topics introduce our pattern language:

➤ Primal Forces
➤ Scalability Model
➤ Pattern Template

PRIMAL FORCES

Software design involves making choices. For example, some of the key choices made when designing software architecture include:

➤ What details to expose and what details to abstract?
➤ What features to include and what features to exclude?
➤ What aspects to make flexible and extensible?
➤ What aspects to constrain and guarantee?

Software design choices are often complex, with numerous issues (or forces) to consider, such as security, cost, adaptability, reliability, and so on. In order to make good choices, it is very important to clarify the context of the decision. Choices can be clarified in several ways, for example:

➤ Separation of concerns
➤ Setting or understanding priorities

To separate concerns, we need to limit the scope of each choice. Partitions in a software architecture can be used to allocate and delineate the boundaries of concerns. Each partition is responsible for resolving a limited set of issues, which simplifies decision-making. The architecture represents the union of the partitions, and provides coverage of all the relevant issues. This separation of concerns is a fundamental role of architecture.

Decisions are also clarified by an understanding of priorities. If we know what is important and what is not, it is much easier to choose what to include and what to exclude in a design. Decisions are difficult because they include some items, and exclude many others, and we must be able to justify such choices. This is another fundamental role of architecture, to explain significant decisions and design choices.

Forces are design concerns (or issues) that exist within a decision-making context. In a design solution, forces that are successfully addressed (or resolved) lead to benefits, and forces that are unresolved lead to undesirable consequences. In any given solution, some forces will be resolved more completely than others. The choice of a design solution establishes a priority on the forces, to the extent that the highest-priority forces are resolved the most completely.

Some forces are domain-specific. Domain-specific forces (called *vertical forces*) are unique to a particular situation due to the domain or problem addressed. Since vertical forces are unique (or local) to one software situation, resolution of vertical forces usually results in unique solutions for each software problem.

Another class of forces, *horizontal forces,* are applicable across multiple domains or problems. Horizontal forces are forces that influence design choices

Risk Is the Universal Force

Risk is a force that is always present in software decisions. Five out of six software projects are destined to fail in one way or another. This figure is essentially unchanged by new technologies and approaches such as client-server and object-orientation. As software professionals, the outlook is grim, unless something significant changes. We believe that significant changes are necessary in the way that software systems are built and the way that risk is managed.

We see risk as a generalized force that is an underlying factor in most other forces. To various degrees, management of risk is a universal force that motivates the patterns and solutions described here.

across several software modules or components. With horizontal forces, design choices made elsewhere will have a direct or indirect impact on design choices made locally. For example, if the horizontal force is design consistency, it is necessary to coordinate software designs across multiple software modules to ensure such consistency.

A certain class of horizontal forces are pervasive in software architecture and development. These are the *primal forces*. The primal forces are present in nearly all design situations, and should be considered part of the contextual forces driving most solutions. One role of the primal forces is to keep architecture and development *on track*. For example, a software decision that seems to be local can have a cumulative impact when there are other software groups making conflicting choices elsewhere in the same enterprise. The primal forces represent the pervasive forces arising from the interrelatedness of software decisions.

The primal forces are an important part of the guidelines presented in this pattern language. Each primal force is horizontally applicable across many domains of software architecture and development. The primal forces represent the common-sense, basic considerations that are necessary for successful software architecture and development. Primal forces comprise a fundamental *value system* for software architects and developers that is independent of particular situational forces.

The primal forces include:

➤ Management of Functionality
➤ Management of Performance
➤ Management of Complexity
➤ Management of Change
➤ Management of Information Technology (IT) Resources
➤ Management of Technology Transfer

The primal forces have different relative importance at different scales. Functionality and performance are critical forces at application-level and finer grains, whereas management of IT resources and technology transfer are enterprise-wide and global in scope.

Management of Functionality

Management of functionality is making sure that software meets end-user requirements. Software provides a mapping from the world of end-user objects to the world of computer technology objects. The functionality of the software provides the mechanism for this mapping, and all of the operations performed on technology objects.

Interoperability is an important part of management of functionality. Interoperability comprises the exchange of information and services between software modules. Interoperability is all about how multiple software modules collaborate to provide functionality.

Management of Performance

The second primal force, sometimes overlooked by software architects, is the management of performance. It is not sufficient for software to meet its functionality requirements; the system must also meet performance needs. End users have changing perceptions throughout the lifetime of a system that can impact these needs. A system is implicitly required to perform at least as fast as comparable systems developed using other technologies.

In the case of CORBA, the performance of an ORB product is limited by the underlying technologies used to implement it. The ORB's built-in client-service decoupling allows for the astute developer to perform many performance enhancements without changing application software. Because the performance enhancements are transparent to application software, they may be phased in over time, or added as needed as determined by the growth of the system. This results in a high degree of scalability in CORBA systems, which has been proven by the success of companies in migrating from prototypes to enterprisewide operational implementations. The best-known performance enhancement supported by CORBA is load balancing. Since CORBA uses dynamic binding to connect clients with services, it is possible to insert algorithms in the binding process to ensure that the services are used optimally. Since many implementations can support an interface, services are often replicated to optimize load balancing.

Managing performance also involves application software optimizations. Application implementations control the details of processing, which is where the greatest amount of flexibility is available to tune the performance of the application. The majority of performance issues involve computationally bound application bottlenecks, not I/O-bound or network-bound performance. Specifically, an application developer controls the application's data structure selection, algorithms, and often language implementation. Performance optimization is an expensive and time-consuming activity. Few projects are willing to incur the additional, often considerable, costs associated with application speed-up.

Management of Complexity

In developing systems, it is important not to lose sight of the value of good software abstractions. Abstraction leads to simpler interfaces, uniform architectures, and improved object models. It is the lack of effective abstractions that results in excessive system complexity. Commonality between components is often not recognized and sufficiently exploited. Without proper design abstraction, needless component differences are exposed, resulting in redundant software and multiple points of maintenance for fundamentally similar objects.

Managing complexity is a matter of analyzing a design and properly identifying the hot spots and problem areas which may be most affected by future changes, for example, the anticipation of changes which have the potential for a performance bottleneck in an implementation. Once hot spots have been correctly identified, a recursive process of redesign revision is appropriate, to provide simplicity and robustness. Developing abstractions that simplify individual interfaces provides cost savings across the system design. This can provide savings in the internal implementation of a software component, and also in each of the clients that access the component services. An effective tool for managing the complexity of a large enterprise is the creation of horizontal interfaces, which is discussed in detail in Chapter 7.

Management of Change

Adaptability is a highly desired but elusive characteristic for software. Most organizations would prefer to have adaptable systems. However, few realize the full implications of what it means to develop a flexible system. When developing a distributed system, it is not sufficient to simply include adaptability as a goal. Rather, the system architect must consider the evolution of the system and decide how and where the system needs to be adaptable. When the system architect designs interface specifications, he or she is making decisions about where the areas of greatest adaptability and greatest stability exist. IDL can be used to define the software boundaries. If properly specified, it is the set of interfaces that provides decoupling between components in the system. A good set of IDL interfaces specifies the exposed functionality of a software component in order to allow multiple implementations to be capable of satisfying the constraints of the interfaces. It is in the software interfaces where system stability and adaptability is realized. A system that can support component implementation changes and still maintain stability is much more

The Price of Adaptability

Of course, adaptability in a system never comes free, and seldom comes cheap. Increasing the flexibility in a system increases the amount of time and resources necessary to develop the system. However, if future extensions are properly predicted, and the design is made robust in anticipation of such changes, the return on premaintenance investment can be realized.

Run-time adaptability is even more expensive. A key technique is the use of metadata (Chapter 7). Run-time adapability can be extremely powerful, as many decisions may be delayed until well after the software is written. Some of these late decisions can benefit from additional information available about the end users and installation environment.

An effective method to reduce the lifecycle is to design for product and vendor independence. A key quality of a good architecture is that it abstracts away implementation detail. OMG IDL is a useful notation for defining product-independent interfaces because it separates interface from implementation. Interfaces should support plug-and-play interchangeability. If interfaces are properly abstracted, it is possible to replace a software component with a new and different component that supports the identical interfaces. In general, it is a good idea to avoid using proprietary product-specific interfaces directly. With proprietary interfaces, there is a risk that the interfaces will become obsolete over time and any interoperability benefits gained from using the interfaces will be lost as new product versions are released. If a large body of code is written to a set of proprietary interfaces, then the cost of updating existing software could be quite significant. Also, most proprietary interfaces are not written for portability to other platforms. Therefore, if anyone ever ported an application to a new platform, the proprietary implementation might not be available, requiring a considerable effort to either reverse-engineer the implementations or to redevelop application code to use an alternative set of interfaces. However, it is not realistic or desirable to never use proprietary interfaces. Rather, recognize the dangers and isolate application code from future changes in product interfaces. A new update from the vendor will inevitably arrive requiring the eventual replacement of application interfaces with some other alternative.

adaptable than a system whose interfaces must constantly be modified to support new component implementations. Minimizing the dependency of clients to particular component implementations is the role of the software architect. This is accomplished by abstracting the key functional elements of categories of components and defining them in an implementation-independent manner. IDL is an ideal notation because it is language-independent. With an ORB, the IDL interfaces can support location and platform independence as well.

Portability is an important aspect of the management of change. Portability is the ability to migrate application software from one product or platform to another. Many standards reduce risk by facilitating portability. Unfortunately, the portability provided by COTS products is imperfect. A number of patterns included here describe approaches to enhance portability, such as object wrapping and profile.

Management of IT Resources

Management of IT resources concerns the impact of large scale on the ability to manage the assets of the enterprise. A typical large-scale enterprise would have many different kinds of hardware (hardware heterogeneity), many different software products (software heterogeneity), and multiple releases of each technology. Managing the large volume of machines and software in a changing organization becomes a major issue in its own right. The management of IT resources involves many aspects, such as hardware/software acquisition, inventory, training, maintenance, upgrade, and support.

The majority of end users are incapable of providing their own technical support, so this burden falls on the enterprise. If the support burden is unresolved there are significant costs associated with lost time and productivity, estimated by *Information Week* in April 1996 to be $40,000 per PC end user per year.

Security is an important aspect of management of IT resources. The secure control of information and services is becoming more important as systems become increasingly networked and interoperable.

Management of Technology Transfer

Management of technology transfer comprises some of the key forces at the external boundary of the enterprise. Management of technology transfer includes the formal and informal relationships established by the use and transfer of software and other technology. Management of technology transfer is also an issue impacting many software developers because of the popularity and the availability of the Internet. It is relatively easy to disseminate technology information across enterprise boundaries through email, the Web, and other services. These information exchanges have an impact on the control of intellectual property and the changing dependencies of internal systems on external technologies.

Management of technology transfer also includes the possibility of creating and impacting standards. In essence, standards are technical agreements between enterprises. Standards represent the minimal technology transfer that occurs between organizations in order to establish commonality and cooperation. CORBA IDL makes the creation of interface specifications accessible to virtually all architects and developers. This same IDL is the accepted notation of the formal standards community and other consortia and alliances. It is now possible for most organizations to create technical agreements for software interfaces as a way to manage the technology transfer environment.

Complexity and Technology Transfer

One of the earlier operating systems was the ALTAIR 8080. It was the first fully functional operating system and was completely configurable to the needs of the user. If it was needed to operate robotic components or control the utilities in the house or monitor satellite telemetry—all that had to be done was a quick rewrite of the operating system kernel in machine language, a speedy redefinition of the instruction table, reconnecting any I/O devices and defining a new instruction set for them, a reboot of the machine, and if everything was performed correctly, the machine would complete whatever the desired task at a speed comparable to the less configurable machines on the market. From an engineering standpoint, such flexibility was a great advantage. The few customers who could figure out how to operate it properly spent years writing programs for it. The company that produced it received rave reviews from their customers for a while until they went out of business. During this time, the more simple and less expensive IBM PC was experiencing record sales. The lesson from the failed system, ALTAIR 8080, was that if something is not simple to understand and use, people are not going to use it.

Differences in technology transfer capability are even more dramatic today, given the ease with which information is transferred over the World Wide Web and other Internet services. Technologies such as Java programming can become household words overnight through mass information and technology transfer.

If an attempt is made to develop a system on a piecemeal basis without an overall architecture, the system will become decreasingly manageable as it evolves due to requirement changes and new technology adoptions. One of the key benefits of architecture is the separation of concerns; rather than tackling all of the problems at once, partition the problem into solvable elements. The Scalability Model separates concerns based upon scale of software solutions. The model clarifies the key levels inherent in software systems and the problems and solutions available at each level.

In a typical small software system, there are two levels of scale (Figure 3.3). The first level is the external model (or *application level*), which directly addresses the end-user requirements. This level includes the user interfaces and associated functionality. The applications are typically driven by interactive user control through GUIs or user commands. The applications implement the external model of the system that interacts directly with the human organization. The applications contain the software needed to address the functional requirements of the organization.

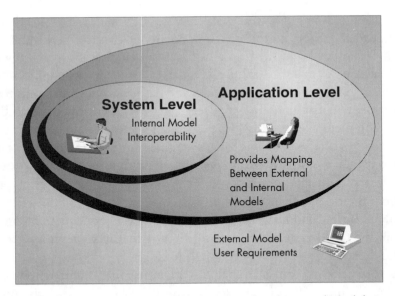

Figure 3.3 The existence of both external and internal models in software systems illustrates the need for multiple levels of software concerns.

The second level is the internal model (or *system level*), which comprises the connections between the applications; it does not directly interface with the end users, nor is it readily observable to end users. The system level provides an architecture for the software system. This level is concerned with providing an infrastructure for the application level, and provides interoperability, communication, and coordination between applications. Access to data stores, auditing, and the management of interprocess resources occur at the system level.

A similar partition exists at several other scales of software implementation. For example, when software solutions span multiple systems across an organization, there is another, related set of concerns at the enterprise level. The Scalability Model explains the differing priorities at each scale and the pattern language includes a set of possible solutions. This resolves a key guidance challenge: ensuring that appropriate solutions are applied at their correct level so that the chance of developing an effective, maintainable system is maximized.

The pattern language is organized by architectural levels that define a comprehensive framework in which to examine the patterns and principles of object-oriented architecture. Although we have identified seven architectural levels, our focus will be on the larger-scale levels of object-oriented architecture (Figure 3.4). The smaller-scale levels have been covered, to various

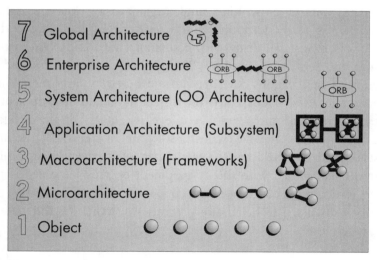

Figure 3.4 The Scalability Model defines several architectural levels corresponding to the scope of software solutions. Richard Helm (1995) was the first to define a hierarchy of architectural levels for design patterns.

extents, by other authors. Specifically, the object level is addressed by the current reusable component libraries and standards such as C++, Smalltalk, the CORBA object model, and CORBA services. At the microarchitecture level, the Gamma Pattern Language and additional design patterns research present the structures necessary to develop component microarchitectures (Gamma et al. 1994). Significant work has also been done at the macrocomponent (frameworks) level. For example, Taligent was quite active in developing software and guidelines at the macrocomponent level in the development of their OO frameworks. Until now, the higher architectural levels have been mostly neglected and, as a result, general interoperability principles across applications, systems, and organizational enterprises have suffered from proprietary solutions and nonreusable, unscalable technological solutions. By defining the Scalability Model, the field of design patterns can be advanced to apply to larger problems, which before now have absorbed significant resources and resulted in less reusable and extensible solutions.

The seven architectural levels are global, enterprise, system, application, macrocomponent, microcomponent, and object (Figure 3.4). The global level contains the design issues that are applicable across all systems. This level is concerned with coordination among all organizations that participate in crossorganizational communications and information sharing. The enterprise level is focused upon coordination and communication within a single organization. The organization can be distributed across many locations and heterogeneous hardware and software systems. The system level deals with communications and coordination across applications and sets of applications. The application level is focused upon the organization of applications developed to meet a set of user requirements. The macrocomponent level is focused on the organization and development of application frameworks. The microcomponent level is centered on the development of software components that solve recurring software problems. Each solution is relatively self-contained and often solves just part of an even larger problem. The object level is concerned with the development of reusable objects and classes. The object level is more concerned with code reuse than design reuse. Each of the levels will be discussed in detail along with an overview of the patterns documented at each level.

Object Level

The finest-grained level is the object level. Here, a software developer is concerned with the definition and management of object classes and object

Design Reuse versus Code Reuse

Design patterns are focused on providing reusable design guidance for developing large-scale systems. The reusability of design itself has a significant effect on the overall development cost of a system, far more than the reuse of individual software components (Mowbray & Zahari 1995). To illustrate this, Figure 3.5a shows a system that is able to take advantage of several reusable components at the framework and microarchitectural level. Note that the overall design of the system still has to occur and that the bulk of the overall tree is in the nodes in the non-leaf node parts of the design. While reducing components does effectively save time in that the prefabricated leaf nodes can be plugged into the design rather than custom-constructed, there is still a large outlay required to build the overall system. However, Figure 3.5b shows a system that is able to reuse much of the design of an existing system. While the system is constrained to the domain of the previously built system, the level of reuse is far greater (Yourdon 1993). By reusing the design, any pieces that are identical to the previous system may be plugged in with minimal modification. However, there are many leaf nodes that must be customized to the new base of users to meet their specific requirements. Note that the cost of changing the leaf nodes is far less than the cost of changing the higher-level design. Therefore, optimizing the amount of design that is reused in a system provides a framework for minimizing the overall system costs far more than if the emphasis is on reusing individual components.

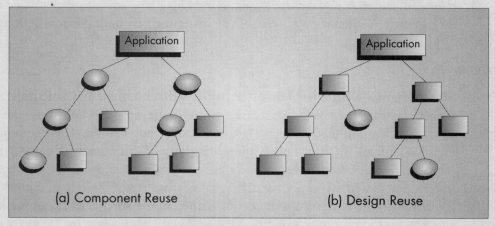

Figure 3.5 Code reuse versus design reuse.

instances. Decisions made at this level include selection of specific object attributes and proper signatures for each operation. At this level, the goal is to build primitive functionality to address application requirements. Secondary goals include reuse of existing software and documentation used in making the decisions about what is included or excluded from the class description. Typically, discussions on the object level are so specific and detailed that they are used only in discussing the specifics of a system's implementation.

At the object level, objects and classes are language-dependent, in the case of class libraries and programming frameworks. Language independence is possible, for example when the class definitions are expressed in OMG IDL. There is a standard object model defined in CORBA that defines the semantics of object interactions. There are also CORBAservices interfaces that define basic object level interfaces for the management and control of objects. CORBAservices include: the naming of objects (Naming Service), the management of object events (Event Service), the management of an object's lifecycle (Life Cycle Service), object persistence (Persistent Service), the relationship between objects (Relationship Service), object transactions (Transaction Service), object externalization (Externalization Service), and object concurrency and locking (Concurrency Service). The CORBAservices are often used as building blocks for larger-scale software components, which may contain policy and rules as to how the services are used by a specific set of components. Language-dependent class definitions are written in a specific programming language, such as C, C++, Smalltalk, Ada, Java, and so on, and are usually not sharable by other programming languages. Language-dependent classes may take advantage of shared run-time libraries so that they are capable of being used by multiple applications.

Microarchitecture Level

The microarchitecture level involves patterns that combine multiple objects or object classes. This level is concerned with the development of small designs used to tackle a limited problem with a software application. The distinguishing characteristic of this level is a limited group of cooperating objects whose interrelationships with other objects are well-defined and understood by the implementor of the component. The goal of patterns at the microarchitectural level is to reuse the encapsulation of components so that they are isolated enough to handle future system changes. The Gamma Pattern Language was primarily concerned with the development of effective design patterns for applications at this level.

Framework Level

The framework level is concerned with the development of design patterns at the macrocomponent level, involving one or more microarchitectures. Often the solution presupposes several architectural issues such as the presence of an object request broker architecture or certain capabilities within a system. At the framework level, the goal is to allow the reuse of both software code and the design used in writing the code. Patterns that are unique to a specific framework model or macrocomponent architecture would be included at this level. Effective patterns at this level can reduce the cost of building applications that share the framework's domain and their maintenance costs. Much of the patterns and guidance from Taligent and Siemens are at this level (Buschmann et al. 1996). Frameworks attempt to use large portions of design and software when applied to solve problems within a specialized domain.

Application Level

The application level is the next scale above frameworks. Applications typically involve numerous object classes, multiple microarchitectures, and one or more frameworks. The application level is concerned with the design patterns used in a single application program. Often, a single developer has control over how an application (at this level) is structured, controlled, and managed. At the application level, the primary goal is to implement a specific set of functionality defined by the software requirements. The functionality must conform to performance goals. This level contains diverse arrangements of structure and design techniques. Because the scope is limited to a single program, there is far less risk involved in experimentation at this level than at larger scales (which impact multiple applications, systems, or enterprises). If the higher scales are built properly, the scope of the impact of changes within an application is limited to a single application program and the data it operates on.

The application level contains programs that implement the external model of a software system. Specifically, the external requirements of the end user are satisfied at the application level; this includes issues relating to user interface and visible system functionality. Application-level software activities include object wrapping of legacy systems and new application development. COTS applications reside in the model at this level. Groups of collaborating frameworks are also included at this level.

Since the finer-grained levels are covered adequately by other works, the pattern language is focused only upon the problem sets that occur at the application and larger scales. The work in design patterns at the application level and higher has been minimal until now; however, it is precisely at these levels where object-oriented architecture is most important.

Application patterns cover a diverse set of solutions. There is also rapid innovation occurring at the application level in COTS software and development support environments. The chosen application patterns in the pattern language include libraries, frameworks, interpreters, event-driven, persistence, and others. This comprises a robust set of application patterns that explain the principles behind most application-level architectures.

System Level

A system comprises several integrated applications. The applications provide the functionality; the system level adds interoperation between the applications. The system is also responsible for managing lifecycle issues, such as system evolution. The system-level architecture is the enduring structure that survives the modification and replacement of component applications over the lifecycle of the system.

The system level is interesting because the forces vary significantly compared to the application level. As we move to larger scales, the impact of change and complexity increases dramatically. Within one application there may be infrequent changes; at the system level these application-level changes comprise cumulative changes with possible systemwide impacts. For example, if a dozen cooperating applications are upgraded once a year on a staggered schedule, the overall system would experience monthly upgrades, with an associated risk of the required changes to existing software impacting the rest of the applications.

Each application may be a complex program with hundreds of classes and thousands of methods. As we scale to the system level, the system complexity increases faster than the complexity of the individual applications. From one perspective, the system resembles a large program that is the union of the individual applications. Since the applications must communicate, there is additional software that implements application-to-application interconnections. If this complexity is not managed properly, the system with N applications resembles a much larger program with N complex modules and $N \times N$ interconnections (Figure 2.6). Complexity at the system level also includes the impact of communications mechanisms and distributed processing.

The apparent complexity also leads to a wide range of diversity in solutions. Many system-level solutions are ad hoc or uniquely crafted for particular application implementations. Within an enterprise, there may be many software systems with varying software architectures. At the system level, the goal is to provide an infrastructure that applications may easily plug into in order to achieve some interoperability benefit. Here, the goal is to reuse architecture so that applications may benefit from commonality between systems, which includes interoperability and software reuse.

At the system level, managing change and managing complexity are the two most important primal forces. Managing functionality and performance have more importance at the application level where they are directly controlled. Complexity is managed through arriving at the right amount of abstraction for a system architecture. Management of change is focused on the development of common interfaces. This defines how services are accessed. Common interfaces allow for component replacement of applications and systems. Good architecture is about matching the right amount of abstraction with the appropriate set of common interfaces.

The system level implements the system's internal model, and provides the cohesiveness needed to allow applications to interoperability effectively with one another (Figure 3.3). Three key principles at this level include horizontal interfaces, vertical interfaces, and metadata. Horizontal interfaces are common interfaces designed to be reused across an organization. For example, horizontal interfaces may contain generic operations for data transfer and access. They can provide mechanisms for reuse, interoperability and management of applications. Vertical interfaces are customized with respect to domain-specific requirements and vertical forces. Providing functionality to end users and optimizing performance are the key motivations behind vertical interfaces. Metadata is self-descriptive information that describes services and data available within a system. Metadata enables system flexibility, with dynamic capabilities for managing change. Together, horizontal and vertical interfaces, along with metadata, comprise a system-level software architecture. These key principles are discussed further in the patterns in Chapter 7.

Within the system level, patterns are categorized into either structural or behavioral patterns. Structural patterns are those that possess a specific structure or set of related components. Structural design patterns at the system level include Gateways, Repository, Component, and Domain OO Architecture. Behavioral patterns define how a system behaves under various conditions. The behavioral patterns are reuse categories, client/server, multitier, and automation.

Enterprise Level

The enterprise level is the largest architectural scale within an organization. Enterprise-level software comprises multiple systems, where each system comprises several applications. Unlike the global level, within the enterprise level an organization has control of its resources and policies. The enterprise is responsible for establishing policies and procedures that are in place throughout an organization. The enterprise-level patterns include guidance for making architectural design decisions that affect the structure, style, and future growth of enterprise software. The patterns help define the necessary policies that need to be in place at the enterprise level, balanced with autonomy at lower levels. The enterprise level is also differentiated from the global level by being limited to a definable scope of influence. The goal of the enterprise level is to provide software access and minimize costs through a consistent set of polices and services usable throughout the organization. By establishing organizational procedure in accordance with the design patterns, many typical enterprise problems in organizations can be minimized. For example, an organization that establishes a policy for particular file formats or network standards can avoid many related problems of procurement flexibility for state-of-the-art products and product incompatibilities without a means of data transfer between them.

At the enterprise level, there are four categories of software information management to consider: the organizational operating environment, distributed interprocess communications, resource management, and organizational profiles. There are additional decisions that must be made at this level that are unique to a particular organization type. Some general characteristics of enterprise-level decisions will be presented as a guide toward identifying and applying some of these less common patterns.

Our model describes the enterprise level in three key patterns, arranged from the most general to the most specific (Figure 3.6). The most general pattern is the standards reference model. A standards reference model is a collection of recommended standards allowed to be used by an organization. The goal of a reference model is to provide a set of target standards to ensure that applications under development or procurement will be compatible with future enterprise environments. Standards reference models are used in many existing organizations. Unfortunately, these models do not provide guidance on how to use the standards, such as implementation conventions, compliance testing procedures, and so forth. This is problematic for organizations attempting to adhere to a reference model, as standards are written so that they have broad applicability.

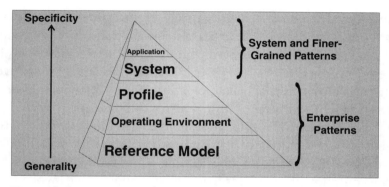

Figure 3.6 The enterprise architecture defines the technology utilization policies, including the standards reference model, the common operating environment, and the application profiles.

Constraining the scope of a broad standard in order to focus on a particular problem is often quite difficult and requires selection of an appropriate subset of a standard, to manage complexity and gaurantee benefits.

The next pattern concerns the establishment of a *common operating environment.* Using the reference model as a guideline, a common operating environment is an enterprise applications suite, based upon a specific set of products and custom applications and systems.

The third key pattern is a *profile,* which contains the additional guidance an organization needs to provide in the use of standards and products. Together, these patterns provide the basis for the key components in developing an enterprise-level object-oriented architecture (Chapter 11).

Included at the enterprise level are the various organizational models, which direct an organization in how to use various standards, for example, organizational policies, security and data access policies, and organizational infrastructure issues, such as the available communication protocols or the location of shared resources.

Global Level

The global level is the largest scale of the architectural levels. The global level comprises multiple enterprises. The key issues addressed involve the impact of software that crosses enterprise boundaries. The global level includes languages, standards, and policies that affect multiple enterprises. The boundaries of global systems are difficult, if not impossible, to define, and include a mixture of de facto and formal standards that are actively in use by the multitude of organizations throughout the world. Global systems and can be jointly controlled by multiple enterprises. The goals of the global level are the joint goals of multiple enterprises. For example, the global level can provide a set of leverageable standards and protocols that benefit organizations by allowing a general means of interoperability and communicating across different enterprises.

The best example of a global system is the Internet, which is defined through a collection of related standards and policies that exist throughout the world to allow the sharing of information. An important aspect of the Internet is the collection of standards that can be supported by anyone who wishes to share and access information in other organizations. Usage is beyond the control of any particular organization and is open to any person or group who wishes to participate.

Also included at the global level are the software standards. There are four major categories of standards in the computer industry: formal, de jure, de facto, and consortium standards. Formal standards are those advocated by accredited formal standards bodies such as International Standards Organization (ISO), American National Standards Institute (ANSI), and IEEE. De jure standards are standards mandated by law and endorsed by a government authority, including such standards as Ada95 and GOSIP. De facto standards are those that enjoy the status of standards through popular use. Currently popular de facto standards include Microsoft Windows and Office, TCP/IP, and the various Internet protocols (WAIS, WWW, etc.). Finally, there are consortium standards, which are created by a wide variety of groups such as OMG and The Open Group. Typically, formal and de jure standards are specifications only, whereas de facto and consortium standards may also include an implementation. The description of global patterns is included in Chapter 12 and 13, including the Internet patterns and Java.

Level Summary

A summary of the levels which are the focus of the pattern language is presented in Figure 3.7. The application level is where the functionality and performance that meet user requirements occur. At the next larger scale, the system level defines the software interconnections between applications. The development of vertical interfaces and horizontal interfaces for interoperability between applications occurs at the system level. Along with the horizontal and vertical interfaces, metadata is defined for run-time flexibility to allow many types of system mod-

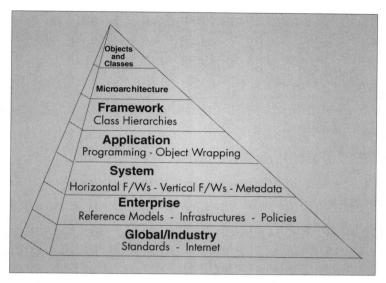

Figure 3.7 The Scalability Model shows the levels addressed in the pattern language.

ifications without requiring changes to application software. The next larger scale is the enterprise level where organizational-level policies, guidelines, and procedures are defined. At the enterprise level, the enterprise controls reference models and operating environments and makes choices to further the needs of the organization. At the global level standards are generated as technology agreements are reached through consensus with other enterprises.

Architectural Scale and Primal Forces

The primal forces are persuasive concerns that influence most software choices. The tradeoffs between these concerns will affect the overall quality of software architecture at all levels. In order to simplify decision making and clarify the separation of issues, we have estimated the relative importance of the primal forces at each architectural scale (Figure 3.8).

On an application level, software developers are concerned primarily with managing functionality and performance when developing software to meet the functional needs of their user base.

The system level is primarily concerned with developing an infrastructure that can effectively manage complexity and change in order to reduce the overall lifecycle costs of developing and maintaining an organization's software sys-

	Application "Programmer"	System "Architect"	Enterprise "CIO"	Global "CEO"
Management of Functionality	1			
Management of Performance	2			
Management of Complexity		2		
Management of Change		1	2	
Management of IT Resources			1	2
Management of Technology Transfer				1

Figure 3.8 The primal forces have varying priorities relative to each architectural scale.

tem. The system-level architect is responsible for providing adaptability and ensuring that the overall system design is sufficient to adapt to the evolving needs of an organization.

On the enterprise level, the emphasis is on managing resources, as large-scale systems often involve thousands of interacting components and services. Additionally, the management of change overshadows other primal forces addressed at lower levels. The management of resources becomes a major concern as the enterprise scale increases.

At the global level, the emphasis is on leveraging existing standards and effectively utilizing the existing base of knowledge to enhance enterprise-level development. However, the enterprise's control over solutions is reduced as an organization has limited influence of external technologies. Keeping up to date on new technologies and use of IT resources are the primary concerns at the global level.

The pattern language will examine the recurring structures at each level and present detailed solutions for the major problems inherent at each architectural scale. Design patterns excel in providing reusable architectural designs that balance the primal forces. A natural side effect of good object-oriented architecture is that overall software development costs are reduced as maintenance costs are reduced, and services can be used during a large portion of the lifecycle.

DESIGN PATTERN TEMPLATE

A design pattern is simply captured expertise. In its most basic form, a design pattern is a problem-solution pair, accompanied by an associated context and an identification of the forces that more precisely define the problem. Along with the context, experience has shown that patterns are more easily remembered and applied if they include a background and an example. The background provides details of the origin of the pattern and additional contextual information. The example demonstrates how the pattern is applied to an instance of a problem within the domain. The nature of patterns is to capture the recurring ideas in software. A discussion of related patterns, within the pattern language and in other works, is important to enhance the value of patterns. Since these are all key elements for a pattern language which deals with distributed computing, they are the basis for the template used to present the pattern language (Figure 3.9).

A visual of the convergence-divergence of a successful pattern is presented in Figure 3.10. Within each design pattern, the applicability section defines the

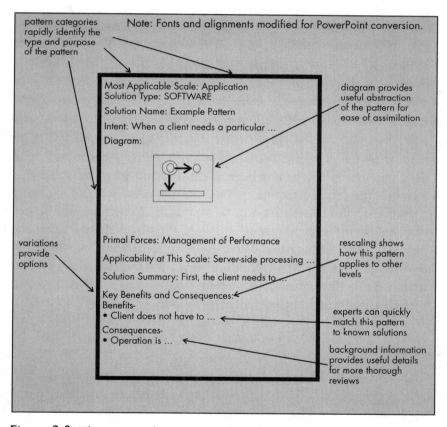

Figure 3.9 The pattern elements are selected to assist in rapid and thorough assimilation of the pattern knowledge.

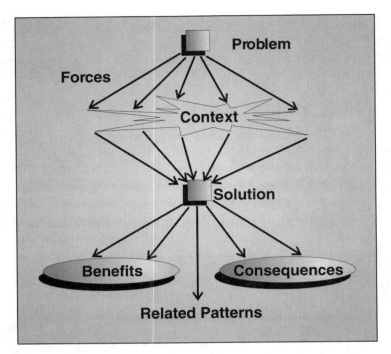

Figure 3.10 Convergence/divergence of patterns.

context of the problem. The background presents a specific real-world example of where the problem has been identified and provides specific instances of some of the forces affecting it. The solution is responsible for bringing a convergence of the issues raised in the applicability section. The forces should be resolved outright, or a tradeoff between the forces should be reached. Following the solution, there is a discussion of the benefits and other consequences that result from how the solution resolves the forces. Often, it is the choice of tradeoffs that distinguishes the pattern from related patterns. The sections of the pattern template will be presented as follows.

Most Applicable Scale

The *most applicable scale* identifies where this pattern fits into the Scalability Model (Figure 3.7). Each pattern is logically placed where its problem is most applicable. A secondary consideration for placement concerns the scale of the resulting solution.

Some patterns define useful solutions at several scales. The forms of the rescaled solutions are also described in the pattern template.

Solution Type

Four different kinds of *solution types* are included in the pattern catalog: software, technology, process, and role.

Software patterns comprise the overwhelming majority of the patterns included in this catalog. Software patterns involve the creation of new software. The vast majority of the *design patterns* currently available in the industry are software patterns.

Technology patterns solve software problems through adoption of a technology (such as Java), as opposed to programming the capability from scratch. Technology patterns are also design patterns in that they result in software design and implementation, although the method of acquisition is different. Technology patterns may involve some programming, for example, creating an object wrapper for a commercial software module.

Process patterns provide a highly effective way to solve a software problem by defining the solution as a decision-making process. Role patterns solve software problems by allocating clear responsibilities to organizational stakeholders. Occasionally, we have found that a simple process or clarification of responsibilities provides the most effective *action lever* for solving a technical problem.[2] Process and role patterns are included because of the significant effect that communication and the human organization have upon software problem solving.

Solution Name

The *solution name* of the pattern introduces new terminology. The name is used for future reference to the design knowledge and principles contained in the pattern. It is important that every pattern has a unique name in order to uniquely identify it. Names are critical as they form the basis for an organization's terminology when discussing and document software architecture and development.

Intent

The *intent* is a brief statement of the problem. A one-line description is ideal, with a maximum of three lines. If the problem cannot be described concisely, it is often best to break it up into its composite parts and discuss them as individual patterns. The problem statement provides a concise, easily recognizable statement of the specific problem the pattern addresses.

[2] Process and role patterns are not design patterns, per se. However, they can provide very effective problem solutions. The overwhelming majority of patterns in this book are software patterns.

Diagram

Each pattern is accompanied by a *diagram* in order to clarify the solution. The diagram is a visual abstraction of the solution.

Primal Forces

The *primal forces* that are addressed or resolved by this pattern are identified. This section provides a rapid way to determine the contextual forces, by relating it to the forces defined in the Scalability Model.

Applicability at This Scale

This section is a list of motivating factors affecting the use of this pattern. If any one or more of the listed factors apply, then this pattern may be applicable to the problem at hand.

The factors listed are relevant in the context of a particular scale. These factors identify the kinds of concerns this pattern can resolve at this scale. It also lists any key preconditions for use of this pattern. The pattern may have applicability at other scales. These variations of the solution are addressed in the "Rescaling to Other Levels" section.

Solution Summary

This section explains a solution that resolves the forces in the pattern identified above. The quality of a particular pattern is determined by the completeness and elegance in which the forces of the pattern are resolved. Just as the intent and applicability define the problem, the solution identifies how the problem is solved by the pattern.

Benefits

The benefits of applying this solution are presented, highlighting the advantages over comparable solutions as well as any positive effects that result from its application.

Consequences

Similarly, the major undesirable consequences of applying the solution are presented, with an emphasis on the difficulties unique to the CORBA environment that may not be obvious to the developer unfamiliar with the domain.

The preceding sections of the template are mandatory and appear in every pattern. The following sections are included in most patterns, where applicable. We have chosen to eliminate some of the following sections from some patterns if there was no particularly useful information to convey.[3] For example, there may not be any significant *variations of the solution* to discuss.

Variations of the Solution

Several of the patterns have common variants, options, and alternative design points. The "Variations" section includes these extensions, which expand upon the capabilities of the solution.

Rescaling to Other Levels

This section describes the relevancy of the pattern to other levels. If a pattern assumes a different name at different levels then it will be mentioned here. Some key questions addressed in this section include: What happens when the pattern is applied at different levels? How effectively does it resolve the forces at the other scales? What new forces are introduced and are they resolved as well, and why or why not? How do the key forces influencing the design patterns change with scale? How do the roles of the key design elements change with scale?

Related Solutions

This section contains references to related patterns within this pattern language and other useful information. The pointers to related patterns are an important aspect of the pattern language. Each pattern resolves some forces and creates new forces. The new forces can be resolved by related patterns, either at the same level or at another level. This section also highlights differences between similar patterns.

This section also includes related terminology, references, and resources. Related terminology is explained for two reasons: in order to distinguish our definitions from other terms using similar names, and in order to connect related concepts that are referred to by different names. These two ambiguities are the

---

[3] This shortens the patterns and eliminates bulky descriptions that may be very time consuming, but not particularly useful.

source of much confusion in software engineering circles. References include well-known terminology, sample technologies, and relevant research. The references are particularly useful to experts who can use this information to rapidly relate this pattern to other known work. If an expert reviewer fully understands one or more of the references, then the core ideas of the pattern are already known by a different terminology.[4] This section serves as both a reference list and an "also-known-as" list of synonyms with respect to other work. Resources include pointers to other kinds of information and organizations that address the problem.

Example

This section contains an example of the solution being applied to a particular problem. In many cases, this is an example of the solution being applied using CORBA. The example demonstrates how the solution is applied to the problem by paralleling the details of the solution.

Background

The background contains further examples of where the problem occurs or general background information that is useful or interesting.

COMPARISON WITH OTHER PATTERN LANGUAGES

The father of design patterns is Christopher Alexander, who developed the concept of design patterns as applied to the design of building architectures. His goal was to improve the quality of architectural designs by analyzing the forces involved in an architectural problem and reusing successful design solutions to the previous similar problems. Alexander stressed the importance of recognizing the various levels of design and identifying the relevant forces at each level, and ensuring that a solution resolved the appropriate forces on each of the levels. Of all the design pattern practitioners who adopted his approach, few, if any, have maintained his sense of scalability and emphasis on recognizing where patterns fit into successively greater levels of complementary patterns.

---

[4] We have encountered this effect in the use of other pattern languages. It sometimes takes significant time to resolve these terminology differences without this useful section.

However, Christopher Alexander was an architect and his patterns were directed toward buildings and city planning rather than the development of software and computer systems. While there is no one equivalent of Christopher Alexander in the software field, progress is being made in developing similar approaches. The importance of an approach that emphasizes numerous levels quickly becomes apparent with the simple truth that dollars will continue to be spent on software systems without a recognition of the big picture. For most organizations, a bottom-up approach of enterprise-level development is not enough, particularly for systems existing in the government or large industries where coordination at higher levels is necessary to be efficient and competitive.

The Gamma Pattern Language (GPL) created the definitive text in the field of software design patterns (Gamma et al. 1994). Their work was focused exclusively at the microarchitectural level and provided patterns for many useful design constructs for use within an application. While many of their ideas scaled exceptionally well, the issue of scalability was not directly addressed, as the emphasis was primarily on the implementation of the design concepts presented. Readers were left to discover any new forces that were introduced at higher levels on their own. The GPL accomplished its mission of providing an indispensable component design guide exceptionally well, as evidenced by its popularity; however, it left room for others to elaborate on interactions between patterns in the collection and on where the collection fit in a larger view of software development.

Richard Helm was the first person to introduce the notion of architectural levels in software design patterns. His model consisted of five levels: the objects and classes, microarchitecture, macroarchitecture, application, and system. The objects and classes level was concerned with the design of classes and class instances. The microarchitecture level dealt with the design of small, lower-level software components with interactions between only a small number of classes. The macroarchitecture level dealt with frameworks and interactions between many classes and subsystems within an application. The application level deals with the development of the software programs. Software programs are composed of one or more components which cooperate to perform a specific set of tasks. Mary Shaw has been actively at work developing design patterns describing software architectures at this level (Shaw 1995). Finally, the system level is concerned with managing interoperability and sharing of data and resources between applications. This was an excellent model for software design patterns; however, in the briefing where the model was presented there was not a detailed discussion of the relevant patterns within each level. Additionally, thus far no one has provided a description of the patterns in each level of the model and how they are related to each other.

The Buschmann Pattern Language (BPL) differs from previous works in that it is a rich pattern language and also provides an architectural model that specifies the interrelationship of the patterns with one another. The BPL model is divided into three categories: idioms, design patterns, and architecture patterns. The idiom level is concerned with objects, classes, and ways to implement them. The design patterns are defined broadly as design techniques used in the construction of applications. For the most part, the model avoids dealing with microarchitectures, choosing instead to greatly leverage on the work documented in the GPL book. Many of their patterns provide a description of how to design higher-level components and incorporate collections and variations of microcomponent patterns described in the GPL book. The architectural patterns provide a means of coordinating activity between various applications. The system level deals with interoperability and the sharing of services between applications and is identical to the system layer described in our model. However, like Richard Helm, the BPL group saw no imperative to complete the model by describing the enterprise level of software development.

Christopher Alexander's pattern language was *generative,* that is, one could apply to patterns systematically to produce an architectural design. The creation of generative pattern languages for software engineering has been an elusive goal for pattern researchers. Though there are some examples of gen-

All Levels	Mowbray 1996 (CDP)	Buschman 1996 (BPL)	Gamma, et al. 1996 (GPL)	Taligent 1996 (TAF)	Garlan 1994 (PSA)
Objects and Classes		Idioms			
Microarchitecture			Micro-architecture		
Frameworks				Frameworks	
Application	Application	Design Patterns			
System	System	Architecture Patterns			Software Architecture
Enterprise	Enterprise				
Global	Global				

Figure 3.11 Relationship of CORBA design patterns with other pattern languages.

erative pattern languages for software (*Proceedings* 1994, 1995), most frequently a truly generative pattern language has a narrow applicability and is focused on a very specialized domain. The pattern language presented in this book does not attempt to be fully generative; we believe that the creation of a generative pattern language of this scope is an inappropriate goal. In order to be generative, the pattern language would have to become an all-encompassing repository of software engineering knowledge. That would bury our key ideas in a large volume of related knowledge. This conflicts with our purpose to identify the highest-payoff, most important solutions, and distinguish them for efficient assimilation and application.

Comparison with Other Pattern Templates

Our template is slightly different than those used to describe other pattern languages. While we recognize the value in developing standard templates, the need to focus on areas relevant to distributed computing was sufficient reason to develop yet another template version. It is assumed that at the enterprise and system levels, the value of a clear separation of concerns and the presentation of sufficient material to create an instance of the pattern solutions in a particular domain is more valuable than a discussion of the code level details required in a concrete implementation. Rather, enough detail is provided to enable someone to take advantage of existing framework and microarchitectural patterns.

BUSCHMANN PATTERN LANGUAGE

The BPL template was not adopted because of the dangers of presenting too much implementation detail in the pattern language. The majority of the patterns being presented are related to the design of IDL specifications to provide for distributed computing interoperability. We assume that, given a solid set of IDL definitions, providing an implementation for them is very straightforward. While this may not always be the case, there is an existing body of patterns geared towards the development of individual applications. Currently, the development of implementations is already detailed by BPL, the GPL, Taligent, and many others, so our focus is on the larger design problems relating to object-oriented architecture. Additionally, many of the development issues unique to CORBA and distributed programming will be discussed in the margins, and are useful for actual application development. Since our primary focus is on developing good architecture and defining the system's interfaces using IDL, a focus on implementation details would risk compromising the emphasis on defining software components and may potentially mask the general applicability of the pattern language. Rather than have a separate section for structure, dynamics, and implementation as is presented in the BPL template, we include a scalability section that details the key design points affecting the ability to implement the design pattern at the different architectural levels.

GAMMA PATTERN LANGUAGE

Similarly, the GPL template was rejected as it was too focused on the micro-component level and the related implementation issues. While the ideas behind the GPL patterns scale particularly well, their implementation sections are not as relevant to distributed computing and could be potentially distracting from some of the underlying concepts.

CONCLUDING REMARKS

The differences between object-oriented architecture in a distributed system versus object-oriented programming in a single application are many. Prior to CORBA, object-oriented tools and approaches were primarily concerned with individual subsystems (i.e., the application level). At the application level, the driving forces are to provide the requested functionality to the user and to maximize the performance of the system. The object-oriented design process is very domain-specific and often involves rather fine-grained objects with many methods, attributes, and behaviors. The focus at the application level is on algorithm design and selection, reusing class libraries, design and selection of user interfaces and storage implementations, and other software development issues. In object-oriented architecture, the focus is on a higher-level system design. Concerns are focused on the management of applications, intersubsystem design and interprocess issues such as interoperability, security, and management. The goal is to manage the complexity of the system to create a system that is easily adaptable to new requirements, new technologies, the integration of new applications, and other changes. An object-oriented architecture should isolate system components to facilitate change and provide for product independence, change management, and future system upgrades.

Due to the very different purposes of object-oriented architecture and object-oriented programming, there is a significant shift in the proper use of the object paradigm in distributed systems. For example, in a collocated system, objects and their data are encapsulated to control data access and protect the object data from other parts of the system. With inheritance, an object can automatically and dynamically use the methods and data of other classes and objects based on the hierarchical relationship. This is very powerful and useful, when the cost of automatically sharing methods and data is low. In a distributed system, this is generally not the case, and data and method sharing is based more on delegation, which allows the sharing to take place explicitly by the developer, for the most part. Rather than inheritance being used to protect a system from other internal system components, the system is protected through containment, that is, having the data in a location that is only accessible through an explicit interface. So when developers are developing systems in a collocated environment, inheritance and polymorphism are emphasized, and when developing in a distributed environment, containment and delegation become the preferred methods of controlling object relationships.

Some software design issues are show-stoppers because they appear to be very important. Feasible solutions are rare and costly, for example computer security and reliability. While show-stopping issues provide high drama to the decision-making process, they draw focus away from fundamental software decisions that are more productive and ultimately more important. We frequently see these high-drama issues dominate software discussions, taking away valuable time from other, more essential, areas. These issues should be controlled through an establishment of scope. If an issue cannot be feasibly resolved, then it is out of the scope of the software project to address it. Project leadership and executives need to establish the project scope and support those boundaries through review processes so that progress can be made in spite of the show-stoppers.

TERM LIST

Most Applicable Scale

Solution Type

Solution Name

Intent

Diagram

References

Applicability at This Scale

Solution Summary

Key Benefits and Consequences

Variations of This Solution

Rescaling This Solution at Other Levels

Related Solutions

Example

Background

Resources

PART TWO

Application Design Patterns

At the application level, the primary role of the developer is to manage the performance and functionality of the application. CORBA is a comprehensive distributed object architecture and is a valuable tool for constructing distributed applications. However, CORBA, like other distributed computing technologies, requires performance overhead for communication with distributed applications. These application patterns describe several ways to mitigate this overhead. The patterns presented were selected to highlight the high degree of flexibility that CORBA provides in performance-tuning applications, which is not readily apparent to most new developers of CORBA implementations.

CHAPTER FOUR

Maximizing Parallelism

The first class of performance patterns describes techniques for maximizing the degree of parallelism in a system. This involves converting sequential operations to parallel operations that can be performed on different processors and ultimately increases the amount of work performed per given unit of time. The performance patterns in this category are summarized as follows.

DISTRIBUTED CALLBACK

This pattern reduces the length of time a client spends waiting for an operation to complete by converting a synchronous operation to an asynchronous operation. The server invokes a callback routine on the client when the operation has been completed.

PARTIAL PROCESSING

This pattern reduces the length of time a client spends waiting for a factory object to create an object instance. The server creates an object reference and just enough associated data to complete the object creation processing after returning the object reference to the client.

INDEPENDENT OBJECT

This pattern reduces coupling of factory objects with the objects they create by spawning a separate process for each object implementation. This decreases the load on the factory implementation and allows for greater flexibility in configuring the object implementations.

Distributed Callback

Most Applicable Scale: Application

Solution Type: Software

Solution Name: Distributed Callback

Intent: A client process needs the results of a service, but cannot afford to wait during processing.

Primal Forces: Management of Performance

Applicability at This Scale

1. The client application must manage one or more activities concurrently, such as the user interface and ORB service invocations.
2. Object operations take a long time and the client application cannot afford to suspend processing waiting for results.

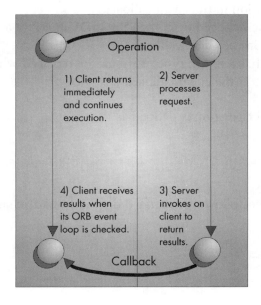

Figure 4.1 Distributed Callback pattern enables clients to replace synchronous OMG IDL definitions with equivalent asynchronous oneway operations.

---

3. A client wants to have several services process operations on its behalf simultaneously and can receive results in any order when processing has completed.
4. It is necessary for a client to continue local processing while sending CORBA requests.
5. The client only wants to accept results, if available, at specific intervals.

Solution Summary

First, define interfaces for the client and server. For each method the client intends to make asynchronous, the client should define a callback object in OMG IDL. The callback should contain parameters for all of the return information required from the server. For increased performance, the client callback should be defined as a CORBA *oneway* operation. Each server operation being converted from a synchronous to an asynchronous call should be converted into a oneway operation with an additional parameter for the callback interface. The conversion is straightforward and is simply of matter of systematically converting interfaces to pass only in parameters with a void return type so it can be defined as a OMG IDL oneway operation. In order to convert any operation to a oneway call, map the in, out and inout allowable OMG IDL parameters type as follows:

1. In parameters should remain the same.
2. Inout parameters should be converted to an in parameter and also added to the list of return information in the client callback.
3. Out parameters should be removed from the OMG IDL interface and added to the list of parameters in the client callback.
4. Finally, if the operation has a return type, it should be replaced with a void and added as a parameter in the client callback interface.

For example, if the initial operation is defined as:

```
interface foo_app {
     string get_info(in string my_name, inout string mood, out string joke);
};
```

Convert the operation to the following interface definition and its associated callback interface:

```
forward interface foo_app_cb;
interface foo_app {
```

```
        oneway void get_info(in string my_name, in string mood,
            in foo_app_cb my_callback);

};

interface foo_app_cb {
        oneway void callback(in string mood, in string joke,
            in string return_value, in boolean successful);

};
```

As illustrated in the OMG IDL signature, when the client invokes the method on the service, it passes its object reference to the server using the new asynchronous foo_app::get_info(). The client continues processing and periodically checks its ORB event queue. The server processes the request and, upon completion, invokes the callback method implemented by the client (foo_app_cb:: callback()), using the callback object reference. The results of the operation are passed back to the client, along with any error information allowed by the interface, completing the transaction. The client must have its own implementation that can be invoked by other objects. The implementation should contain the actions to be performed at the completion of the service. Since the client returns immediately, the server is unable to pass exception information back to the client, if an error occurs in processing the operation. Additionally, the server cannot send exceptions back to the client as part of the callback invocation, as it is a client to the callback interface and therefore is not allowed to pass in exception information. Any error information must be included as part of the client callback interface.

Benefits

➤ Client does not have to wait for the server to complete the operation.
➤ Client can receive the results when the server completes.
➤ Client can handle multiple callbacks in any order.
➤ If the client is already processing ORB events and servicing requests from client applications, the amount of additional overhead is minimal.

Other Consequences

➤ Error handling is primitive, as exceptions become less useful with oneway calls.

- ➤ The effect of operations is more difficult to ascertain in the case of errors or failure because there is no exception condition on the initial invocation.
- ➤ Client must provide a callback implementation.
- ➤ Client must accept ORB callbacks or check for ORB events periodically.
- ➤ No way to check for partial results and progress status, but this can be added as an additional operation.

Variations of This Solution

A useful addition to the solution is an additional signature for the client and object implementation to exchange progress information. For example, the client can use this information for display to the end user. The progress operation can be implemented as either a client call to the service (pull mode) or status update callbacks to the client (push mode).

Rescaling This Solution to Other Levels

The consequences of using this pattern become more severe at higher levels. In particular, the lack of a guaranteed response becomes a more serious concern. Also, the inability to use exception information to convey error information is a deterrent to usage of this pattern at the system, enterprise, and global levels.

Related Solutions

- ➤ OMG Event Service—This is the CORBAservice responsible for event management. It provides a standard method of notifying producing and consuming events.
- ➤ Notification—This pattern is similar to the Push model described in the OMG Event Service. The OMG Event Service decouples clients from object implementations, whereas this pattern increases coupling. At the application level, the simplicity of a custom solution may provide greater benefits in terms of understandability and performance than using the OMG Event Service. At the system level, however, performance is less of an issue than the management of change (which benefits from looser coupling). In such cases, the OMG Event Service will most likely provide the greatest benefit.
- ➤ Multithreading—This technology only partially resolves these issues. Server multithreading has no direct impact, except to potentially provide better service response times. If the client is single-threaded, then there is a strong

motivation for this pattern. Client multithreading resolves the issue of process blocking, but does not resolve the issue of status monitoring, which requires a live thread and additional operations, as suggested in the pattern.

➤ DISCUS peer-to-peer asynchronous operations—A set of horizontal interfaces for providing asynchronous communications between client and services. A similar solution is proposed by Mark Roy in Patrick & Roy (1995).

➤ X Windows callbacks—This was an early use of callbacks in the development of graphical user interfaces.

Example

The OMG IDL for a callback mechanism has two parts: the OMG IDL for the service being invoked, which must include the object reference for the callback object to be invoked after the operation completes, and the OMG IDL for the callback object itself. Following is an example of such an OMG IDL definition.

```
module DC {
    forward foo_callback;

/* This interface defines the server object and operation of interest to */
/* the client. It is defined as a oneway operation to allow the client to */
/* continue processing while the server performs the operation. A */
/* oneway operation returns to the client immediately, which does not */
/* allow the server an opportunity to return an exception in its */
/* implementation. */

    interface foo {
            oneway void op1( object dataobj, foo_callback client);
    };

/* This interface must be implemented by the client */

    interface foo_callback {
            oneway void op1_cb(object dataobj, long status);
    };
}
```

In the implementation of foo_op, the last call should be an invocation on foo_callback, using the object reference passed into the foo_op invocation. The server may optionally want to check for an exception in case the client no longer exists, or it may just wish to ignore it. Also, by convention, if the client is not interested in receiving the results of the operation, it can pass in a NULL object reference, in which case the server would not invoke on the object reference upon operation completion. Often, the callback routine should continue some sort of status information. The oneway operation does not allow the server to convey status or error information to the client. Exception checking is necessary in a distributed environment because there is always the potential for communication failures.

Background

If a client is using synchronous messaging, server-side processing can entail significant delays. For example, a client application needs to guarantee a reasonable response time to a user. A user interface program must have continual awareness of user events and respond accordingly.

Sometimes a user loses interest in waiting for the results of a transaction and wishes to cancel a request. CORBA does not automatically provide an operation that allows a client to forcibly interrupt a server. A client may want greater control over how it waits for a transaction to complete, how the transaction is progressing, and when it accepts transaction results; this pattern provides such a mechanism.

The pattern was developed as a way to improve the current asynchronous mechanisms in a data interchange framework. Initially, asynchronous calls were implemented using a synchronous call, which returned immediately while processing continued in the server, followed by a synchronous getResponse() method, which periodically polled the server for the results of the operation. The getResponse() method was called within a loop with the expectation that if the results were not ready it would return an exception, giving the client the opportunity to perform other tasks before trying to invoke getResponse() again.

Although it seemed a good idea at the time, experimentation showed that while the client was able to perform other tasks between the asynchronous call and the getResponse() call, the server only responded to the initial getResponse() call after it had finished processing its current task and checked the ORB event loop. The resulting effect on the client was that rather than receiving an exception and continuing after invoking getResponse(), the client was forced to wait for the server to check its ORB event queue before continuing. Of course, when the server did respond it was always with a successful completion as it did not check the event loop concurrently with processing a request. Realizing that this defeated the benefits of asynchronous operations, we redesigned the asynchronous portions of the framework.

The new design was based on a peer-to-peer model, where the client implements a callback routine from an OMG IDL-defined specification, creates an object reference for the callback object, passes the object reference to the server application, and returns from the invocation immediately. When the server has completed its processing, it is responsible for using the object reference passed by the client to invoke on its callback, passing the results of the operation. Both the initial server invocation and the client callback use the CORBA oneway keyword to ensure asynchronous behavior in all CORBA implementations.

Partial Processing

Most Applicable Scale: Application

Solution Type: Software

Solution Name: Partial Processing

Intent: To improve the performance of a CORBA-based application by optimizing the amount of parallelism.

Primal Forces: Management of Performance

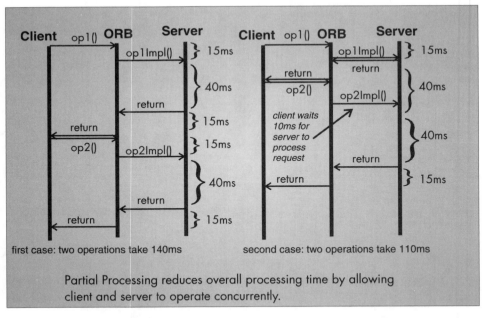

Figure 4.2 Partial Processing patterns increase the amount of parallelization in a system and reduces client blocking.

Applicability at This Scale

1. The time to create an object is excessively long.
2. The latency time of the network invocations is greater than the server-side processing.
3. There is a need to minimize the amount of time the client blocks in execution operations.
4. There is a delay between object creation and subsequent object accesses.
5. Performance gains are needed in a multithreaded environment
6. Server operations take too long to complete and results are necessary for the client to proceed.
7. The return parameters are referential types, such as object references or other identifiers.
8. Using a synchronous invocation mechanism, such as CORBA.

Solution Summary

If all the parameters for an operation are in parameters, then having the client wait for the completion of the operation may be unnecessary. In such cases, it is desirable to return to the client as soon as possible. To optimize performance, perform the minimal processing necessary to return valid results to the client. After returning control back to the client, complete the processing of the operation in the implementation before processing the next ORB event. This processing can take place independently from the client. If any further requests are made of the implementation, the corresponding ORB event will be processed after the current operation has been processed. This technique can also be applied if an object reference or some other referential data type is returned.

The first step in implementing this pattern is to generate the return values for the operation. Often, this entails creating object reference and other referential types before the creation of the data they refer to. For example, if an object reference is created with several properties and attributes, create the object reference first, and delay the creation of its attributes and properties until after returning the object reference to the client.

Next, record any information needed for subsequent processing in an area accessible after the method completes. For example, if the interface contains additional information about how to create the object such as secondary type, location, and so on then that information needs to be retained for later. After any needed information has been stored, complete the object method, returning the requested information to the client.

After the client has returned, the server needs to complete the processing of the initial request. This is done by inserting additional processing before processing the next service request. Before processing the next ORB request, the server needs to create the information underlying the referential data (object reference, etc.) sent to the client. For example, the server may need to create and/or initialize properties and attributes needed by an object's implementation, perform database requests needed to initial objects, or establish event channels and connections for future object requests.

After the initial request has been fully processed, it is time to process the next ORB event. This allows the client and server to operate in parallel, thereby maximizing the benefit of working in a distributed environment.

Note, however, that this technique may not be desirable if an error occurs in the processing performed after the return to the client, as there is often no means to provide error information, or even the fact that an error occurred, to the client. For this reason, if part of the processing is likely to return an error (for example, if it involves memory allocations or database calls), these portions must be completed first before returning to the client. An alternative approach may be to use the OMG Event Service or some other mechanism to propagate the error to the client separately from the client invocation.

Benefits

➤ Maximizes parallel processing between client and server.
➤ Decreases the length of time client spends waiting for results.

Other Consequences

➤ Requires creating and maintaining intermediate results.
➤ Server is unavailable while creating object instance, unless it is multithreaded.
➤ Object instance will not be accessed until the server has completed creation of it. May be difficult if object implementation resides in a different process.
➤ Parallel implementation may be more complicated and harder to maintain.

Rescaling This Solution to Other Levels

This pattern can be applied to implementing shared services at both the system and enterprise level. However, the complexity it adds to the implementation may not be worth the gain in performance for system and enterprise code that is expected to have a long lifecycle.

Related Solutions

➤ Distributed Callback—This pattern is similar to Distributed Callback, except that this pattern does not use a oneway operation so that it can return a reference to partially processed results.

➤ Independent Object—This is an excellent companion to Partial Processing as the processing can be the establishment of a noncollocated implementation. The additional overhead of the Independent Object pattern is greatly neutralized by the Partial Processing pattern.

➤ Fine-Grained Framework—This pattern is another method of greatly improving application performance. In some cases, the Fine-Grained Framework pattern can be used to hide partial results being returned to the client and the processing being completed within the client stub on the client machine.

➤ Lazy Evaluation—This is the technique of delaying the initialization or evaluation of a variable until it is actually accessed. If an object is much more likely to be created than accessed, it may be beneficial to delay object initialization until its data is actually requested by a client application.

➤ Parallel Patterns for Synchronization on Shared-Memory Multiprocessors (McKenney 1995)—This pattern language contains techniques for improving performance of programs on parallel architectures.

Example

Using Digital ObjectBroker v2.5's C binding, first modify the default mechanism of handling ORB events in order to allow the explicit handling of ORB events only. This provides the control over ORB event handling that is necessary for this pattern. In ObjectBroker, there is a function, ORB_main_loop(), called by a server implementation that can either force the server to wait for client events, dispatch invoked methods and return to the ORB event loop, or the server can return immediately if no events are present and perform some other processing between ORB event checking. By replacing the standard event handling code with the code below, events are processed explicitly, one at a time, with a processing step taking place between each event. Details are given as follows:

1. Modify the default handling of events to allow processing between checking for each ORB event.

   /* *Used to create the structures used to store intermediate results* */

```
      printf("Setting up partial results table");
      setup_partial_results();
```

/* *Continue processing events until program terminates* */
/* *ObjectBroker code to process events. You can either wait for an event to be processed or you can choose to return immediately if there is not an event currently in the ORB event queue, as in this example* */

```
      for(;;){
              OBB_BOA_dispatch(CORBA_DEC_BOA_OBJECT,
                      &Ev,OBB_BOA_DISPATCH_MAYBE_ONE);
              if (status !=OBB_SUCCESS){
                      printf("Error from OBB_BOA_dispatch()\n");
              }
```

/* *If there is a partial event pending, process it, otherwise, return right away. As mentioned above, at most one event is processed before checking for partial results. If they exist, processing is completed immediately before checking for the next ORB event.* */

```
      status = process_partial_results();
```

/* *Note that status is not checked here as the client has already returned from the operation invocation. Therefore, it is imperative that any serious errors are checked for before returning to the client because once partial results are processed, the server has no way of returning an exception for the operation. It is possible to inform the client of errors through an event channel or a callback routine, if such a mechanism is properly designed, however.* */

```
      }/*end for*/
```

/* *Given the about loop, this function will never be called, however, if an ORB based termination routine does exist (as with the ObjectBroker ORB), a cleanup routine may be inserted there to ensure its invocation before program termination.* */

```
      printf("Cleaning up partial results table");
      cleanup_partial_results();
```

2. Provide a structure or class to contain the partial results prior to processing:

```
      enum CommandType{NONE, CREATE, SET, GROUPSET};

      struct partial_info {
          boolean is_empty;
          object dataobj;
          union OpData switch (CommandType){
                  case CREATE: string    create_type;
                  case SET: NamedValue    set_value;
                  case SETGROUP: sequence<NamedValue> groupset_values;
                  case NONE: long noValue;
                  default: long errorValue;

          }
      } PARTIAL_INFO;

      PARTIAL_INFO results;
```

3. Provide initialization and cleanup routines or methods for the partial results structure.

```
void setup_partial_results () {
        results.is_empty = TRUE;
        results.dataobj = CORBA_OBJECT_NIL;
        results.OpData.CommandType = NONE;
        results.OpData.noValue = 0;
};
```

4. Define how the partial results are processed between ORB events. Remember that partial results are not expected to occur very frequently in comparison to the number of ORB events handled. If the main ORB event loop waits on an ORB event (perfectly reasonable behavior), then partial results will occur much more frequently in comparison to ORB events processed, as much time is spend in idle waiting. Overall system performance can be dramatically enhanced by minimizing the amount of busy waiting in the system.

```
void process_partial_results(){
        if (results.is_empty != TRUE){
                switch (results.OpData.CommandType){
                        case CREATE:
                                create_object(dataobj,
                                        results.OpData.create_type);
                                break;
                        case SET:
                                set_prop(dataobj, results.OpData.set_value);
                                break;
                        case SETGROUP:
                                set_prop_group(dataobj,
                                        results.OpData.groupset_values);
                                break;
                        case NONE:
                        default:
                                fprintf(stderr, "Invalid case statement reached
                                        in process_partial_results\n");
                                break;
                };
                cleanup_partial_results();
                setup_partial_results();
        }
};
```

By default, CORBA invocations are synchronous. This implies that the client thread blocks while the server performs the desired operations. Often, the operations are lengthy, and it may be undesirable for the client to block. This is especially true when there are either few return parameters, or when the return parameters are simply a reference to a more complex structure. In general, partial processing is desirable because it reduces the amount of time the client waits for an operation to be performed. Even if client multithreading is available, there are many applications where the availability of a reference to a result will suffice for continued processing.

One of our customers was using a data interchange framework as the basis for a system that was to eventually handle thousands of objects. As a result, maximizing the performance of the operations was a major concern. Their pattern of use was to create a large batch of objects, initialize sets of properties on each object, and then respond to user events. An analysis of system performance for a session revealed that a large amount of time was being spent in data object creation and therefore, it was a major candidate for optimization.

A detailed examination revealed that the data objects were created in a batch and then used much later, after the construction of various control objects and the initialization of various data servers. After examining the creation code, it became apparent that if the object reference of the object being created could be returned before the properties were initialized, then the factory server could finish setting up the properties after control was returned to the client application but before the factory server processed the next ORB event. If the implementation of the object being created lived in the same process and was controlled by the same event loop, then as long as processing was completed before processing the next ORB event, this approach should be successful. If the object lived in an outside process, then the new process would need to be informed that the object was either in use or was not yet fully constructed in order to force it to wait until the object creation processing had completed.

5. Finally, in the implementation of the methods of the object, the server must check for major errors and populate the partial results structures/classes with sufficient information to allow later completion of the operation (may involve the creation of object references and associated object reference data) before returning to the client application. Conditions that may result in catastrophic failure (memory allocation, secondary storage access, etc.) must be checked before returning to the client so an appropriate exception can be raised. Continuing with the above example is the implementation of an object's set method utilizing the Partial Processing design pattern:

```
void dtImpl_set(CORBA_Object object, CORBA_string propname,
    CORBA_any *value) {
        results.is_empty = FALSE;
```

```
        results.dataobj = object;
        results.OpData.CommandType = SET;
        fill_NameValue(propname, value, &results.OpData.set_value);
        return;
};
```

While some time is taken up copying the necessary data into the partial processing structures, if the time to perform the actual operation is much greater (for instance, if locating the property was far more time-consuming than copying the value), then partial processing could potentially save quite a bit of time.

Mapping Void Pointers to OMG IDL

What's all this nonsense about OMG IDL not allowing pointers? Absolutely not true! It's just that OMG IDL forces you to define pointers as pointers *to* something. For example, if you want to define an OMG IDL interface that accepts a pointer to a long where the value coming in matters as well as the value returned by the implementation, then declare the parameter of the operation as an inout long. The C and C++ bindings will map to a pointer to a long. While very similar to regular C/C++ code, now you clearly define what the pointer is pointing to, and also the OMG IDL defines whether or not the value passed in is used (out vs. inout), which is important information to a client making a request.

In C and C++, void pointers are often used to creatively violate the type checking mechanisms of C and C++ in order to either allow one of several or any type at all to be passed as an argument in a method's interface. Additionally, void pointers can be used to pass around an object without having to be explicitly aware of its type. When mapping such interfaces to OMG IDL, there are separate techniques to handle each instance. If a void pointer is used to express one of any number of types, an equivalent OMG IDL interface could use a CORBA any instead. The CORBA any is self-describing and can contain any type in its value field as long as its TypeCode is included in the _type field of the any. If the void pointer was used to pass a generic type without being explicitly aware of its specific type, define an interface for the object being passed and pass it as a first-class object using an object reference. An object reference can be passed as a CORBA_Object with intermediate interfaces knowing which specific type is being handled. The object that does need to know the specific interface of the object can use the self-describing ORB interfaces to retrieve the interface from the Interface Repository.

Background

Once implemented, the client and server could live on different machines. This immediately provides the application with a performance gain as now two or more processors can work independently to accomplish the work on behalf of the client. When implemented, a noticeable improvement in performance was indeed obtained with a significant improvement in client response times.

Independent Objects

Most Applicable Scale: Application

Solution Type: Software

Solution Name: Independent Objects

Intent: To resolve processing bottlenecks due to tight coupling of implementations, such as separating the factory implementation from the objects that it creates.

Primal Forces: Management of Performance, Management of Complexity

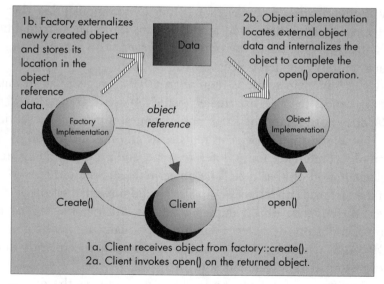

Figure 4.3 The Independent Objects pattern separates the implementation of objects from the factory implementation that created them.

Applicability at This Scale

1. The factory process contains the implementations for the objects that it creates.
2. The factory process has become a performance bottleneck in the system.
3. Separate object implementations are desirable to allow greater flexibility in object activation and the location of implementations.
4. There are many objects created in the system; however, only a few are accessed.
5. There is a need to have a centralized factory, but object implementations need to be located near the clients that access them.

Solution Summary

First, limit the role of the factory solely to object creation and preparation of newly created objects such that their implementations may be accessed independently of the factory. In many factory implementations, the factory server also contains the implementation of the objects it creates. While it is convenient to collocate the factory with its objects in order to allow the factory server to manage objects created by the factory, objects implementations can, and frequently should, manage themselves. In order to accomplish this, there needs to be a separate object implementation defined for the objects created by the factory. The factory still creates the objects; however, it no longer serves as a valid implementation for created objects.

Many ORB implementations require an ORB to register as an implementation of an object in order to create a valid object reference for it. However, CORBA does not require the same implementation instance to service created objects. Therefore, the factory can register as an implementation of an object, create an object reference for an interface type, and promptly deregister itself as an implementation of that type. The object reference should remain valid even though the factory is no longer eligible as a valid implementation of that object. However, the separate object implementations will be able to manage subsequent invocations on the object reference. Optionally, it may be possible to use the CORBA::BOA::change_implementation() function to explicitly direct object invocations to a new implementation.

After creating an object reference, the factory creates the data necessary to manage the object implementation. As before, the factory continues to handle all the details of object creation. After a valid object has been created, the object is externalized in such a manner that its data is available to other implementations of the object, and specifically to the implementations designated to replace the implementation that once existed in the factory. If this pattern is used in conjunction with the Partial Processing pattern, then it may be necessary to provide a method of concurrency control to prevent the object implementation process from internalizing and accessing object data before the factory has completed its creation and externalization.

Now that the object has been created and externalized, all subsequent invocations on the object will be directed to registered object implementations rather than the factory. If no such implementation is active, then the implementation repository is responsible for activating the implementation. In order for the implementation to properly service client requests on the object, it must be capable of locating the object (often using the Instance Reference pattern), and internalizing it, thereby relocating it into a separate process from the factory. By configuring the implementation repository, it is possible in most ORB implementation to direct where the implementation is located and determine the activation policy of the service (see CORBA 2.0 specification section 8.2 BOA Interface).

Usually it is not desirable to internalize an object during each method invocation, so some additional sophistication is required by object implementations to determine when an object needs to be internalized and when the instance of an object is already available within an implementation.

Benefits

➤ Provides greater flexible in configuring implementations; specifically, an implementation of an object may be located separately from where it was created.
➤ Easier to replicate implementations.
➤ Locate object implementations locally and keep centralized factories, if desired.
➤ By decoupling implementations, they are more maintainable and easier to extend and replace.
➤ Eliminates bottleneck at factory.

Other Consequences

➤ More difficult to implement.
➤ Initial invocation on externalized object may be expensive.

➤ Creation of object reference occurs in a separate process from the object implementation. May not be possible in all CORBA implementations.

Rescaling This Solution to Other Levels

Separating the objects from the factory that creates them is a technique that could be applied at all levels. It is increasingly important at higher levels of the architectural model as factories are more likely to be potential bottlenecks if the same process is responsible for both creating and managing objects. If threads are available at the system level and objects can be accessed from multiple processes, then the need to separate factories from other object implementations is reduced.

Related Solutions

➤ OMG Persistent Object Service—The Independent Objects pattern will often need to store a persistent image of the object that can be accessed separately by an implementation other than the factory. Therefore, using the OMG Persistent Object Service is one method of externalizing the object in the process of relocating it elsewhere.

➤ OMG Externalization Service—This CORBAservice could be used independently of the OMG Persistent Object Service to move the object implementation to a separate process.

➤ Instance Reference—This pattern supports the Independent Objects pattern by providing information about the object that will allow it to be activated by any implementation, not just the factory that created it.

Example

The ability to implement this pattern is dependent upon the capabilities of the underlying ORB. Specifically, the ORB has to be able to create an implementation and object reference separately from the registration of an implementation with the Object Request Broker. This is a key element, as a factory needs to be able to create object references for an implementation without registering itself as a provider of the implementation. If an implementation needs to be registered in order to create an object reference, then the factory should register an implementation for the object, create the object reference, and then subsequently deregister itself as an implementation prior to processing additional ORB events.

A detailed example of a possible implementation of this patterns follows.

1. The factory must be able to create the object reference and externalize the object in a location that is accessible by the process that will manage the object's implementation.

    /* Call database to return create an object of specific type and to return the Persistent Identifier (PID), table name, and database */

    ```
    create_object("DATABASE 19", "IMAGE_OBJECTS", &PID);
    ```

    /* Create reference data with PID, table name, database */

    ```
    ORB_ReferenceData id;

    sprintf(impl_id_string, "%d %s %s", PID, "IMAGE_OBJECTS",
            "DATABASE 19");
    ```

    /* Add Instance Reference to CORBA reference data. */

    ```
    id._buffer = strdup(impl_id_string);
    id._length = id._maximum = strlen(impl_id_string) + 1;
    ```

    /* Perform a BOA create with the reference data */

    ```
    object_ref = CORBA_BOA_create(CORBA_DEC_BOA_OBJECT, ev, &id,
            DS_dt_OBJ, dataobj_impl);
    ```

2. The implementation must be able to internalize the object instance when the object implementation has been activated by the ORB.

    /*Return PID, tablename and database from object reference */

    ```
    id = CORBA_BOA_get_id(CORBA_DEC_BOA_OBJECT,&ev,
            object_reference);
    if(lid._buffer) { fprintf(stderr, "Object_Not_Found\n");
    sscanf(id._buffer, "%ul, %d %s", &PID, tableName, databaseName);
    ```

    /* Call database and get object pointer using PID, table name and database */

    ```
    image = get_object(PID);
    ```

    /* Use object pointer to complete implementation */

    ```
    image->convertToSunRaster();
    ```

3. The object implementation must ensure the integrity of the object instance in the event of failure. In this example, the object is retrieved from the database each time a method is invoked. An alternative implementation would check to see if the object is already in memory before retrieving it from the database. In such a case, care must be taken to periodically commit any changes to the object to the datastore so, in the event of a failure, the client

is aware of the current object state. In this example, it is assumed that in the underlying object representation, which is hidden from the client, the object has a commit() operation, which syncs its current state with its persistent image stored in the database.

```
image->commit();
```

Background

It is often desirable to provide an object implementation that exists separately from the factory that creates objects. Frequently, if objects are collocated with the factory that creates them, a performance bottleneck may occur at the factory server. A developer may want to bring up separate implementation in close proximity to the client application for performance reasons. This allows each client to invoke on an object implementation that is separate from the implementations being invoked on by other clients.

When initially developing objects with CORBA implementations, there are two readily apparent basic approaches to object creation. The first approach is to have objects create themselves and publish their object reference in a place where it can be located by client applications (files, OMG Naming Service, OMG Trader Service, etc.). This approach is the most common of early users of CORBA. However, in non-object-oriented language bindings, confusion arises in later distinguishing between the object implementation and the objects themselves. The second approach uses a technique similar to the one described in the OMG Lifecycle services, where a factory creates objects and returns them to client applications. Since an implementation is required in order to create an object and generate an object reference, most frequently, the factory that creates the objects shares a process with the object implementation of its created object references. However, if the factory is heavily used and generates lots of objects that are accessed frequently, it may be desirable to completely decouple the creation of objects from their access and use. In addition, this decoupling could allow a more optimal placement of the implementation of unshared objects (used by a single user or group) rather than requiring them to be collocated with the factory implementation.

Initially, the need to separate objects from their factory occurred in an effort to eliminate a performance bottleneck at the factory. Originally, the factory and all of the implementations for its objects existed in the same process. This resulted in one process handling all requests for object creation along with all object access for every object in the system. As the system grew, some means of separating object creation from object access and manipulation was desired. Also, while it was desirable that object creation remained centralized, clients wanted to bring up object implementation for their objects on their local machine.

Through experimentation, it was realized that if the factory created an object, but was not available as an implementation for that object, then the object reference was still valid. Furthermore, when the client invoked on the object, the ORB would search for registered implementations for that object type. If a registered implementation was not available, it would proceed to start whichever program was registered in the implementation repository as containing the implementation for that object type. Once started, the method would be located in the newly activated implementation and executed. Within the method, the object could be located, or if not currently in use, it could be internalized using the information contained in the reference data of the object reference. When new objects were accessed by a client, they could be treated in an identical manner, locating the object in the implementation if it was already in use, or internalizing the object, if accessed for the first time in a particular session.

By decoupling the implementation in this manner, the ORB implementation would permit the activation of an implementation on behalf of the client making the request. This allowed the configuration of the ORB implementation activation process to bring up the implementation on the local machine of the client and also, by not allowing clients to share object implementations, made it possible for each user to have his or her own separate implementation. While the particular desired effect was possible due to a specific vendor's ORB implementation features, by decoupling the object implementation, the source code was still portable across the same CORBA binding with no adverse effects to the clients. Furthermore, if other vendors had similar configuration features, they could be used without adverse consequences.

CHAPTER FIVE

Improving Object Implementations

The second set of patterns modifies the implementation of objects in order to better manage system complexity. Included in this section are patterns that highlight possible uses of lower-level object services within an object implementation. Many of these patterns require complex changes to the object implementations, but such complexity is hidden from the client applications. Many of the CORBAservices are at this architectural level, such as the OMG Lifecycle, Persistent Object, Property, and Externalization Service. When creating implementations from these patterns, an emphasis should be placed upon using the CORBAservices to ease their creation and to provide a common, standard basis for application development.

DYNAMIC ATTRIBUTES

This pattern reduces the need for large numbers of attributes in OMG IDL, which greatly increases the complexity of a system.

INSTANCE REFERENCE

This pattern maps from the object implementation to a specific object instance in a non-object-oriented CORBA binding.

OBJECT WRAPPER

This pattern allows the integration of legacy applications into an object-oriented architecture.

LOCK

This pattern provides for access control between clients and details the use of the OMG Concurrency Control Service.

> Keep data types and user-defined structures shallow. Clients will not be fond of "going deep" to set and retrieve data from complex types. Provide convenience functions to set and retrieve values from complex user-defined data types to provide fewer points of maintenance for such application hot spots.

Dynamic Attributes

Most Applicable Scale: Application

Solution Type: Software

Solution Name: Dynamic Attributes

Intent: To change the attributes of an object without being forced to recompile the object's OMG IDL.

Primal Forces: Management of Functionality

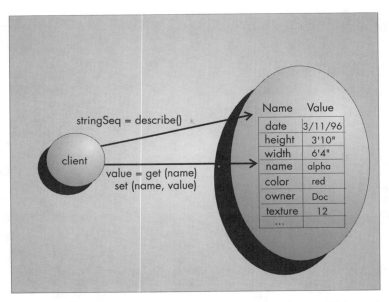

Figure 5.1 Dynamic Attributes pattern enables the modifying of object attributes at run-time.

Applicability at This Scale

1. Multiple attributes are exposed in the OMG IDL. For example, these attributes may include domain-specific information.
2. There are multiple uses of the OMG IDL or the implementations, some of which may use different attributes.
3. Changes to the OMG IDL require recompilation. Developers indicate that they have concerns about the frequency of recompilation.
4. The attributes change from time to time based on changes in the requirements or other factors.
5. Multiple software modules are dependent upon the OMG IDL definitions.
6. There is a need to reduce the number and complexity of the interfaces used by client applications.
7. There is a need for a notion of type, or secondary type, separate from the OMG IDL interface type.

Solution Summary

Refrain from defining large numbers of attributes in the OMG IDL. Defining large amounts of attributes in an object's OMG IDL definition will result in the generation of large numbers of interfaces in the language binding. Frequently, if an object has a large number of interfaces, it will be harder to understand and require a larger effort to implement and to maintain over time. Furthermore, any changes to the object attributes will have an effect on all clients written to use the IDL definitions. Instead, limit the attribute OMG IDL definitions to a few that are fundamental to the object definition and are unlikely to ever change, such as the specification of secondary types.

Define in the OMG IDL a general accessor function to attribute values. Leave the management of attribute values up to the object's implementation. This allows attribute values to be updated in the implementation without necessarily changing existing client and server applications. Only the clients that rely on the newly defined attributes need to be changed in order to accommodate new attributes in the system. Furthermore, the overall number of interfaces is greatly reduced, making the system easier to understand and more flexible in its ability to handle changes in its attribute definitions.

Often, supporting interfaces may need to be defined to support generic accessor functions. For example, it is frequently desirable to provide methods that permit the retrieval of attribute names and types from an object. Also, if it is desirable for the client to dynamically alter the object definitions, then supporting interfaces can be provided (i.e., add, remove, change). Generic accessor methods and supporting functions are essential in developing intelligent clients capable of adapting system changes.

Benefits

➤ Fewer interfaces are generated.
➤ Attributes can be modified without changing the OMG IDL.
➤ Interfaces are more stable, increasing the robustness of the architecture.

Other Consequences

➤ The OMG IDL no longer lists what an object's attributes are. One has to examine the object's implementation or provide some other means to retrieve an object's attributes.
➤ Objects are no longer definable by a Data Definition Language (DDL)—State information is no longer just the value of attributes. More work is required to map from object state to DDL, for example, in order to work with the Direct Access Protocol of the OMG Persistent Object Service.
➤ Any service based on object attributes being defined in OMG IDL will no longer be compatible with objects defined in this manner.

Variations of This Solution

The OMG Property Service is a CORBAservice for dynamic attribute creation and modification. For many CORBA developers, the OMG Property Service will be a popular, commercially available solution addressing the need for dynamic properties. However, for some vertical domain frameworks it may be desirable to encapsulate the OMG Property Service interfaces with a set of interfaces tailored for a specialized set of applications. In such cases, it would be best to use the OMG Property Service interfaces in the implementation of a more specialized set of interfaces.

A variant of this pattern is to create an object for the encapsulation of tabular data. This variant is most often used in conjunction with relational databases where a need exists to represent the cells, rows, and columns that match a relational query. This variant includes accessor functions similar to the original pattern, with property names being replaced by one or more row-column fields. It is expected that the eventual standardization of the OMG Collection Service will provide an ordered collection object, thereby eliminating the most obvious need for a table object. This variant may still have some utility where the self-describing nature of the describe() operation is desired in order to detail the internal schema of a tabular object.

Rescaling This Solution to Other Levels

This pattern is generically useful at all levels. In particular, it is optimally useful for all implementations where attributes are apt to change. The ability to obtain attribute information at run-time using interfaces like the describe() operation enables the development of flexible architectures that can be applied to a wide range of domains.

When a client is likely to set/get many attributes in a session, the overhead of repeatedly accessing the remote object over a network may become an issue. By having the attributes exist in the object implementation rather than in the OMG IDL specification, it is easy to greatly increase performance by adding a set of operations to get and set many attribute values at the same time. For example, complementary operations to the following operations:

```
any get (in string attributeName );
void set (in string attributeName, in any value);
```

would be the following:

```
typedef sequence <string> NameList;
typedef sequence <any> ValueList;

ValueList get_many(in NameList);
void set_many (in NameList names, in ValueList values);
```

Of course, care must be taken to have a well-established convention for returning exception information. Many implementations define an exception structure on a set that returns a list of the attributes for which the operation fails, with the assumption being that the attributes not returned were set successfully. On a multiple get it may be advantageous to avoid returning an exception, so at least some values are returned. In the event that the data is unavailable for one or more of the attributes, a value may be defined to indicate that the data was not available and by convention the client could test for unavailable data after retrieving the attribute list from the object.

Related Solutions

➤ Component Architecture—This pattern provides for generic access to a collection of system services. The generic accessor functions to object attributes could also be the basis for a generic means of accessing information in all system objects.

➤ OMG Property Service—Also provides a means to associate and modify object properties at run-time. If available, this service could be used to implement the Dynamic Attributes pattern or potentially replace it, if its capabilities are sufficient for a particular environment.

➤ OMG Collection Service—This service could provide a place to store Named Value pairs at run-time.

Example

Consider an OMG IDL framework that defines a general container class with dynamic attributes. There is a single OMG IDL attribute type that defines a secondary type of the container object. The actual properties depend on the implementation of the container class and may be changed via the container class interfaces. The main factory (ft) contains an implementation of container class (dt) objects and a factory that creates container objects. In the actual implementation, the type attribute is one of several predefined types of IMAGE, MAP, TEXT, and so on. By making "type" a string rather than an enumeration, the implementation may support the creation of dt objects with new secondary types at any time. Each of the secondary types is associated with a lengthy list of named attributes. The list is currently compiled into the factory although they could also be stored in a database accessed during run-time.

The OMG IDL for the dt object in the framework is shown in the following:

```
interface imageObject {
        exception NOT_FOUND {};
        exception BAD_TYPECODE {};
        typedef sequence<NamedValue> attrList;
        readonly attribute string objType;


        any get (in string attributeName)
               raises ( NOT_FOUND );
        void set (in string attributeName, in any value)
               raises (NOT_FOUND,BAD_TYPECODE );
        attrList describe ();
};
```

In the implementation of the imageObject interface, a list of attributes would be managed using the get and set interfaces, with a describe interface to allow a client to examine the available attributes at run-time.

Background

Many objects have one or more data attributes associated with them. OMG IDL allows developers to define the data attributes for a class in the OMG IDL definition. The OMG IDL can provide accessor operations for the exposed state of an object. Object attributes are less reusable and prone to change far more often than the other interface information. If the objects have many attributes, these changes cause substantial modifications to the interface and application software. Modifying OMG IDL can be a cumbersome process that necessitates modification of multiple programs that depend upon a single interface. Some means of altering an object's attributes without recompiling the OMG IDL is desirable.

This pattern was first discovered when developing a CORBA 1.1 layer on top of Digital's ACAS product. There was no OMG IDL compiler or method to automatically generate marshaling code, so we had to develop the marshaling code ourselves. Rather than develop our own OMG IDL compiler and stub generator, we agree on a fixed set of interfaces and developed code to marshal only the stable set of interfaces. To allow the addition of attributes for different object types, we defined interfaces to define a general accessor mechanism using DS_dt_get. The specific attributes which were available were defined within the implementation and could be changed without affecting the clients or the marshaling code for the operation. A method to retrieve the attributes was also provided (DS_dt_describe), as well as methods to dynamically add new attributes (DS_dt_Add) and to remove attributes that were added at run-time (DS_dt_delete). When ORB products matured so this was no longer necessary, we realized that having stable interfaces greatly increased system interoperability and so we maintained the implementation of Dynamic Attributes.

Instance Reference

Most Applicable Scale: Application

Solution Type: Software

Solution Name: Instance Reference

Intent: To optimize performance of object instances through shared server implementations. To provide a mechanism of mapping from the implementation of an object's interface to a specific object instance.

Primal Forces: Management of Performance, Management of Functionality

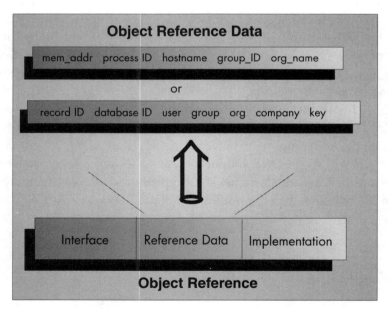

Figure 5.2 The Instance Reference pattern helps preserve an OMG IDL object model in a non-object-oriented language binding.

Applicability at This Scale

1. The programming language used is not object-oriented, such as C, COBOL, or others.
2. Multiple object instances are needed or desirable.
3. CORBA is used as the infrastructure mechanism.
4. For performance reasons, it is desirable to implement multiple object instances per server process.

Solution Summary

The CORBA specification allows the insertion of Reference Data into an object reference as part of the BOA_create call. The reference data is an identifier defined by the object implementation prior to the creation of the object reference. In a non-object-oriented binding, it is the responsibility of the implementation that receives an object reference to determine which object instance is being referred to. Therefore, an implementation has to put whatever information it needs to locate object instances into the reference data so that in later calls when an object reference is received, the object instance can be located and the requested operation completed. An explanation of how to create object instances, and thereby object-oriented implementations, is detailed in the following.

When creating objects, create information on how to access the particular object instance. This information should provide enough information such that any implementation of that object should be capable of locating the object instance. Therefore, any references to in-memory data or areas not accessible by all implementations should not be used. References to files or database identifiers may be useful if they are always available to all object implementations. Often, many location elements are combined into a single string that is later parsed out by object implementations.

Store this information in the object Reference Data of an object reference. Reference Data is a standard CORBA type and is a part of the CORBA object reference. It is a parameter to the CORBA::BOA_create() operation, used to create object references. It is important to remember that the Reference Data is set when the object reference is created and is immutable, and cannot be changed at a later date. So, the selection of useful Reference Data is a critical part of designing implementations that can handle *stale* object reference. Stale object references are those for which a valid object instance no longer exists.

In each object method, within a non-OO language binding, each implementation method needs to provide a mapping from the object implementation to the object instance. In the current non-OO bindings, an object reference is passed to an object implementation as part of method invocations. The object Reference Data can be extracted from the object reference using the CORBA:: BOA::get_id() operation on a specified object. This is the same reference data used to create the object, and is intended to be used by implementations to map to specific object instances. Therefore, in each object method, the reference data should be extracted and used to access the object instance. The object instance data should then be used in completing the object invocation.

For objects with many interfaces, this mapping can be encapsulated in a convenience function, as discussed in the Library pattern.

Benefits

➤ Allows for multiple implementations for an interface.
➤ Provides a mapping to an object instance.
➤ Allows you to approximate OO programming in a non-OO environment.

Other Consequences

➤ Increased code complexity.
➤ Danger of requiring a specific implementation.

Rescaling This Solution to Other Levels

This solution is rather specific to the application level. It could also be used whenever you need a finer-grained identification mechanism than the one provided by the application interfaces.

Related Solutions

➤ Fine-Grained Framework—This pattern will often require support from the Instance Reference to dynamically detect whether or not a server access is needed to locate the information stored within the object being invoked upon.
➤ OMG CORBA C binding—Provides the details of the binding and how the reference data may be used for mapping to object instances.
➤ Digital C's ObjectBroker v2.5 System Integrator's Guide—Provides some details on how to implement object implementations using the C binding.

Example

Here is an example of how using this pattern in the C binding uses ObjectBroker v2.5:

1. Create the object and its associated data:

   ```
   object_memory_ptr = create_new_object();
   ```

2. In the creation of the object, create an Instance Reference. Remember that the reference data is permanent and cannot be changed throughout the lifetime of the object. By referring to a specific host and process id the object can be tied to the lifetime of a particular process. If another implementation receives an object reference with reference data that it did not create (for example, different pid and/or host), then it recognizes that the object reference is stale (object it refers to no longer exists) and can return the proper exception.

   ```
   ObjectDataList **impl_ptr;
   ORB_ReferenceData id;

   impl_ptr = (ObjectDataList**)malloc(sizeof(ObjectDataList*));
   *(ObjectDataList**(impl_ptr = object_memory_ptr;
   gethostname(hostname, MAX_HOSTNAME_SIZE);
   sprintf(impl_id_string, "%ul %d %s", impl_ptr, getpid(), hostname);
   ```

3. Add Instance Reference to CORBA reference data.

   ```
   id._buffer = strdup(impl_id_string);
   id._length = id._maximum = strlen(impl_id_string) + 1;
   ```

4. Use Reference Data in creating the object reference.

   ```
   object_ref = CORBA_BOA_create(CORBA_DEC_BOA_OBJECT,ev,&id,
                   DS_dt_OBJ,dataobj_impl);
   ```

5. Define a way to map from the implementation to the object instance when the object reference is passed by the client.

   ```
   ObjectDataList* GetObjectPointer(CORBA_Object object_reference) {
         ORB_ReferenceData id;
         ObjectDataList *object_impl_pointer;
         long pid;
         char* hostname;
         CORBA_Environment ev;

         id=CORBA_BOA_get_id(CORBA_DEC_BOA_OBJECT,&ev,
             object_reference);
         if(!id._buffer) return ((ObjectDataList*)NULL);
         sscanf(id._buffer, "%ul, %d %s", &object_impl_ptr, &pid, hostname);
         if (pid != getpid()) return ((ObjectDataList*)NULL);

         return((ObjectDataList*) *(ObjectDataList**)object)impl_ptr);
   }
   ```

6. Insert a mapping routine in server skeleton.

```
void fooImpl_set(CORBA_Object object, CORBA_Environment *ev,
        CORBA_string propertyname, CORBA_any *value) {
    ObjectDataList *node_list;

    if(!(node_list = GetNodePointer(object))) {
        CORBA_set_exception(CORBA_DEC_BOA_OBJECT, ev,
            CORBA_SYSTEM_EXCEPTION,
            ex_CORBA_INV_OBJREF, NULL);
        return;
    }
}
```

Background

In non-object-oriented language bindings, the CORBA specification does not map as cleanly as it does in an object-oriented language. For example, in the C language bindings, the CORBA interfaces map to independent functions, whose first parameter indicates the object/interface the operation is being invoked upon. As an implementor of a CORBA implementation in a non-OO environment, it is critical to be aware of the intent of certain portions of the CORBA specification. In particular, in a C implementation of the CORBA specification, a client is only mapped to an implementation. It is up to the developer to complete the mapping of an object reference to a specific object within an implementation. CORBA provides an object reference data for exactly this purpose. When an object reference is created, it is the responsibility of the object creator to provide enough information in the reference data so that an implementation of the object can locate the specific object created during an invocation. CORBA does not force the use of the reference data, nor does it provide guidelines to aid in performing this mapping. Experience has shown that this mapping is critical to mimic object-oriented behavior in order to provide consistency of programming styles across the various CORBA language bindings. Providing an Instance Reference to map to a specific object simplifies implementation development and allows the sharing of component designs across languages.

For example, in the C language CORBA binding, one of the most common mistakes made by naive CORBA-based application developers is to confuse an object's implementation with the object itself. Many new developers begin working with CORBA by defining one or two classes in OMG IDL and examining the interaction between a minimally implemented client and server application. With the C binding, a client invocation will map to a method in an implementation and execute whatever code is defined within the server method skeleton. Without a proper understanding of the larger picture, a developer will simply insert within the server side whatever code he or she wants the client to invoke. For a single object, this method works just fine. The problem arises when additional objects are added to the system. If the implementation is confused with the object, a developer would be tempted to either define a new class in OMG IDL, so the client can access a different object, or provide a different implementation of the class and put the code for the new object in the new implementation. While this approach works for small systems, it works by treating CORBA as a simple communication mechanism and ignores the intent of the CORBA system architecture in a non-object-oriented environment. New developers will frequently develop a mistaken belief that they understand the CORBA model because they can control which code set is being executed.

Introducing the use of reference data to define and support separate objects within an implementation at this point is difficult, as there may be a tendency for a developer to use the working application as proof that they somehow got the use of CORBA right. However, as the system grows and many objects are introduced, the system quickly becomes unwieldy and impossible to manage. Having dozens of implementations supporting a mere dozen of objects rapidly degrades the performance of a CORBA-based application and creates a system that is extremely difficult to manage and maintain. By having code that does not match the intended model of CORBA implementations in non-object-oriented language bindings, application development becomes confusing and increasingly more difficult, leading developers to erroneously question the quality of the binding, or the feasibility of using CORBA. However, by properly understanding how non-object-oriented bindings are managed and the proper use of the Basic Object Adapter (BOA) reference data in object creation and subsequent accesses, such tragedies can be easily avoided.

Digital's ObjectBroker was one of the early products to support the CORBA C binding. When reading through the earlier manuals of ObjectBroker, it quickly becomes apparent that, on the server side, there really is no notion of objects. The ORB is responsible for mapping a client's request to a specific implementation; however, managing the object instances is entirely up to the server developer. When receiving a request, the server receives an object reference and has to provide the requested information back to the client. If no means of distinguishing between the object references is provided by the creator of the object reference, then the server has no choice but to respond to all requests for instances of a class in an identical manner. Since one of the fundamental notions of object-oriented-ness is that objects encapsulate state, this is rarely acceptable for any but the most basic of applications. If the realization that the server developer has to provide a mapping to object instances is not made, then a naive CORBA developer may mistakenly believe that object instances must be defined in OMG IDL and that the object implementation is indistinguishable from the object itself. The object identifier pattern provides a clarification of the differences between implementation and object in a non-object-oriented binding. It also provides a description of a general mechanism for storing instance information within the reference data of an object reference, which can be used by server implementations to map to a specific object instance.

Object Wrapper

Most Applicable Scale: Application

Solution Type: Software

Solution Name: Object Wrapper

Intent: To integrate legacy applications into an object-oriented architecture, and perform this integration in an inexpensive and timely manner. The resulting integration should be functional and robust.

Primal Forces: Management of Functionality, Management of Complexity

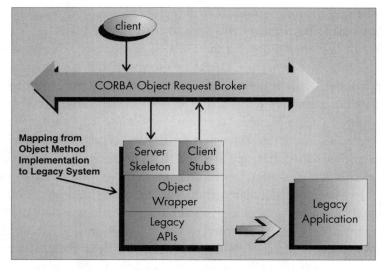

Figure 5.3 An Object Wrapper is an essential tool for developing migratable systems using a mix of underlying applications and services.

Applicability at This Scale

1. An object interface is desired for applications without an OMG IDL interface.
2. Developer has limited control over the existing application.
3. Legacy applications may have additional constraints or execution prerequisites, for example, proximity to a database may be required.
4. Application documentation and source code are not always available.
5. Unable or unwilling to change the internal implementation of the application.
6. Desire a large amount of flexibility in migrating the legacy application to a new system over time.

Solution Summary

Define an OMG IDL interface for the legacy application. This interface describes an object-based front end for the legacy system and should conform to the current domain object model. The OMG IDL interface should only expose those attributes and operations that are needed by other CORBA clients and services. The interface should be defined to represent the ideal object-based interface desired for the system and should be at a high enough level of abstraction to allow for many implementations to potentially provide the service described. It is counterproductive to directly model the existing behavior of the legacy system as the goal is to provide a useful object interface, not to minimize the effort in mapping from the interface to the existing system.

Provide an implementation for the OMG IDL interface. This implementation provides a bridge between the CORBA environment and the legacy system. The implementation should be collocated with the client interfaces to the legacy system. The wrapper communicates to the legacy system using its native communication facilities. CORBA clients communicate to the application via its OMG IDL interfaces. Client applications and application services view the legacy system as a standard OMG IDL-specified CORBA object, or perhaps as operations on a larger distributed object, depending on the OMG IDL definitions used.

The object wrapper implementation can be quite involved. However, it is important that the implementation maintains the encapsulation of the legacy system behind the OMG IDL interface. It is the encapsulation of the implementation details that allows the legacy system to be utilized as a replaceable component in a distributed environment. For some systems, it may be desirable to have many object wrappers, or to only define interfaces for the control of legacy applications. For example, if a legacy application has access to substantially faster transfer rates than are available through an ORB, an object wrapper may provide an object-based interface for the control of the underlying application, which manages the actual data transfer through proprietary communication mechanisms.

Benefits

> ➤ CORBA clients can access the legacy system through an object-oriented interface.
> ➤ Existing application functionality is unchanged.
> ➤ Object operations can be provided by the legacy system or a new method implementation without affecting the client. This allows the migration to occur gradually, even on a per-operation basis.

Other Consequences

> ➤ Implementation of the object wrapper can be an involved process and require detailed knowledge about the behavior of the legacy system. Developers must provide the complete mapping between requested operations and the legacy system.
> ➤ Object wrappers may inherit the limitations of the legacy system; for example, they may be constrained to execute on a particular file system or host in order to execute the client code to communicate to the legacy application. At least, however, the clients of the object wrapper will not share the legacy application constraints and can access the object wrapper as a normal CORBA object without concern for its physical location or specific implementation.
> ➤ Provides a layer of indirection from the client application to the legacy system, which could potentially impact performance.

Rescaling This Solution to Other Levels

Object wrappers are applicable at all levels. It is an invaluable tool for providing a well-architectured interface to preexisting non-CORBA-compliant applications.

Related Solutions

> ➤ Gateway—A variant of an object wrapper, which is used to provide an object in one object model or domain with the interfaces of another model or

domain. The implementation serves as an object proxy that communicates with the object in its native domain in order to provide the requested service.

➤ Layered Architecture—A large-scale use of object wrapping principles to provide a layer of abstraction and encapsulation over a set of interfaces.

➤ *The Essential CORBA:* Chapter 8, "Object Wrapping" (Mowbray & Zahavi 1995)—Details a wide range of examples of using object wrapping with other technologies.

Example

Object Wrapping has been detailed extensively in other works, such as Chapter 8, "Object Wrapping" in *The Essential CORBA*. An example of object wrapping is an object-based interface to a file system such as the following interface definition:

```
interface FileDatabase {
        typedef sequence <octet> octetSeq;
        exception NOT_FOUND { string errorMsg; };

        octetSeq getFile ( in string filename )
                raises ( NOT_FOUND );
}
```

While the OMG IDL interface is a poor example of abstraction, it does provide an object-based representation for a file system. Once a client obtains a reference to an object with a FileDataBase interface, it invokes the getFile() method and obtain a sequence of octets containing the binary representation of the file. The implementation of the FileDatabase object contains code to map the filename string to the command used to obtain a file in the underlying file system, and also code to map the file into a sequence of octets, which is returned to the client application. While such code is not completely trivial, it is substantially simpler than the implementation of a complete file system.

> As much as possible, interfaces should be decoupled from one another. This increases the flexibility of the system by allowing the implementations to be placed in disjoint locations.

Background

Object wrapping was an early technique for developers of object-based systems to leverage existing technology in an object environment. The goal of object wrapping is to make existing systems appear to be objects in a system regardless of how they may be implemented internally. While it takes some amount of effort to create an object wrapper, generally the effort required to map from an object interface to the legacy system is a fraction of the cost of redeveloping the legacy system using object technology.

Lock

Most Applicable Scale: Application

Solution Type: Technology

Solution Name: Lock

Intent: How to manage concurrent access to objects, avoiding concurrency problems such as race conditions and deadlock.

Primal Forces: Management of Functionality

Applicability at This Scale

1. In a distributed environment, it is possible for one or more clients to attempt to access an object simultaneously. There are some operations that must be performed atomically in order to preserve data integrity.

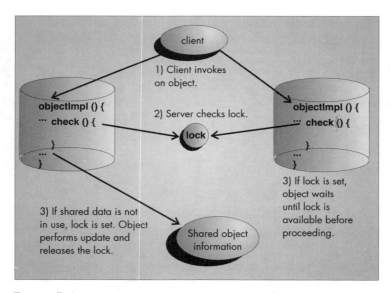

Figure 5.4 A Lock provides a useful tool for object implementations to control access to shared data and services.

2. A method of concurrency control is needed to control access to certain objects or object data in order to guarantee that only one client may have access at a time. The client application should not be concerned with access control policies.
3. Within the implementation of an object, a service may need to control access to some portions of its data to ensure that only one process may write or modify a data segment at a time.

Solution Summary

To coordinate access between object implementations and shared information in a CORBA environment, use a lock object that is independent from the processes involved in accessing the shared information. One such lock to manage concurrency control is provided by the OMG Concurrency Control Service, specifically, the parts that refer to the handling of non-transactional clients.

It is important to understand that the lock referred to in the OMG Concurrency Control Service is itself an object, rather than being a constraint placed upon another object. It is up to the implementation to set the lock to the appropriate values and to verify that the lock is appropriately checked before access is allowed to the protected data.

The OMG Concurrency Control Service is an ideal service to implement, if it is not provided by an ORB vendor, as it is small and its documentation is very straightforward. In practice, there is seldom any reason to ever expose the interfaces of the OMG Concurrency Control Service to the clients of other objects, as its primary purpose is to coordinate actions between object implementations.

Benefits

➤ This pattern uses the standard OMG Concurrency Control Service.
➤ Allows for different processes to execute in parallel and coordinate in accessing critical sections of code.

Other Consequences

➤ This pattern is not currently available on all ORB implementations; however, it is easy to implement.
➤ The use of locks entails a significant performance hit, especially if critical sections are accessed often. Parallelism is often a compensating gain, but it has its own side effects.

Rescaling This Solution to Other Levels

Concurrency is primarily an object implementation concern, so it is unlikely to have any applicability at higher levels where the emphasis is on architectural and interface-level concerns.

Related Solutions

➤ Repository Architecture—This pattern could be used as the system-level equivalent of Object Locking. The Repository Architecture is often implemented by using the OMG Concurrency Control Service to coordinate data access between processes.

➤ OMG Concurrency Service—This CORBAservice is the standard way to manage object-level locking and is described quite well in the OMG Common Object Services Specification (COSS) documents.

➤ Semaphores, Critical Sections—Object locking has been around for a while. The OMG Concurrency Control Service provides an object-oriented specification that embodies existing locking techniques.

➤ Coordinators: Using Access Patterns for Parallel Programming (Jurgen Knopp, PLoP '95)—A pattern language for architecture-independent concurrency control in a parallel system.

Example

A simple use of the OMG Concurrency Control follows the standard sequence of operations listed in the following:

1. Obtain the object reference for the OMG Concurrency Control Service LockSetFactory from the OMG Naming or Trader Service.
2. Invoke the LockSetFactory::create() operation to get a lock for the object. Maintain this lock in a variable that can be accessed from everywhere where the object needs to be locked, unlocked, and destroyed.

   ```
   foo = LockSetFactory::create();
   ```

3. To lock the object, invoke the lock method on the lock with the appropriate mode:

   ```
   foo::lock( lock_mode::read );
   ```

4. Before accessing any critical or protected sections of code, check the status of the lock by invoking the try_lock method:

   ```
   foo::try_lock(lock_mode::read);
   ```

If the lock returns TRUE, then it is safe to access the critical section of code. Otherwise, the client must either wait and try again later or perform some other action such as throw an exception or attempt to use some other object.

5. After exiting the critical section, the client needs to unlock the critical section by freeing the lock using the unlock method:

```
foo::unlock( lock_mode::read );
```

Background

The OMG Concurrency Control Service is used to provide locking of critical sections of code and shared application data. The OMG Object Management Architecture Model defines a lock object that an implementation must check before allowing access to an application's data. The service defines many modes of access to allow for differentiating between read, write, upgrade, intentional read, and intentional write access.

CHAPTER SIX

Modifying Client Stubs and Other Tricks

The next class of performance-related patterns involves modifying either the object interfaces or implementations in order to reduce the number of calls across the network in a distributed system. Network calls have important performance consequences. System performance can be increased by minimizing the number of network calls; therefore, reducing the number of calls is a key form of performance optimization. A brief synopsis of patterns in this category is presented in the following:

LIBRARY SKELETON

This pattern details the modification of client stubs in order to eliminate unnecessary network calls for operations that do not require distributed processing.

FINE-GRAINED FRAMEWORK

This pattern simulates fine-grained objects using caching and shared implementations transparently. This optimizes management of object implementations in order to minimize the number of calls across a network.

LIBRARY

This pattern and the next one provide a detailed justification for commonly used structures in application development. The Library pattern provides a means to enhance code maintainability and reuse in applications.

FRAMEWORK

The Framework pattern provides a means to reuse objects and code through specialization. The pattern allows modification of code for new functionality without changing object abstractions.

Library Skeleton

Most Applicable Scale: Application

Solution Type: Software

Solution Name: Library Skeleton

Intent: To limit the amount of network calls by collocation of clients and object implementations.

Primal Forces: Management of Performance

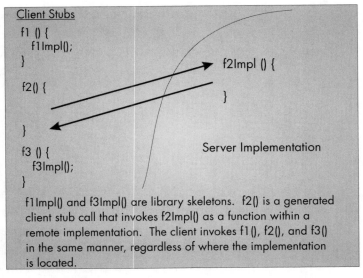

Figure 6.1 The Library Skeleton pattern maintains client-side transparency while providing needed flexibility to application implementors.

Applicability at This Scale

1. There is a need for an increased performance in the client application.
2. Significant time is spent making distributed calls across the network.
3. Some of the functions invoked by the client applications code could potentially be executed anywhere, because they do not require data that resides at a specific location.
4. Some of the functionality and data being requested from the remote object may be available on the client machine.

Solution Summary

First, generate client stubs and server skeletons from OMG IDL definitions. The client stub files will contain the client code necessary to invoke operations on objects. The server skeletons contain the functions called in response to a client invoking a client stub operation. Most, if not all, ORB implementations have an OMG IDL compiler that creates client stubs necessary for invoking operations in remote object implementation. However, for performance reasons, it may be necessary to modify client stubs on a case-by-case basis in order to avoid unnecessary client invocations by performing some of the operations locally.

Remember that objects defined in OMG IDL do not necessarily have to be distributed. In order to improve performance, a developer may remove the marshaling code from one or more generated client stubs, and replace it with the code used on the server side in the object implementation that implements the object operation. In particular, all operations that are implemented as empty functions or can be implemented within the client stub should be moved there. This includes any operations that have predictable, static operations and are not dependent on data that is stored remotely. In practice, the bulk of the operations will need to perform a remote call to the distributed object implementation. However, network calls tend to be expensive enough that even slightly reducing the number of remote calls will result in greatly improved performance.

Clients that use the client stubs maintain implementation transparency as they are invoking on an operation interface identical to the one pregenerated by the IDL compiler. Specifically, when the client invokes a operation in the client stubs, then the message will call the local implementation of the operation, instead of the default behavior of invoking on the remote object. As far as the client is concerned, the client stubs interfaces still provide an architectural software boundary and can later use the pregenerated client stubs without any source code modifications, if desired.

Of course, unlike a completely distributed object implementation, the client will now need to be modified if the library skeleton operations are modified. A prominent danger is that if a remote object is changed to provide new implementations for the library skeleton operations, then the new operations would never be invoked by the client application, which would continue to utilize the client library skeletons. Ideally, the configuration management of the applications would aid in tracking the local and distributed portions of objects. Another benefit is that objects can use Library Skeleton to exist completely in a local implementation. This allows the use of normally distributed objects locally, without the presence of an ORB. This is useful in maintaining software boundaries in applications that may eventually become distributed. Additionally, a library skeleton may be used for debugging in order to isolate errors locally.

Benefits

➤ Allows object implementor flexibility in locating methods remotely or locally.
➤ Increase performance by only making network calls that are absolutely necessary.
➤ A library object adapter is of great benefit in testing code locally before distributing the code to separate processes.
➤ Given the lack of debuggers capable of tracking the changes that occur in the course of an ORB invocation, testing code locally with a library skeleton may be the only method of catching some of the more obscure errors.

Other Consequences

➤ Will need to modify code rather extensively whenever new client stubs are generated, as most ORBs do not currently support local OMG IDL-based application development.

Rescaling This Solution to Other Levels

This pattern is useful wherever OMG IDL definitions are used; that is, everywhere throughout all levels.

Related Solutions

➤ Library—The code to implement library skeletons can be placed in a library to facilitate its replacement with standard distributed calls in order to have a fully remote object implementation.

➤ Framework—Testing and debugging frameworks can combine with the Library Skeleton pattern to provide local testing of CORBA applications.

➤ OMG CORBA Core—The description of the Object Request Broker is a collection of interfaces for the underlying communication mechanisms. The ORB interfaces are much more descriptive and much less complex than the numerous lower-level interfaces they are based upon.

Example

An example of using the Library Skeleton pattern for a simple interface definition follows:

```
interface Envelope {
        exception NOT_OPENED {};

        void Open();
        void Close();

        void Stuff(in string letter)
                raises(NOT_OPENED);
        string GetLetter()
                raises(NOT_OPENED);
};
```

If it is known that the Open() and Close() operations are to be implemented as empty functions (NOPs) in all server implementations of the Envelope interface, then rather than use the default client skeletons, which will invoke the server side Open() and Close() NOPs, modify the client stubs by removing the code created by the OMG IDL compiler and replacing it with the code contained in the server-side implementation, an empty function call, in this case.

Background

When CORBA 1.1 first came out, it was immediately apparent that OMG IDL had many architectural benefits even without the use of an ORB. In order to illustrate the location transparency of an ORB, we developed two identical versions of the framework, one built on top of ACAS 2.1, which was intended to be distributed, and a NO_ORB version, which could be run without an ORB. Essentially, the no-ORB version was a library adapter where the server-side code was compiled and executed locally within the same process in the client. Once CORBA implementations began to appear and after realizing that location of the code was transparent to the client, it became clear that there are some operations that could benefit greatly from being executed locally, whereas others had to be run remotely to be useful (access to shared data stores, etc.).

Therefore, the notion of selectively moving parts of the distributed skeleton code back into the client stubs came about from realizing that 1) it could be performed transparently to the client applications by using shared libraries, 2) there was no risk if it did not work (trivial to change it back) and there was the potential for substantial performance gain (greatly reducing network traffic), 3) not everyone had our experience with library adapters and some may not realize that it was a valid option, and 4) the framework had many operations that were implemented as NOPs but needed to be called in order to preserve the architectural integrity of the framework. Eliminating network traffic on such calls was highly desirable. Therefore, many of the framework classes were split up between local library calls performed within the client stubs and the standard ORB client stub invocation calls to remotely call the operation in the object's implementation. The performance gain was quite large and greatly improved client response time.

> Map integers to explicit longs or shorts, using longs if the length needed is indeterminate.

Fine-Grained Framework

Most Applicable Scale: Application

Solution Type: Software

Solution Name: Fine-Grained Framework

Intent: To define and use fine-grained objects in a distributed system without incurring prohibitive costs in terms of performance and system complexity.

Primal Forces: Management of Performance

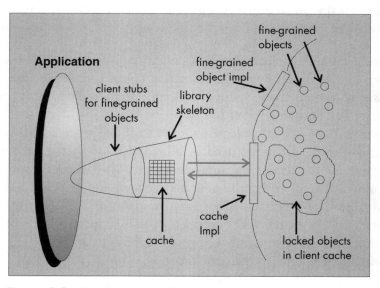

Figure 6.2 The Fine-Grained Framework pattern provides a possible solution in implementing fine-grained objects while lessening the performance penalty of distributed invocations.

Applicability at This Scale

1. There is a large number of object instances that must be implemented or represented.
2. There are performance issues: either with the server implementation, the ORB, or both.
3. The performance problems may be caused by the large number of objects or the large number of invocations.
4. The behavior of clients accessing these object instances is known.

Solution Summary

The default behavior of an OMG IDL-defined fine-grained framework is to invoke a distributed client method for each remote object. In practice, the network overhead of object invocations is sufficient to reduce the performance of applications below acceptable levels. There are two areas where performance concerns can be addressed in the implementation of fine-grained frameworks, in the server-side and the client-side invocation of fine-grained objects.

The first set of techniques is applied at the server. Admittedly, when implementing fine-grained objects, there is little that can be done in the server implementation, as the greatest delays are usually due to network latency. However, some gains can be obtained from the following:

1. Provide multiple objects within a single implementation. A shared server policy and an object implementation that contains multiple object instances is usually a more efficient use of system resources than a server-per-object policy or an unshared server policy.
2. Locate multiple object implementations in a single process. This helps reduce the number of processes needed, allowing more system resources to be available for the remaining implementations. Also, if threads are available, additional threads to handle multiple requests are generally less expensive than additional processes. Most early examples of CORBA use convey the impression that each object implementation is supported by its own process. While this is often convenient, there is nothing to prohibit collocating several implementations in the same process.

The next set of techniques for increasing the performance of a fine-grained framework involve modifications to the client application, specifically the client stubs. It is critical that in providing client-side enhancements that client-side transparency is strictly enforced. A client should always access fine-grained remote objects as if they were remote objects. Any modifications should occur behind the client software boundary, which is specified by the interface to methods in the client stubs. If transparency is maintained, optimizations may be performed within the client stubs, which leverage existing fine-grained object optimization techniques or techniques unique to the CORBA environment.

First, the Library Skeleton pattern may be used to reduce the number of network calls. For example, if some of the operations can be performed locally, then the client stubs can be modified to avoid a remote invocation. Similarly, coarser interfaces can be defined, such as the get_many() operation shown in the Dynamic Attributes pattern, and the client stubs can be modified to perform one coarse operation rather than several smaller operations. Of course, this is only effective if an immediate response of data or operation success is not required. Rarely is this the case.

More commonly, the Library Skeleton pattern can be used to manage an object cache that works in conjunction with a separate cache OMG IDL interface that shares the same server process as the fine-grained objects that it manages. For example, to organize a cache on the client and server side, first organize the object instances into working sets in the object implementation, where objects likely to be used together are in the same set. Next, define an OMG IDL cache interface that allows for a single retrieval operation to retrieve one or more working sets of objects and a single update operation to update one or more working sets of objects. This interface should be used exclusively by the caching mechanisms implemented within the client stubs. Also, if more than a single client is expected to access objects within the implementation at a time, then the object implementation will require concurrency controls to ensure cached object instances are not available for other clients to access simultaneously.

On the client side, within the Library Skeleton, the client stub will have to perform considerable processing in order to manage the object cache. For each object invocation, the following operations will need to be performed, at a minimum:

1. When an object is invoked, the client stub will need to check to see if the object already exists in the object cache. If not, the stub will need to invoke upon the object cache interface to retrieve the requested object and make it available in the local object cache.
2. Once the object is available locally, the client stub can perform the requested operation on the cached object rather than performing a remote invocation.

3. To ensure the integrity of the server-side objects in the event of a client failure, periodically update the server-side objects with the values stored in the Library Skeleton object cache.

Benefits

> Increased expressiveness of domain objects.
> Increased performance when using fine-grained objects.

Other Consequences

> Caching of objects could result in uneven performance from ORB depending on how often objects are in current cache.
> Complexity of cache management is introduced.
> Modifies client stubs, which increases configuration management.

Rescaling This Solution to Other Levels

This pattern only deals with low-level objects and would not scale to the higher levels of software architecture. It is primarily a technique to use existing caching techniques in a CORBA environment.

Related Solutions

> Instance Reference—This pattern details the use of the object reference data, which is a key component in creating an implementation flexible enough for the complex needs of cache management and other techniques of managing fine-grained objects.
> Flyweight Pattern (Gamma et al. 1994)—This pattern details an elegant method for coordinating the control of large numbers of fine-grained objects.

Primal Forces

Management of Performance, Management of Functionality

Example

An excellent example of handling fine-grained objects is the caching mechanisms used in the first distributed prototype of a data interchange framework.

From the beginning of project development, the goal was to maintain CORBA compliance and provide distributed capabilities, even though an ORB was not currently available. Client stubs were provided that invoked library routines. In the case of ft and dt objects, the client stubs provided local object management, and, in the case of the ap, the client stubs provided access to distributed ap implementations. The ap operations transparently migrated the dt objects created by the local factory to the remote ap implementation, before the invocation of the remote operation, and back to the local client, after the conclusion of the operation invocation.

The basic OMG IDL framework consisted of the following objects and their associated operations:

```
ft {
        create_dat(in string type, out dt dataobject)
}

ap {
        exchange(inout dt dataobject)
        convert(in string propertyname, in string desiredFormat,
              inout dt dataobject)
        query(in queryStruct query, out dt dataobject)
        execute(in dtSeq inDataobjects out dtSeq outDataobjects)
}

dt {
        open()
        close()
        destroy()
        get(in string propertyname, out any value)
        set(in string propertyname, in any value)
        describe(out propertyNameSeq names, out propertyTypeSeq types)
}
```

The ft is the framework factory whose sole responsibility is the creation of dt objects. The dt is responsible for managing data that is passed to various system services (ap objects). The ap objects are application services. For the most part, all of the ap objects are distributed services that accept a dt object from the client application, perform a set of operations on the dt object and return it to the client. Each of the dt objects has a set of attributes stored in the implementation that are accessed via the accessor functions (see Dynamic Data Attributes pattern).

In the original framework implementation, the factory client stubs maintain a list of local data objects. When create_dat is called, a new dt is added to a local list of data objects. When any dt operation is called by the client application, the client stubs check the local list to see if the data objects exists. If the data object does not exist, then it returns an exception. Otherwise, the operation is executed locally without accessing the object request broker. The only distributed object is the ap object. When one of the ap objects is accessed by the client (which passes the server a dt object), the dt object is moved from the local application and reconstructed within the remote ap implementation. Any ap accesses to the dt operations are performed on its local dt object. When the dt object is transferred to the ap object, it is removed from the local client. At the conclusion of the execution of the ap method, the dt object is transferred back from the ap implementation to the local client. The client can again access the dt object, and also once again all accesses to the dt object are performed locally.

The key advantage of this early implementation is that the most commonly used operations were performed locally, with the performance advantages of local operations, with only a few key operations requiring remote invocations. Despite the rather large overhead of object migration, the overall performance gain by having two-thirds of the operations performed locally was significant, since the majority of the clients only required remote access once or twice in a particular session. Furthermore, the fact that the dt and ft operation were local objects and the ap objects were distributed remained completely transparent to client applications. Changing the location of the object implementations could have occurred by swapping out the migration-based client stubs with a different set of client stubs generated by an ORB vendor's OMG IDL compiler, without requiring any modification to the client application code.

Background

Often, there is a need for an application to use many fine-grained objects to represent data in a domain. The large number of objects may all be of the same or similar type or may each represent a unique type of objects. Providing an individual implementation for each type of object requires the ORB to maintain a large number of implementations simultaneously. Managing large numbers of objects of the identical type requires a huge number of OMG IDL invocations, which may potentially be across the network, and results in performance becoming a major concern. Often, the object accesses occur in predictable working sets or are accessed in some nonrandom order, such that they could benefit from caching and ordering techniques. The server is overwhelmed by the large number of object accesses, while the client has resources that are not being fully used.

In non-object-oriented language bindings of CORBA, the object implementation developer is typically responsible for providing the mapping between an object's implementation and the specific object being referred to by the client application. In OO bindings this mapping is automatic with few configuration options available. However, sometimes a similar mapping can be created manually by using proprietary replacements to the Object Reference Data maintained by the BOA. At any rate, the pattern of performing this mapping is key for new developers of CORBA and provides many opportunities for performance tuning and optimizations.

Library

Most Applicable Scale: Application

Solution Type: Software

Solution Name: Library

Intent: To establish a single software module for maintenance and extensibility. This module is reused by multiple client applications.

Primal Forces: Management of Functionality, Management of Complexity

Applicability at This Scale

1. It is advantageous to reuse code developed for one application in other applications.

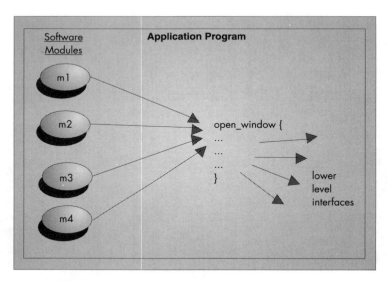

Figure 6.3 The Library pattern introduces an essential tool for managing the complexities of using numerous sets of OMG IDL in application development.

2. There is a need to shorten development timelines or reduce costs through reuse.
3. Many systems reimplement the same functionality.
4. Similar functionality is implemented incompatibly in multiple systems. There is a need for interoperability or portability between systems. There is a need to eliminate unnecessary redundancy and complexity.
5. Development, testing, and maintenance of multiple versions of overlapping software is difficult and expensive.

Solution Summary

First, separate reusable code into its own section. Use language constructs to package the code into easily identified and well-named units. Constructs in C are called functions, in Pascal they are called modules, in Ada they are called packages, in C++ they are called classes, and so on.

Provide a well-defined interface to the code section. Often, the units are small and are called locally for maximum performance. In fact, they are often so small that they are not even software components in their own right but helper functions used to implement components. Therefore, an OMG IDL interface for such code is rarely desired or useful. Additionally, these functions are often closely bound to the operation system or language, making OMG IDL interfaces potentially inappropriate.

Once created, access the library code through its interface, from whichever sections of code you need to access the unit's functionality.

Benefits

➤ Single point of maintenance, reuse of code.
➤ Provides a logical named grouping of lines of code.

Other Consequences

➤ Harder to customize functionality.
➤ Modifying code could have widespread effect.

Variations

Sometimes an OMG IDL interface to software libraries is desirable in order to have clearly defined software boundaries and to allow for future migration of application components.

Rescaling This Solution to Other Levels

At the system level, the same design pattern relates to the reusability of system services, for example, factoring common services out of individual applications into a single shared service. Theoretically, an application can consist of nothing more than a specific arrangement of remote services. At the system level, OMG IDL-defined interfaces are very important as they facilitate remote access and provide a well-defined and accessible interface to the application services.

At the enterprise level, this directly relates to the sharing of system resources. When a service is no longer a convenience but an integral part of an organization, it needs to have a stable set of interfaces and an implementation that is responsive to large numbers of applications and users.

Related Solutions

➤ Profile—Developing a set of libraries within a domain is one piece in a complete profile that should be in place in any enterprise during serious software development.
➤ Framework—This pattern is an organized collection of cooperating libraries and classes. Application Frameworks are more complicated but also far more powerful in developing software applications.
➤ Naming—The example in the Naming pattern provides an identically named set of functions that provide additional flexibility by allowing the Naming Context to be specified. It is useful to compare whether the simplicity of the example presented in the Libraries pattern is more valuable than the flexibility in the Naming pattern. Such tradeoffs are the stuff object-oriented architecture and software development are made of!

Example

One example of this pattern is a pair of convenience functions that access the OMG Naming Service. Normally, to access the OMG Naming Service, a client needs to be familiar enough with the OMG specification to know how to manipulate NameComponents, NamingContexts, CORBA exceptions, CORBA sequences, and other CORBA objects. For many classes of developers, that is an excessive amount to learn in order to perform what are very basic operations, that of storing and retrieving name and associated object references. By using the convenience functions below, all a client needs to know is the name of the object in order to retrieve it, and can store an object simply by passing the object and its name to a convenience function. Such abstraction is a basic component for managing the complexities of distributed object development.

This example differs from the one given in the Naming Pattern (system-level) example in that it does not require the passing of a NamingContext variable to specify where to store and retrieve the name. Rather, a default value is maintained with the convenience function itself, making it less flexible than the one in the Naming example. Often, a developer of library convenience functions will be forced to make a tradeoff between a simple interface with limited functionality versus a more complicated interface with correspondingly greater functionality but also a correspondingly larger learning curve.

```
CORBA_Object getReference(char* objectName) {
      CORBA_Environment ev;
      COSNaming_Name name;
      COSNaming_NameComponent name_comp;
      CORBA_Object object;
      NamingContext ctx = DEFAULT_NAMING_CONTEXT;

      name_comp.id = (char*) strdup (objectName);
      name_comp.kind = NULL;
      name._length = 1;
      name._maximum = 1;
      name._buffer = &name_comp;
      object = CosNaming_NamingContext_resolve(ctx, &ev,
            &name);
      if((ev._major !=CORBA_NO_EXCEPTION) || (CORBA_Object_is_nil(object))) {
            return (OBJECT_NIL);
      }
      return (object);
}

void storeReference( char* objectName, CORBA_Object objref) {
      CORBA_Environment Ev;
      COSNaming_Name name;
      COSNaming_NameComponent name_comp;
      CORBA_Object object;
      NamingContext ctx = DEFAULT_NAMING_CONTEXT;

      name_comp.id = (char*) strdup (objectName);
      name_comp.kind = NULL;
      name._length = 1;
      name._maximum = 1;
      name._buffer = &name_comp;
      CosNaming_NamingContext_rebind(ctx, &ev, &name, objref);
      if (ev._major != CORBA_NO_EXCEPTION) {
            fprintf(stderr, "Failure adding name to Naming Context.\n");
      }
}
```

Background

Often, a developer has a recurring need for a particular functionality in a piece of code. Often, time is spent developing a set of data structures or a way of accessing system functions (i.e., time, shared memory) and, rather than reinvest an equivalent amount of time developing a new code set with the same functionality, a developer would like to reuse the same code in another location. Also, if the same, or nearly identical, code exists in different places already, a developer may want to propagate modifications such as corrections or extensions to all the places where the code is used. If the code is in different locations, this could be a very expensive task. It is desirable from a developer's standpoint to have a single point of maintenance and place for future extensions and improvements because less work is required to maintain the code, and furthermore it reduces the overall complexity of the software.

Also, often a developer has a need to minimize the complexity of a set of interfaces. If a set of interfaces is frequently accessed as a group in a recurring order, it may be advisable to encapsulate them into a single grouping as a method of hiding the underlying complexity of the operations. Often the functionality offered by the interfaces is not required for an application and the need to minimize complexity in development is far greater than the need to change the way a set of interfaces is used for each invocation throughout an application.

Most programmers are already using libraries and looking for ways to reuse useful functions and structures. However, many new developers have some difficulties recognizing the importance of how libraries and reusable code affect the overall maintainability of a software application. Also, the use of libraries to abstract away from complicated and lengthy interfaces is a less common application of libraries that needs to gain more attention in the current software development environments.

The OMG Persistent Object Service is not the only way to provide persistence in a CORBA environment. A factory may create objects whose persistence is transparent to the client application. Also, a specialized BOA may provide persistent objects.

Framework

Most Applicable Scale: Application

Solution Type: Software

Solution Name: Framework

Intent: To provide for software reuse and customization, for software modules incorporating a high level of functionality.

Primal Forces: Management of Functionality, Complexity, Technology Transfer

Applicability at This Scale

1. Some recurring solutions involve several objects and a complex array of interactions and interrelationships between them.
2. It requires a considerable investment of time and effort to develop code that sets up and utilizes a detailed object model, and it would be desirable to maximize the return on this investment by reusing this code.

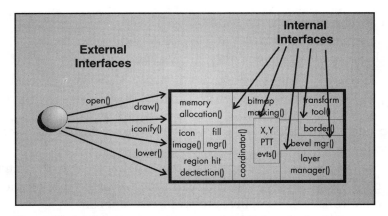

Figure 6.4 The Framework pattern highlights the logical separation of a framework's internal and external interfaces.

3. Making use of such complex code requires understanding a large body of code in some detail and extreme care must be taken to map the framework solution to a particular problem.
4. After reusing a large body of interdependent code, it would be ideal if there is a single point of maintenance and placement of future extensions.
5. Libraries may be an insufficient solution for providing dynamic changes in an application.

Solution Summary

Separate out all of the objects and provide an interface that encapsulates much of the complicated details of how objects are related. Define an external interface to each of the framework components that allows clients to access the functionality of the component. Define internal interfaces that are used within the software component to allow the cooperation of subcomponents in providing the functionality of the external interfaces. Encapsulate the internal interfaces and only allow client access to the external interfaces.

Once the framework components are implemented, provide concise design rules and guidance in how to reuse, customize, and tune system. Provide hooks to allow new functionality without changing interfaces. Anticipate future changes to object hierarchy and provide document and software support for system evolution.

Benefits

➤ Reuse of classes, objects, and code.
➤ Easy to specialize and extend, very dynamic and modifiable.
➤ Reusable over the development of many applications.

Other Consequences

➤ The primary drawback to application frameworks is that they are very expensive to develop.
➤ Costs for framework development occur up front, with the intention of recouping the initial investment through the repeated reuse of the application framework in new applications within the domain.
➤ While there is the potential for reuse, it may not be realized if the framework is poorly understood and developers do not take advantage of it.

Rescaling This Solution to Other Levels

There can be application frameworks at all levels of software development. However, the likelihood that the expense of developing an application framework will be recouped in future developments is highly dependent on the number of future projects developed using the frameworks, which tends to decrease at higher levels.

Related Solutions

➤ Library—A nonhierarchical, less extensible method of code reuse.
➤ Taligent Guide for Reusable Code (Taligent 1994)—Details the creation of object-oriented frameworks
➤ Framework Patterns (Andreas Ruping—PLoP '95)—Describes the construction of reusable frameworks that preserve flexibility and still guarantees consistency.

Example

A well-known example of an Application Framework is the Motif toolkit built upon the Xlib and the Xt interfaces. Unless care is taken to provide an extensible set of library and classes, an application written directly to the Xlib interfaces is likely to be difficult to understand and nearly impossible to extend in order to manage the changing requirements of most systems. The introduction of widgets provided a higher level of abstraction than the base Xlib interfaces and allowed for the extending and specializing of widgets to meet the demands of graphical application development. The hooks are provided in widgets to dramatically alter the functionality of an application with relatively few, if any, modifications to the base classes. Furthermore, the widgets can be extended with a very low probability of affecting widgets currently in use by other parts of the application.

While the widgets contain well-defined hooks for future modifications and extensions (external interfaces), there are many internal interfaces that provide the glue for the management of information encapsulated inside the widget object. Developers can use the Motif libraries by only being aware of how to use a small number of interfaces and by following simple rules of widget construction. The internal complexities of the underlying event management (hit detection, etc.) are hidden beneath a well-designed set of abstracted interfaces.

Background

A library often needs to be completely rewritten to provide extensive specialization of a routine. If object-oriented techniques are used, libraries are cumbersome in providing the inheritance-based specialization with complex interactions between several other classes and objects. Also, libraries are difficult to modify without breaking a large portion of application software. Frameworks are designed for future modification and specialization, and are more robust as classes and code are modified over time. There are two classes of interfaces in an application framework: client interfaces and internal interfaces. The client interfaces are provided for client access and can be easily plugged into an application. The internal interfaces are tightly coupled and are usually not intended for direct client access. The client interfaces represent the well-thought-out abstractions for the client to use and modify in application development.

Modern software development involves the integration and collaboration of thousands of cooperating classes. Even with libraries, there is an overwhelming need for structures that serve to reduce the overall complexity of the system and can be easily configured to meet the changing requirements that mark the software landscape of today. Application frameworks are a collection of objects and interfaces that provide a simplified access to a more complex collection of interfaces. Unlike libraries, they can be hierarchical and are usually designed for extension through both aggregation and inheritance.

TERM LIST

Most Applicable Scale

Solution Type

Solution Name

Intent

Diagram

References

Applicability at This Scale

Solution Summary

Key Benefits and Consequences

Variations of This Solution

Rescaling This Solution at Other Levels

Related Solutions

Example

Background

Resources

PART THREE

System Design Patterns

System-level software design is different from application-level design due to the increased need to manage change and complexity. Systems comprise the integration of a number of applications (or subsystems). Most software applications are complex. Object-oriented applications typically have hundreds of classes and thousands of methods. If we integrate the system by exposing internal application details, then our system resembles a very large application with aggregated complexity. Such a system would be difficult to develop and maintain due to this complexity. In addition, exposing application details creates brittle interdependencies between subsystems. If we change one application, the change may require corresponding changes in several other subsystems. Avoidance of consequential changes is a key goal of system-level patterns.

Other authors (Shaw 1996; Buschmann 1996) choose to call the system level *software architecture*. This use of the term architecture appears primarily in academically oriented literature. In the academic model, software architecture comprises the partitioning of the software system into modules, module interfaces, and module interconnections. In a CORBA-based distributed object model, the connections are supported by the object request broker (ORB). These connections are transparent to application software, so connections are not a key consideration in CORBA-based software architectures.

In our reference model (the Scalability Model), there is a need for architecture at every level of granularity. Architecture is the abstraction that explains how the software modules are put together. This definition is chosen to directly address a time-consuming activity in software: system discovery. System discovery is said to consume up to half of all programmer time (Coplien 1994). At the system level, the need for architecture becomes clear; the forces driving application-level programming are superseded by the forces of system-level change and complexity.

CHAPTER SEVEN

Principles of Object-Oriented Architecture

At the system level, a system architect is primarily concerned with managing the complexity of the system and with planning for future changes in the system components. In the CORBA environment, a system architect can leverage the benefits of OMG IDL to develop well-defined boundaries to software components, which enables the easy migration of the underlying implementations that support the components.

This section focuses on the key issues and recurring patterns in developing system-level software solutions in an organization. At the system level, the major forces are coordinating between applications to enable interoperability and to allow for future extensions to cope with changing requirements and technologies.

HORIZONTAL-VERTICAL-METADATA

This pattern is a blueprint for the development of superior software architectures.

METADATA

This patterns enables the delaying of architectural decisions until run-time and permits the dynamic discovery of objects and services.

ARCHITECTURE MINING

This patterns enables the discovery and reuse of existing architectural components.

Horizontal-Vertical-Metadata

Most Applicable Scale: System

Solution Type: Software

Solution Name: Horizontal-Vertical-Metadata (HVM)

Intent: To design interoperable, flexible, and reusable software systems, as opposed to brittle, special-purpose designs.

Primal Forces: Management of Change, Management of Complexity

Applicability at This Scale

1. When interoperability is a key priority, proper application of HVM makes interoperability relatively easy to achieve.
2. When adaptability is a goal, HVM creates the design hooks that make adaptability possible.
3. When reuse is a goal, HVM assures that the subsystem interfaces will be defined to support software reusability and interchangeability.

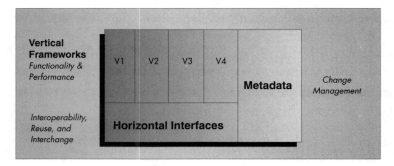

Figure 7.1 Balanced use of horizontal, vertical, and metadata in system-level architecture designs leads to enhanced interoperability, flexibility, and reuse.

Solution Summary

There are three key principles to apply when designing system-level interfaces: the use of horizontal interfaces, vertical interfaces, and metadata. Most system-level designs are almost entirely vertical, making the systems noninteroperable, brittle, and nonreusable. This pattern describes how and why it is important to employ horizontal interfaces and metadata.

In first-generation object-orientation, object designs were based almost completely on domain analysis, which led to specialized, domain-specific interfaces that we call *vertical interfaces*. Vertical interfaces also result from direct use of internal subsystem interfaces, use of proprietary product-dependent interfaces, and many other frequently encountered sources. Vertical interfaces have the disadvantage of being specialized to a single need, and therefore very specific to one implementation. By default, most software interfaces are vertical interfaces, and are therefore not particularly suitable for supporting interoperability, reuse, and adaptability.

When each individual subsystem is considered to be part of a larger class of subsystems, it is possible to define interfaces that apply to the entire class of potential subsystems, not just one instance (see the Architecture Mining solution). Interfaces that apply to an entire category of subsystems are called *horizontal interfaces*. If there are several subsystems in this same system that can be categorized together, then there is an immediate benefit of interoperability and interchangeability (a form of adaptability). If the horizontal interfaces are utilized in other system developments, then there is reuse. Because the horizontal interfaces are not dependent upon internal implementation details, it is possible to make local changes to subsystems without impacting the overall system (another form of adaptability).

Vertical interfaces and horizontal interfaces define static structure of the system. *Metadata* is self-descriptive information that defines the dynamic structure of the system. Metadata defers some design decisions until run-time, such as the number and location of services. Key forms of metadata include: white pages directories (such as the OMG Naming Service), yellow pages directories (such as the OMG Trader Service), semantics and constraints (such as the future OMG Meta-Object Facility), and service-specific metadata (such as DISCUS server metadata).

The effectiveness of metadata is closely related to the prevalence of horizontal interfaces. Metadata enables the discovery of services and their characteristics. The use of horizontal interfaces allows clients to integrate with a wider range of object implementations with less software than if every implementation only supports vertical interfaces. The use of horizontal interfaces makes the metadata description of services simpler and more consistent. When metadata is complex and inconsistent (i.e., has vertical qualities), it becomes very difficult for clients to utilize effectively.

Vertical interfaces also have their place in a well-balanced HVM solution. Vertical interfaces can capture specialized functionality and performance needs not accessible through generalized horizontal interfaces and metadata. The vertical interfaces should be used with the understanding that they compromise the reusability of the software relying upon them and potentially the overall adaptability of the system. An important convention is that all subsystems should be written to interoperate fully using only horizontal interfaces and metadata, and only then should vertical interfaces be integrated to support specialized functionality.

Benefits

➤ Interoperability between subsystems and other systems.
➤ Adaptability of the system-level solution, including run-time flexibility from metadata, and the ability to support localized changes, subsystem replacement, and the addition of new subsystems.
➤ Reuse of software between systems.
➤ Reuse of functionality between subsystems.
➤ Isolation and loose coupling between subsystems.

Other Consequences

➤ Coordination of horizontal interfaces and metadata between multiple unique subsystems is a technical and political challenge that requires great discipline and common vision.
➤ System extensions must be well coordinated and consistent with the HVM architecture design and vision.
➤ Generalization of interfaces and metadata information may make it less convenient to access specialized vertical functionality than if all interfaces were customized (vertical).

Rescaling This Solution to Other Levels

Horizontal interfaces have a role at the application level in providing abstract common interfaces among finer-grained application-level objects. Use of horizontal interfaces at this level is the structural solution behind the intentions of many design patterns (Gamma et al. 1994).

At the enterprise and global levels, metadata has an increasingly important role in managing resources, making their discovery possible. Horizontal interfaces at these levels allow applications to access diverse implementations without specialized code.

Related Solutions

➤ OMG Distributed Document Component Facility—a set of horizontal interfaces for the creation and management of compound documents, based on OpenDoc.

➤ Microsoft OLE—a set of horizontal interfaces for desktop interoperability based on their Component Object Model (COM).

➤ Data Interchange and Synergistic Collateral Usage Study (DISCUS)—a horizontal and metadata-based reference architecture.

➤ Architecture Patterns (Mowbray 1995a)—A description of the patterns of system-level software integration.

Example

An interesting example of how HVM architecture can provide dramatic benefits occurred on a system integration project. The project comprised the integration of seven legacy applications using a set of horizontal interfaces with metadata. Concurrently to this integration, a separate project created a point-to-point vertical integration of two of these seven systems. At the conclusion of the prototypes, it was found that the integration of the seven systems had only cost about half as much as the vertical integration of the two systems. It was also discovered that the quality of integration was superior in the HVM solution. The HVM solution had the advantage of being extensible to add additional capabilities and applications through leverage of the existing integration software, whereas the vertical solution did not.

Metadata

Most Applicable Scale: System

Solution Type: Software

Solution Name: Metadata

Intent: To enable dynamic discovery and reconfiguration of object implementations in order to defer selected design decisions until run-time (for flexibility and extensibility).

Primal Forces: Management of Change

Applicability at This Scale

    1. Enable dynamic discovery and management of resources.

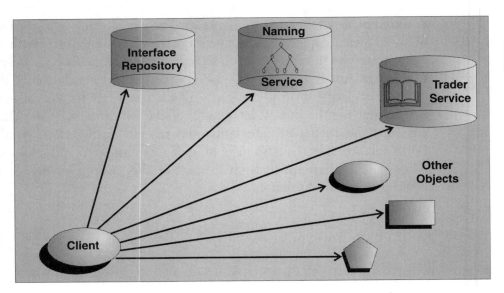

Figure 7.2 Metadata enables dynamic service discovery and reconfiguration.

2. Adaptability—dynamic reconfiguration, relocation, and installation of services.
3. Deferral of commitment of design decisions until after system installation or indefinitely.

Solution Summary

Provide an architectural solution such that the system objects are self-describing. Define well-known interfaces and well-known descriptive formats that objects support in order to describe themselves. Make interfaces accessible to clients so that they may examine the self-describing data. Advertise services in well-known repositories to allow clients to access public metadata. Private metadata that is only accessible to privileged clients should be maintained by object implementations, using a common format (ideally, a format that is consistent with the public metadata). There are several CORBA standards for public metadata, including the OMG Interface Repository, the OMG Naming Service, the OMG Trader Service, and the future OMG Meta-Object Facility.

Benefits

➤ System adaptability—the flexibility to reconfigure, change, and extend the system without software changes.
➤ Reduced software maintenance—change metadata instead of rewriting software.
➤ Software that can take advantage of dynamic information and discover new capabilities and resources, as opposed to software that needs to be reprogrammed for each new capability.

Other Consequences

➤ Maintenance of the metadata information whenever changes occur.
➤ Additional software to access and use metadata versus hardwired solutions that assume system configuration decisions.

Variations of This Solution

Metadata is most effective when it is simple and shares a common representation across a wide variety of resources. Examples include the OMG Naming

Service, OMG Trader Service, and DISCUS metadata (Mowbray & Zahavi 1995). The usefulness of metadata is strongly related to abstraction. If a wide range of resources can be described simply and consistently, then their metadata access can be implemented consistently by clients. Whenever metadata becomes specialized areas, it requires client specializations to use unique features.

Vertical metadata standards, such as Federal Geographic Data Committee (FGDC) and Special Data Transfer Service (SDTS) for Geographic Information Systems (GIS) applications are only useful for special-purpose vertical market applications because they are very complex and industry-specific.

Rescaling This Solution to Other Levels

Metadata is commonly used at the enterprise and global levels in order to facilitate discovery and management of resources, for example, Internet and intranet directories, as well as file server and printer directories (such as the Mac Chooser).

Related Solutions

> ➤ Horizontal-Vertical-Metadata—Provides the overall framework for how metadata may be best incorporated into a large system.
> ➤ Naming—This pattern provides the simplest form of metadata—the simple association of an object with a name.
> ➤ Trader—This pattern provides a minimal metadata capability by allowing a set of attributes to be associated with an object reference. However, the implementation of the Trader controls which attributes are used in order to store and retrieve an object based on its properties.
> ➤ Other Examples—Switchboard, Interface Repository, ODP Trader, OMG Naming Service, OMG Trader Service, OMG Meta-Object Facility Reflective OO Systems, Macintosh Chooser, Yellow Pages, Internet Directories, X.500, DCE Cell Directory Service.

Example

Suppose there is a need to create a flexible system with a dynamic set of services. The following steps are an example of how the metadata might be created and used in a Trader Service-based metadata solution.

1. Characterize the services in terms of some common types of attributes: What kind of information do they manipulate or visualize? What domains do they support? What software interfaces do they support? What are the different qualities of service that are available? What data formats are utilized? What platforms do they run on? Does it have a front end and/or a back end? And so forth.
2. Create a Trader schema by partitioning the services with respect to the interfaces supported. Use common attributes for each interface type. Coordinate the common attributes across interface types, so that there is a high level of uniformity in the metadata representation. Document the Trader Service schema for the purposes of system installation and maintenance.
3. For a particular installation, register each service offer with the Trader Service using the common attribute schema.
4. Whenever the system configuration changes or a new application is installed, update the Trader Service tables to reflect the changes.
5. Monitor usage of the Trader Service and the common attributes. Verify that the Trader Service is actually used, that the schema contains the right information, and that the attributes are used as intended or for other unintended purposes.
6. Update the schema or installation as needed to reflect the lessons learned.

Background

Metadata is on-line, self-descriptive information contained in an information system. It is available for application software to reference in order to discover and select system resources, as well as to determine the attributes and characteristics of these resources.

Architecture Mining

Most Applicable Scale: System

Solution Type: Process

Solution Name: Architecture Mining

Intent: A way to reduce design risks, accelerate design processes, and produce high-quality, robust system-level designs.

Primal Forces: Management of Technology Transfer, Management of Change

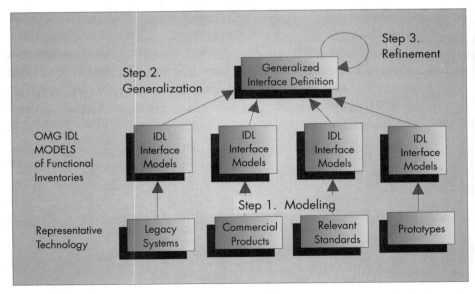

Figure 7.3 Architecture Mining is a bottom-up design process that exploits the existing system knowledge used to design robust new systems.

Applicability at This Scale

1. For risk reduction, to amass knowledge and confidence to create low-risk designs.
2. To save time and cost of design reinvention, through design reuse.
3. For expertise and knowledge transfer, when existing systems or experts can be used for important design contributions.
4. When additional knowledge of the problem and potential solutions are needed for system-level architecture design.
5. When there are overlapping legacy systems.
6. When legacy-system modules must be integrated into the target architecture.
7. When designing high-risk or widely used designs.

Solution Summary

Mining is a bottom-up design approach, incorporating design knowledge from working implementations. Mining can incorporate design input from top-down design processes too, so that there can be both top-down traceability and bottom-up realism.

Before mining starts, it is necessary to identify a set of representative technologies that are relevant to the design problem. Technology identification can be done by various means, such as searching literature, interviewing experts, attending technical conferences, and surfing the net. All available resources should be pursued.

The first mining step is to model each representative technology. Technology modeling produces specifications of relevant software interfaces. We recommend using OMG IDL as the interface notation because it is concise and free from implementation detail. OMG IDL is also a good design notation for the target architecture because it is language-independent, platform-neutral, and distribution-transparent. By modeling everything in the same notation, we create a good basis for design comparison and tradeoff.

In the modeling step, it is important to describe the as-built system, not the intended or desired design. Frequently, relevant design information is not documented as software interfaces. For example, some of the sought-after functionality may only be accessible through the user interface. Other key design lessons may be undocumented. It is useful to capture this design information too.

In the second step, the mined designs are generalized to create a common interface specification. This step entails more art than science. The goal is to create an initial strawman specification for the target architecture interfaces. It is usually not sufficient to generate a lowest-common denominator design from the representative technology. The generalized interfaces should resemble a best-of-breed solution that captures the common functionality as well as some unique aspects inspired by particular systems. Unique aspects should be included when they create valuable features in the target architecture or represent areas of known system evolution. A robust assortment of representative technologies will contain indicators of likely areas of target system evolution.

At this point it is appropriate to factor in the top-down design information as one of the inputs. Top-down information is usually at a much higher level of abstraction than bottom-up information. Reconciliation of these differences involves some important architecture tradeoffs.

The final step in the mining process is to refine the design. Refinements can be driven by the architect's judgment, informal walkthroughs, review processes, new requirements, or additional mining studies.

Benefits

➤ Rapid way to assemble required knowledge to create complex or risky designs.
➤ Risk reduction because new designs are based upon proven systems.
➤ Robust and stable designs because they are modeled on a range of technologies, not just one system or isolated group of designers.
➤ The real product of mining is the edification of the OO architect. With a mature understanding of the problem and previous solutions, the OO architect is well-prepared to make good architectural decisions.

Other Consequences

➤ Must have access to detailed design information about legacy systems and relevant commercial technologies.
➤ Access to human experts is usually much more valuable than documentation; access to human experts may take key people away from other important tasks. On the bright side, a focused study may require only a day or so of the time of any given expert.
➤ Most object-oriented methodologies do not provide ways to assimilate mined information.

Rescaling This Solution to Other Levels

Mining may be applicable at the application level for certain complex design problems. In some cases, it may be less expensive and risky to exploit existing expertise than to create new code without exposure to preexisting solutions. Mining is applicable at enterprise levels, but less so at global levels, given the reduced access to information resources.

Related Solutions

➤ Common Interface—The creation of a common interface is a typical goal of an architecture mining process.
➤ Architecture Mining (Mowbray & Zahavi 1995)—A detailed description of the architectural mining process.
➤ The Software Productivity Consortium (Reston, VA) proposes architecture farming (see "Background") and mining as design approaches for software architecture.

Example

Suppose we are designing an application for a large end-user organization. The end user has four existing systems, all of which are independent, but highly overlapping. The end user would like to reduce the cost and time to build new systems. They believe that object-orientation and code reuse may be possible answers. Given these indications, we determine that architecture mining would be an applicable process to gain understanding of existing systems before considering the design of a new system.

Technology identification is straightforward because the identities of the existing systems are well known. It is valuable to consider mining of additional systems from outside the organization if technology access is possible, for example similar systems that are commercially available, competitor's systems, or applicable standards.

For each legacy system, we need to identify the available expertise and resources. Review all available documentation to determine which parts of the system might be applicable for mining study. Inquire as to who are the best available human experts regarding the key parts of the system. One of the key challenges in architecture mining is influencing the organization to obtain access to these experts.

The preferred way to interview a legacy system expert for architecture mining is by walking through an existing design document, such as an Interface Control Document (ICD). The legacy ICD contains the written documentation of the system interfaces. This documentation is often out of date because many organizations do not update their documentation to the as-built state. (Note: This is an important question to ask.) The documentation may also be ambiguous because legacy ICDs often use informal notations that are less rigorous than OMG IDL. The human expert can explain these gaps and provide essential rationale and insight into the legacy design.

It is useful to encode each legacy ICD into OMG IDL. This step gives all the mined information a common notation and a comparable level of formal description. The important information at this step is not the OMG IDL code, but the knowledge gained by the architects performing the mining.

The generalization step involves integrating this knowledge into a unified design. It is useful to work iteratively. Producing the first design iteration is perhaps the biggest challenge. It is useful to ignore the written mining documentation in the production of the first draft, since preexisting designs may tend to overconstrain the problem.

After the initial design is on paper, it is useful to compare the draft design with the legacy systems. This is a quality-enhancing step that allows one to carefully review the approach and pick up essential design details from the legacy, such as missing parameters.

The mining knowledge becomes a useful tool of the architect. The architect can use this knowledge to defend the design. The architect can also use the knowledge to explain how the new design maps back to the legacy design for the purposes of system integration.

Background

Mining is a way to quickly create successful OO architectures: robust, product-independent, reusable, and extensible. Most OO design approaches assume that design information is invented as the process proceeds. In a top-down process, design information is generated from requirements, which may be represented as OO analysis models. Requirements-driven architecture design is called *Architecture Farming*. In a spiral process, design information is invented during each iteration. As the spiral process proceeds, architects invent new design information as they learn more about the application problem. It is fair to say that these approaches *reinvent* much of their design information.

Precursor designs exist for most information systems applications and problems. These designs are in the form of legacy systems, commercial products, standards, prototypes, and design patterns. In our experience, it is not difficult to identify a half dozen or more precursor designs for any given application problem. Valuable information is buried in preexisting designs, information that allowed earlier architects to build useful systems. Extracting this information for use in OO architectures is called *OO Architecture Mining*. OO Architecture Mining is a bottom-up design approach. It exploits historical design and implementation experience to create new OO architectures. Because we are relying on successful previous designs, there is substantial risk reduction. The challenge of OO Architecture Mining is to discover, extract, and refine the nuggets of design knowledge. Because there is often a great deal of implementation detail to review, the process is analogous to mining the earth for precious metals.

How does an OO architect gain sufficient knowledge to design and defend a good architecture? Knowledge can come from years of experience of designing similar architectures. Alternatively, the learning process can be greatly accelerated by explicit mining of design knowledge from existing technologies and experts.

In my observation, most software architectures are designed in a vacuum. It is easy to ignore or reject preexisting designs when confronted by a new design problem, but there are serious consequences. "Design-in-a-vacuum" invariably produces immature, custom designs with minimal potential for interoperability, reuse, and adaptability. Because technology transfer between multiple architectures rarely occurs in practice, the positive effects of OO Architecture Mining can be quite dramatic.

CHAPTER EIGHT

Fundamental Structural Patterns

The fundamental structural patterns are commonly used to manage the complexity of a system through the separation of concerns within a system.

REPOSITORY ARCHITECTURE

This patterns allows shared data to be accessed by one or more independent processes with a minimum of coordination mechanisms.

GATEWAY

This pattern allows for information to be accessed natively from different object models.

COMPONENT ARCHITECTURE

This pattern maximizes the decoupling of objects by providing a minimal common interface for all software components.

Layered Architecture

Layered architectures are multitiered structures for large-scale systems (Figure 8.1). The layering provides a way to manage complexity and reuse software. There are major products and whole books dedicated to this topic, which we do not attempt to replicate here.

Layered architectures are often used for larger scale systems, where there is a strong motivation to manage the change and complexity of a system. The layering is applicable when a system is divisible into areas of concern with well-defined boundaries. Often, it is undesirable for application developers to know all the details of every software tier in the system, due to complexity, multiple software packages, and platform differences. Layering provides the architectural boundaries that manage complexity for individual developers.

A layered architecture can provide a well-thought-out model of an information system that reflects the scale and depth of the application-level services. The layered architecture separates the application models into discrete tiers such that lower levels have no need for access to services defined at higher levels.

(*Continued*)

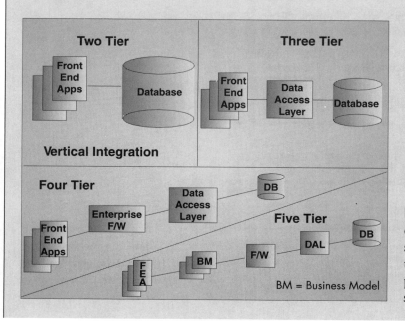

Figure 8.1 The Layered Architecture is a system-level structure that reduces the complexity of a large-scale system.

The three-tiered layered architecture is the most common solution. The bottom tier is dedicated to data access and isolates the rest of the system software from direct dependency on the back-end implementation. This allows for system extension and upgrading of databases and storage management. The top tier is intended for user interface and presentation logic. There can be several instantiations of the top tier for different platforms and user environments. The role of the middle tier is reusable application software. There may be multiple versions and frequent changes in the top and bottom tiers; the middle tier provides a stable reusable set of application software that provides a common enterprise model and leverages application development.

Additional tiers are sometimes added to layered architectures to provide additional benefits. An additional top tier can provide isolation of user interface programmers from the complexity of the middle-tier model. Additional layering at the back end can provide isolation from the data storage mechanisms, providing more system extensibility and reduced complexity.

In layered architectures, it is important to verify that the constituents of each level are complete, particularly in the bottom and middle tiers. Omissions at a lower tier

(Continued)

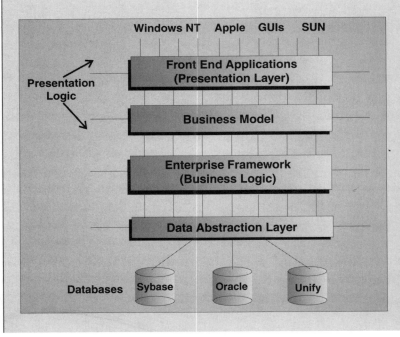

Figure 8.2 Interface layering increases system reuse and insulates the system from change.

can lead to software changes at multiple levels. For example, if a new data element is needed at the user interface, it may require changes to software at all tiers if the information was not present at the database level and modeled in the middle tiers.

When there are multiple data sources in an organization, it is useful to define a single data abstraction layer for all the data sources so clients are not aware of the differences in the protocols in accessing the various databases. The data abstraction layer is responsible for receiving the request for data from the client applications and transparently identifying the physical databases the data resides in and making the product-dependent database calls to retrieve the data from the database. By defining a data abstraction layer, clients do not have to know the syntax of how to access each of the physical databases. Furthermore, if a database is replaced or physically restructured, the clients will not have to be modified, if they restricted their data access to the data abstraction layer. Similarly, if the Enterprise Framework only accesses the data abstraction layer, it receives the identical benefit, being a client of the data abstraction layer. This allows the Enterprise Framework to be portable across various databases as long as they share an identical data abstraction layer. While the Enterprise Model uses the data abstraction layer, it is completely decoupled from the physical databases. Also, the Enterprise Model can change without affecting the underlying data abstraction. As we move to other abstraction levels, we see that the Enterprise Abstraction Layer of the system is completely decoupled from the Data Abstraction Layer, and the Presentation Layer is completely decoupled from the Enterprise Framework layer. Additionally, changes at any of the higher levels have no effect on the levels beneath it. This decoupling increases the potential for reuse of each layer and insulates the system from change.

In large application systems, there needs to be a way to manage the complexity of the system such that application developers do not need to know all of the details of every portion of the system. Ideally, they need only be concerned with the portions that directly affect their level of development, and should interact with the rest of the system only through minimal higher-level interfaces that describe the underlying tasks in very general terms (Figure 8.2). By limiting the knowledge of the system to appropriate levels and spheres of responsibility, a developer can more quickly add new features and system extensions, as well as fix any software problems, unhindered by dependencies on unrelated parts of the system.

Repository Architecture

Most Applicable Scale: System

Solution Type: Software

Solution Name: Repository Architecture

Intent: To provide shared access to a large number of objects (or data elements). To provide a uniform and flexible organization to the shared objects and the surrounding system.

Primal Forces: Management of Change, Management of Complexity

Applicability at This Scale

1. There are many distinct programs that need access to the same data set for processing.

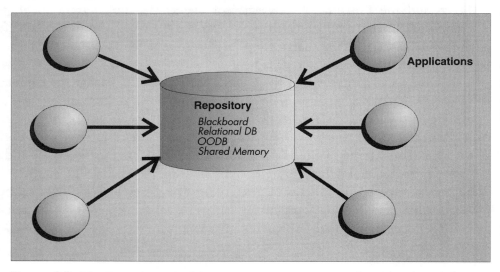

Figure 8.3 The Repository Architecture separates processes from the shared data on which they act.

2. As the data changes, the programs need to be aware of the changes so they can operate on the most recent data in real-time.
3. Programs have little interaction with each other except in obtaining the most recent results of changes made to the shared data.
4. Programs generally cannot access one another's address space in a safe and predictable manner.
5. There may be any number of programs that may also need to access and potentially update a data set.
6. To simplify application software by leveraging commercial database software.

Solution Summary

In a repository, the shared objects are centralized in well-known locations external to all applications. The shared objects may be primarily data or a combination of data and associated shared programs. The data must be accessible by all participating applications throughout their lifetimes. A repository is encapsulated by a data access layer. This layer provides both access to the shared data (and programs) and a means of concurrency control. One application may update a portion of the repository at a time. The repository must only allow applications to access and manipulate the data through the encapsulation.

Although the repository concept is simple, repositories have several well-known forms, as discussed in the following "Variations" section.

Benefits

➤ Any number of applications may access the repository supporting extensibility.
➤ Changes to data are reflected immediately and available to all applications.
➤ Applications are integrated with the repository, not with each other. This enables reuse of repository software and isolation of applications.
➤ The repository hides the implementation details of the shared information and associated access methods. This may provide significant reduction in the complexity of the overall system and individual applications.

Other Consequences

➤ Changes in the repository can have systemwide impacts.
➤ Need to provide for concurrency control in the data access layer.

- No way to provide or receive notification for data changes.
- Accessing shared data may be expensive due to external location.

Variations of This Solution

The repository solution has several forms. Some common forms are a database architecture and a blackboard architecture.

A *database architecture* is typically implemented using a commercial database product. In the case of a relational database, the repository stores a structured collection of tabular data. The data is accessed through query language statements. The use of the query language hides the complexity of the sophisticated processing required to implement queries. It has been estimated that to program the functionality of a state-of-the-art commercial database from scratch would cost on the order of $100,000,000.

Choosing a database architecture is an obvious but significant solution. With object-oriented approaches it is commonplace to design sophisticated object schemas. Frequently, a much simpler database solution can be substituted. Regarding the choice between object-oriented databases and relational databases, Brodie and Stonebraker (1995) recommend using a relational database approach unless you are doing something very specialized. The distinction between these OO and relational databases is blurring as the industry moves to unify the query languages and APIs through standards activities.

A *blackboard architecture* is a collection of shared objects with public access methods. Blackboards are often implemented in shared memory for efficiency. In a blackboard architecture, the applications are called knowledge sources. Knowledge sources are controlled and scheduled independently based upon the content of the blackboard. Each knowledge source can read and update the blackboard contents, providing some value-added knowledge to the overall system. Knowledge sources communicate only indirectly through the state of the blackboard, not through direct interaction other knowledge sources.

A blackboard architecture is a good choice for a research environment where frequent experimental software changes are anticipated, but the shared state information is relatively stable.

Rescaling This Solution to Other Levels

The repository architecture is a fundamental structure in a distributed computing environment for managing complexity and change. Its key characteristic is the isolation of a large number of shared objects from client applications that use the data.

At an application level, the repository solutions can be scaled down to a set of shared collections. The OMG Collections Service is a potential candidate for the interfaces. Global variables (sometimes called common areas) are a degenerate form of this solution.

At the enterprise level, the probability of repository transaction failures and their resulting consequences are significant; a greater level of robustness is required. *Transaction monitors* are a technology that assures consistent state changes in large-scale repositories. The OMG Transactions Service is a common interface specification for CORBA-based transaction monitors.

Related Solutions

➤ Notification—Can be used to coordinate between processes.
➤ OMG Concurrency Control Service—Can be used to provide concurrency control.
➤ The Repository Architectural Pattern (Shaw 1995)—This pattern describes several system-level architectural patterns.
➤ Shared Repository (Mularz 1994)—This pattern describes the repository architecture in a distributed environment.
➤ OMG Query Service—This is an example of a repository architecture that coordinates access to an underlying database management system.

The relationship of the Concurrency and Transactions services is discussed in the preceding "Rescaling" section.

Example

The OMG Query Service is an example of a repository interface that encapsulates a data store for use by multiple applications. The purpose of the OMG Query Service is to allow arbitrary users to invoke queries on a collection of objects and to receive the query results. As in all repository architectures, the access to the data is separated from the processing of the clients and any number of client applications can concurrently access the OMG Query Service with a guarantee that the query service will properly coordinate data access.

Creating an Object Model for Your Domain

It is important to realize that it is up to the implementor to define the object model for the domain at the system level. Using OMG IDL and CORBA, the system architect is not constrained by the nature of the underlying applications in establishing the object model. Actually, the reverse is true, as CORBA allows the specification of the object model to be independent from how its implemented. A single application may service operations in many independent object interfaces. For example, a conversion program need not be modeled as a conversion server, but may instead be used as a backend service used to implement the getRepresentation() operation for many different classes. Conceivably, many classes may use other means to implement a getRepresentation operation, but such details are all implementation issues that the system architect need not be concerned with in the development of the overall object model.

When a new set of services is introduced into the domain, perhaps providing new capabilities to an existing system, it is up to the system architect to decide whether to expose the interfaces of the new services to client application developers, or extend the vertical domain model and hide the interfaces of the new services in the implementation of the extended domain model. If the system architect wishes to require client applications to only code to the domain model, he or she attains the flexibility of changing the source of the underlying services without breaking the clients. However, if clients are allowed to develop directly to interfaces outside of their domain, then either a commitment must be made to maintain the non-domain-specific interfaces or clients must accept the risk that they may need to be eventually modified in response to changes outside of the domain.

Gateway

Most Applicable Scale: System

Solution Type: Software

Solution Name: Gateway

Intent: To provide seamless interoperability between two disparate systems, domains, or object models.

Primal Forces: Management of Complexity

Applicability at This Scale

1. An object or its information needs to be interchanged between disparate systems.
2. An object needs to exist in one or more different object-oriented environments.
3. A client needs to be isolated from explicit knowledge of foreign systems and needs to access foreign data transparently

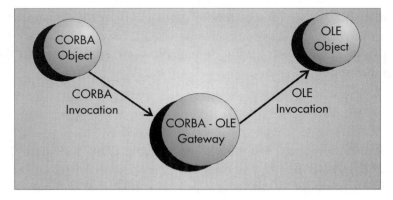

Figure 8.4 The Gateway pattern is a fundamental technique used to reconcile differences between object models.

Solution Summary

When software needs data from another system, often the data is accessed using an unfamiliar set of operations and formats. Ideally, a client program would not need explicit knowledge of how the information is accessed or stored natively, but rather can access the information in a form similar to how it would access information within its own domain. Gateways are an intermediate program that allows a data set to appear to be in native form, regardless of how it may be accessed or stored in its native environment.

In creating a gateway from one domain to an object in another domain, there are three basic steps. The first step is to create an object representation, or *proxy*, for the foreign object in the local domain. This proxy should appear as a native object in the local environment. For example, in the case of a native CORBA environment, the proxy object should have an IDL interface that defines logical operations that make sense in the CORBA domain.

The second step is to provide an implementation for the local proxy object. The implementation of the proxy object will be responsible for mapping to the remote object and associated services in the foreign domain. When the proxy object is invoked by the client, it translates any information from the local domain to the data types of the foreign domain and invokes the actual object in the foreign domain to perform the requested operation. The proxy object differs from a local domain object in that it does not actually contain the object data but is a vehicle for obtaining the information from the actual object.

Finally, when the operation is complete, the results are sent back to the object proxy implementation. The implementation translates the results from the foreign data types to appropriate types in the local domain and returns them to the client. In many implementations, it may be necessary to request services from one or both of the domains in converting data into the appropriate return types.

Benefits

➤ Client only needs to know how to access objects in its domain. No special knowledge is required by the client.
➤ The implementation of the object proxies can change without affecting the clients.

Other Consequences

➤ Care must be taken to avoid creating redundant proxies. Need a method to verify a proxy for an object already exists rather than create one each time.
➤ Requires object to maintain a representation in two disparate systems.

Related Solutions

➤ The CORBA-COM Interoperability Specification—Defines a standard gateway between OMG's CORBA and Microsoft's COM.
➤ The Proxy Design Pattern: Revisited (Rohnert 1995)—This pattern describes the definition and use of proxies that can be used to develop gateways.

Example

The following example shows how a gateway between CORBA and the World Wide Web can be created by creating a CORBA proxy for the data represented by a URL.

In order to create a gateway to a specific Web page, there needs to be an OMG IDL-defined interface for the proxy representing the page. The following OMG IDL definition is an example of a interface that can be used to model a specific page in CORBA:

```
interface HomePage {
        typedef sequence <octet> octetSeq;
        typedef sequence<octet> image;
        typedef sequence <image> imageSeq;
        exception NOT_FOUND {};

        string getText()               /*returns the text from a page*/
             raises (NOT_FOUND);
        imageSeq getImages()      /*returns sequence of images on page*/
             raises (NOT_FOUND);
        octetSeq getBinary()          /*raw data-an HTML stream*/
             raises (NOT_FOUND);
        void display()
             (BAD_BROWSER);
        void changeBrowser(in Browser currentBrowser)
             raises (NOT_FOUND);
};
```

When a HomePage object is created, its URL is stored as private data within its implementation. Since the URL is considered private data in this example, it is not defined in the OMG IDL and no accessor methods will be created to allow clients or other objects to access it. When a client receives an object reference to the HomePage object, it can retrieve the text from the home page, a list of images that are on the home page, or the raw data of the home page itself. Notice that a CORBA client only views the HomePage as a standard CORBA object and receives data from the home page as standard CORBA types. Furthermore, the HomePage CORBA object is not intended to be the actual object (although it appears as one to CORBA objects), but is a proxy for the object stored within the WWW environment. The gateway is responsible for receiving CORBA requests for the WWW home page through the CORBA HomePage object proxy and converting it into the WWW protocols corresponding to a request to the HTTP server for the specific home page. Furthermore, upon receiving the home page, the gateway must convert the HTML file received into the appropriate CORBA types necessary to complete the CORBA client's request. The fact that the WWW communication is transparent to the CORBA client is critical in maintaining interoperability between the object environments by preserving the environment boundaries. This example only presents a single CORBA-to-WWW mapping. A WWW-to-CORBA mapping is presented in the section on Internet design patterns. In order to create a bidirectional gateway, it is necessary to create a WWW proxy to the CORBA object.

Background

Today, there are many different and competing object models in use throughout the industry. While CORBA has the largest backing by vendors, many of the competing models are extremely valuable either in niche markets or in meeting the functional needs of specialized platforms. Also, even in the CORBA environment, many CORBA implementors do not support the CORBA 2.0 IIOP protocols and consequently are not interoperable with other CORBA implementations. When objects need to interact with other object models it is frequently desirable to have objects simultaneously represented in two different object models. One approach to achieving this level of object interoperability is to construct a gateway.

> Keep names short and be aware of the complete binding (at least of the target language) of the names used. Nested modules add considerably to the name lengths. Strive to eliminate redundant and uninformative tags.

Component Architecture

Most Applicable Scale: System

Solution Type: Software

Solution Name: Component Architecture

Intent: To provide for flexible substitution of software modules. The substitution can be both static (compile-time component replacement) and dynamic (run-time dynamic binding).

Primal Forces: Management of Change

Applicability at This Scale

1. Software system has many services that are available to client processes.
2. A client wants to have every service accessible by an standard, well-known interface.

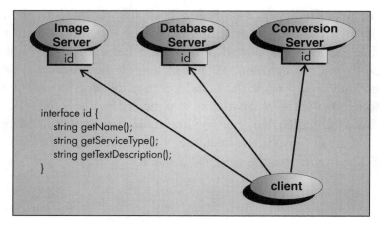

Figure 8.5 The Component Architecture pattern promotes interchangeability and run-time configurability of systems.

3. All components need to be loosely coupled so that replacing one component with another has no effect on the other components in the system.
4. It is expensive or otherwise undesirable to change clients to use new interfaces.
5. Many clients only need a base level of functionality from applications and would like to be guaranteed that one or more applications will be capable of supporting the base level of functionality throughout the system lifecycle.

Solution Summary

Decide upon a base level of functionality that the majority of applications should support. In general, the base level should be small and focus upon a single aspect of interoperability, such as data interchange, or conversion.

Define a set of OMG IDL interfaces that support this base level of functionality. Most services will have an additional interface to express finer-grained functional needs, so the component interface should be small.

Add an implementation for this base set of functionality to all existing implementations in the system. Having a base level of functionality guaranteed to all clients in the domain encourages the development of intelligent clients that work well with existing and future services without modification. Furthermore, having numerous implementations available increases the robustness of clients as they potentially have many options in fulfilling their service request.

It is quite likely that many applications will have clients that are written to the more specialized interfaces. These clients should remain unaffected by the addition of the new component interfaces. Clients that require only the base level of functionality can be written to the horizontal interfaces, which should be more stable and easily supported by new or other existing applications. The horizontal interface should hide via abstraction all the lower-level details of a component and only provide the base-level functionality. The client should be written to handle whatever datatypes are indicated by the interface in order to support any future interchange of the horizontal component implementations. For example, if an "any" is returned, the client should be capable of handling all user-defined types that the any may contain.

Benefits

➤ Components are easily replaceable.
➤ Clients are decoupled from services implementation, making the clients less affected by changes to services implementation.

Other Consequences

> ➤ Clients cannot assume the existence of a particular application.
> ➤ Clients are restricted to limited functionality.
> ➤ Interfaces are static, freezing application functionality and capability.
> ➤ Not useful when exposure to underlying application functionality is desirable.

Rescaling This Solution to Other Levels

At the application level, the need to accept detailed functionality of a specific implementation may make a component architecture undesirable. This is especially true when access to new and changing functionality is critical to a particular application. At the higher levels, there is a greater need for stable interfaces and less of a need to be concerned with the detailed functionality of applications. Therefore, at higher levels, a component architecture is likely to be increasingly desirable. Also, if some common service that is guaranteed by a large group of components is necessary, then utilizing a component architecture is an easy and effective means to provide it.

Related Solutions

> ➤ Standard—A standard is highly desirable for a commercial component architecture. Otherwise, the component interfaces are proprietary, and therefore, entail risk for the consumer.
> ➤ Layered Architecture—Often uses a Horizontal Component Architecture for stable interfaces where the implementations are intended to be easily replaceable. "Horizontal Architecture" (Mowbray & Zahari 1995), Chapter 7 in *The Essential CORBA,* describes the DISCUS component architecture.

Example

A component object architecture can be defined in a CORBA environment by requiring a group of services to support the same interface, with their own unique implementations. If the client retrieves the object reference for a desired service at run-time, for instance, by using the OMG Naming or Trader Service, the specific service accessed by the client can be altered by changing the stored object reference. Consider the following OMG IDL:

```
module foo {
    interface sameForAll {
```

```
             exception DIV_BY_ZERO {};
             long add(in long a, in long b);
             long subtract(in long a, in long b);
             long multiply(in long a, in long b);
             float divide(in long a, in long b);
                    raises(DIV_BY_ZERO);
        };
    }
```

A component object environment would require that every service in the environment support the foo::sameForAll interface. From the point of view of a client that relies on the foo::sameForAll interface, each service has an implementation for the interface that it uses. Any service in the environment could potentially meet the needs of the client, although some of them might be better than others (faster results, greater precision, etc.). However, as long as there is at least one service that supports the needed interface, the client can be expected to function.

Background

Sometimes applications are developed with the expectation that they will have a long operational lifecycle. Even though the application may rely upon components that could potentially change over time, the application has no desire to access any new functionality; rather, it simply needs the same constant functionality over its lifetime. Such applications require stable interfaces that should be present through its lifetime. A mechanism of writing to stable interfaces and determining which interfaces are stable is necessary for managing change.

CHAPTER NINE

Advanced System Design Patterns

The OMG Object Services provide most of the basic services used by an application. Furthermore, as the technology gains even more maturity, a variety of applications frameworks based on the OMG CORBAservices and OMA are expected to arise. However, there are many less obvious methods of configuring systems services and of developing system-level applications that could improve the performance or increase the robustness of CORBA applications. Many of the system-level design patterns involve the application of larger-scale architectural principles than those presented at the application level, or are only useful in coordinating behavior between one of more CORBA applications. However, before using these techniques as building blocks for advanced CORBA software constructs, an awareness of the cost of many of these patterns must be taken into account. Specifically, many of these advanced patterns require a greater level of complexity in configuration management and in the implementation. Current-generation configuration management tools provide little help in addressing the specific intricacies of the CORBA environment. Unless extensive care is taken, the implementation of these patterns may increase development costs and especially maintenance costs. It is important to weigh the pattern's benefits against its liabilities carefully to determine if the benefits are worth the price to be paid over the lifetime of the system.

ARCHITECTURE ENFORCEMENT

This pattern demonstrates how to enforce the design intent of a layered architecture through selectively controlling the client stubs compiled into the applications at each of the client layers.

REPLICATION

This pattern increases the performance and reliability of a system by producing multiples copies of an object implementation.

AGENT

This pattern delegates operations to be performed to an external process that performs the work on the client's behalf.

ARCHITECTURAL FRAMEWORK

This pattern demonstrates how to manage the complexity of a system by creating a framework defining meaningful abstractions for system components.

Architecture Enforcement

Most Applicable Scale: System

Solution Type: Software

Solution Name: Architecture Enforcement

Intent: To provide mechanisms to enforce the separation between interfaces representing different architectural layers or partitions.

Primal Forces: Management of Change

Applicability at This Scale

1. A system's interfaces have been partitioned into a layered architecture.
2. No other mechanism is available for enforcing the boundaries of a layered architecture.
3. One or more interfaces are conceptually unavailable to certain categories of applications.
4. An application may obtain an object reference for an interface, even though the interface should conceptually be unavailable to the application's particular layer.

Solution Summary

In most CORBA implementations, clients and servers do not have to share the same interface repository in order to communicate. It is quite possible to have the interfaces available to client applications be a subset of the interfaces whose implementations are available from the server. Therefore, if possible, provide separate interface repositories for client and server applications. If all implementations of a service are intended to be available only to backend programs, then it should not be available in the interface repository used by clients. Therefore, if a client tried to construct a request to a backend service, the ORB will

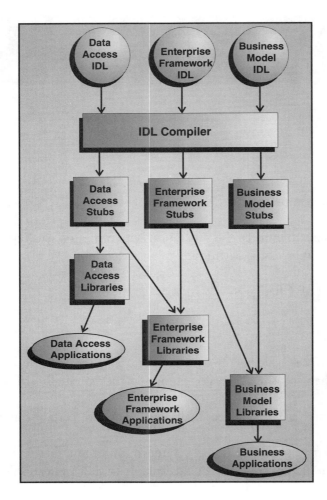

Figure 9.1 Architecture Enforcement provides a technique for ensuring that the conceptual layering used to design the OMG IDL interfaces is maintained in application development.

not see it in the interface repository and should not recognize it as a valid request. However, backend services are not constrained, as they have a full OMG IDL set available for the construction of requests.

The most common way of a client making requests is through the client stubs. Even if multiple interfaces are available for a client to use, they do not have to be compiled into a single set of client stubs. Rather, each module can be compiled to separately generate a corresponding set of client stubs for each module. This will then allow a means to control which interfaces can be invoked by a client by controlling which sets of client stubs are made available. Therefore, if the CORBA DII is not being used by client applications, interface access can be controlled by selectively compiling the generated client stubs into applications such that only the client stubs mapping to allowable interfaces are made available to client applications at a particular level.

The third method of controlling access to architectural layers is through the intelligent management of namespaces. If a module is a supporting module for a set of OMG IDL and is not meant to be invokable by any way outside another module, then the module should be included inside the module it supports. This will clearly indicate that the two modules are related and that the supporting modules are not completely independent from the supported modules. When generating client stubs for the supported module, compile the module as is. When generating client stubs for modules outside of the supported module, then exclude the nested supporting module. This will result in no client stubs being generated for the nested interfaces, making the supporting OMG IDL interfaces unavailable to client applications.

Benefits

➤ Layering can be enforced.
➤ OMG IDL information can be made opaque to clients who do not need to call it.
➤ By separating the OMG IDL into different sets, they can be maintained, developed, and compiled independently.

Consequences

➤ The ability to enforce architectural levels is highly specific to CORBA implementation. All techniques may not be possible in a given implementation.
➤ Some relationships are complex enough that a successful compilation may not be possible without having most of the supporting OMG IDL defined at compile-time.
➤ Adds substantially to the configuration management complexity of maintaining separate sets of OMG IDL and Interface Repositories (IRs). Can easily escalate into a maintenance nightmare.

Rescaling This Solution to Other Levels

This solution can also be used at the enterprise level as it is highly effective as a means to separate enterprise-level OMG IDL from system- and application-level OMG IDL.

Related Solutions

➤ Layered Architecture—This is an architectural pattern that describes abstraction layers within a system. The following is a list of layered architectural patterns described in other sources:

A Pattern for Generating a Layered Architecture (Rubel 1994)

The Layered Architectural Pattern (Shaw 1995)

The Layered Architectural Pattern (Buschmann et al. 1996)

The Levels of Abstraction Pattern (Hopley 1995)

➤ Vendor Reference Manuals—The reference manuals for a specific CORBA implementation provide the best source for the detailed information needed to implement this pattern.

Example

Consider the following set of OMG IDL, which defines the Pin Setter in a bowling alley:

```
module US_Bowling {

        enum PinState { UP, DOWN, MISSING };

        interface PinSetter {
                enum PinNumber { ONE, TWO, THREE, FOUR, FIVE, SIX,
                    SEVEN, EIGHT, NINE, TEN };
                exception HW_MALFUNCTION;
                exception MISSING_PIN;
                PinState GetPinState(in PinNumber pin);
                void SetPinState(in PinNumber pin, in PinState state);
                void Reset()
                        raises( HW_MALFUNCTION, MISSING_PIN);
        };

        interface Pin {
                attribute current_state;
        };

    }
```

In the US_Bowling module, Pin and PinSetter are the only two interfaces defined. The designer of the Pin interface defined it in IDL, rather than within the implementation of PinSetter, so that the Pin objects could be distributed independently from the interface PinSetter. The intent is to allow PinSetter to invoke the Pin interface through its IDL; however, the designer does not want anyone else to invoke the Pin interface. Applying the techniques outlined in the solution, it is possible to configure the interface repositories to enforce this intent. In the above example, the proper way to control access is to compile the IDL into a set of client and server stubs that are compiled into the implementation of PinSetter. Also, if the interface repository of PinSetter is not shared with its clients, then add the IDL to the PinSetter interface repository. Next, remove the definition of "interface Pin" from the above IDL. Then, compile a new set of client stubs for client of PinSetter. Distribute this new IDL to the client of PinSetter, if the interface repository is not shared by the PinSetter implementation. This configuration will allow the client application to access the PinSetter interface without revealing or enabling the invocation of the Pin interface. The PinSetter implementation, however, can still access the Pin interface as usual. Also, if the Pin interface was located outside of the same module as the Pin Setter interface (module US_Bowl), then an additional step of relocating the Pin interface into the same module as the PinSetter interface that invokes it would have been necessary. The intended purpose of the interfaces is now enforced by the configuration of the client stubs and interface repositories.

Background

In a CORBA environment, it is possible to have many sets of interfaces defined in the environment. CORBA provides no mechanism for making an OMG IDL set private, or usable only from within the implementation of another specific interface. All interfaces may be accessed by any client that has an object reference to that interface. This is not desirable if you wish to define supporting services that can only be used by certain prespecified supporting services. Currently, CORBA does not have built-in capability to provide for the explicit layering of OMG IDL interfaces by controlling access between layers and ensuring that layering constraints are enforced.

This pattern was inferred from using similar techniques to address three different situations that occurred in helping clients extend an OMG IDL framework. The first situation arose when we had many developers working on an evolving set of OMG IDL. It quickly became apparent that it was not desirable to have every client and server in the system recompile every time the OMG IDL was modified. Rather than create separate environments for the testing of applications and the testing of new OMG IDL definitions, a baseline set of OMG IDL was agreed upon and application clients and servers were written to this baseline. Additionally, new OMG IDL definitions could be added and removed from the common interface repository as long as the baseline definitions remained. Furthermore, the generation of client stubs and server skeletons was modified so that rather than generate new definitions from scratch, the baseline definitions were maintained, with new information only being generated for modified definitions. This allowed existing clients and servers to work normally, despite having client stubs that did not reflect the complete set of interfaces accessed via the interface repository. As long as the new interfaces were not used by the client, the clients remained oblivious to their presence. While the new interfaces were inaccessible by the stable clients, new client stubs could be generated, compiled, and used by the new test clients.

The second use of generating different client stubs for different layers of an architecture came about in developing an object-oriented front end for a relational database. The architectural intent was to not allow client applications to access the relational database directly, but to use the objects defined at the enterprise object model defined above the data access layer. The data access layer was to be accessed within the implementation of enterprise object only. There were several developers working on the project, and there were problems that made it desirable to verify compliance with the original architectural intent. Initially, all levels were compiled with the same set of client stubs, which allowed all server object interfaces to be accessed by all clients. By reconfiguring the system and compiling the clients that were not also object implementations with only the OMG IDL for the enterprise object model, clients who violated the architecture by communicating directly with the data access layer were quickly identified and corrected, as the data access layer interfaces were no longer available for their use.

The third development activity that led to the limiting of client stubs to some clients was the search for available security mechanisms in the CORBA environment. This work predated the standardization of the OMG Security Service and provided valuable insight as to how configuration management could be used to provide at least some basic level of security. While separating client stubs from applications provided for some small measure of access control, it was inadequate for all but the most minimal of security requirements.

Solution Name: Defining Exceptions

Intent: To provide exceptions that allow clients to determine the source of the operation failure.

Applicability at This Scale: The core CORBA specification defines nearly 30 standard exceptions that are general enough to cover a large range of explanation of system failure. CORBA allows clients to use the predefined system exception when an implementation is unable to service a request. However, most ORB vendors also utilize the standard CORBA exceptions to return failures within the ORB marshaling layer. As a client invokes an operation, the identical exception could be received from either the ORB or the object implementation, if the object implementation also returns the standard CORBA exceptions. CORBA does allow the definition of user-defined exceptions, and the implementor of the object has complete control over which exceptions are returned in the event of an error.

Solution Summary
1. Define, either globally or in each module, exceptions corresponding to the general system exceptions defined by CORBA.
2. In server applications, refrain from ever returning a CORBA-defined system exception. Always return user-defined exceptions in applications.

Benefits
➤ Clients can easily determine whether the failure originated in an application or within the ORB.
➤ Exceptions returned by the server cannot possibly conflict with mechanisms used by the ORB. Less likely to encounter problems with ORB implementations.

Other Consequences
➤ Developers are creating exceptions that are redundant with the CORBA system exceptions.
➤ Excess exceptions may be confusing to future developers/maintainers of OMG IDL.

Replication

Most Applicable Scale: System

Solution Type: Software

Solution Name: Replication

Intent: How to provide improved performance and reliability by replicating an object in multiple distributed locations.

Primal Forces: Management of Performance

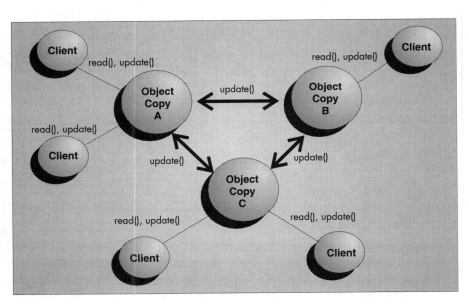

Figure 9.2 The Replication pattern allows multiple clients to access shared data with improved performance and reliability.

Applicability at This Scale

This pattern is applicable when:

1. Performance is inadequate for shared data access in a distributed system.
2. There are multiple client users of some shared objects or data. For example, there may be a groupware application that needs enhanced performance.
3. Client read accesses are more frequent than client update accesses to the shared data.
4. There is a need for shared data access, even when some nodes or the network is experiencing failures.
5. There are multiple distributed host machines with local clients and significant performance difference between local and remote access. The distributed machines have available disk space and underutilized processors.
6. Resolution of performance issues is a high priority, sufficient to counterbalance the additional complexity, computation, and storage requirements due to replication.
7. One of the following two conditions is true of the shared data: a) Updates are relatively small and inexpensive compared to copying the data, and b) it is more efficient to copy the shared data than to propagate updates.

Solution Summary

Create multiple copies of a shared object, that is, replicants. The replicants should be located close to the client software, performancewise (probably on the same machine). When clients read the shared data, they do so concurrently to the replicants. When a client updates the shared data, the changes are reflected throughout the replicants. The replicants share a private communication with each other to initialize, update, and recover.

The insertion of replication into an application should be relatively transparent to the client software, that is, each client should be able to interact with a replicant in the same simple way that it could interact with a single, centralized copy of the shared data. This gives the developers and maintainers the ability to fine-tune the solution by increasing or decreasing replication as needed to optimize performance or resource use.

Benefits

➤ Enhanced performance for local data access and updates.
➤ Ability to transparently tune performance, without changing client software.

- Parallel access for read-only operations by clients.
- Enhanced reliability and availability in case of network outages and server crashes.

Other Consequences

- Additional development and maintenance of the replication solution can be complex and costly.
- There is the possibility of inconsistency between replicated copies.

Variations of This Solution

One key set of variations involved different kinds of guarantees on the coherence of the updates. In some domains, it may be acceptable to have some asynchrony in the update and some inconsistency in the client views, for example, in a groupware application with a shared canvas. Some domains may require atomic update, so that all clients have an identical, coherent view of the data, and all replicants need to complete an update before further client access can proceed, for example, in a groupware application for an object-oriented drawing space. Some installations may require rigorous coherence guarantees equivalent to the ACID properties (Atomic, Consistent, Isolated, Durable), where all updates must be committed reliably. For example, this may apply to an On-Line Transaction Processing (OLTP) application where inventory or credit is being exchanged. The solutions vary in the kinds of protocols used between the replicants: asynchronous, concurrency-controlled (that is, the OMG Concurrency Control Service), or transactional (that is, the OMG Transaction Service).

Another key variation deals with the tradeoff of whether one propagates the operation or copies the data when doing updates. In operation logging, the replicants propagate the instructions for modifying the data whenever there is an update operation, and the operations are recomputed in every replicant. In value logging, the replicants exchange the modified data, and the update operations occur only in one replicant. Operation logging is used when there is a significant amount of data or the performance cost of recomputing updates is relatively small. Value logging is used when the cost of transmitting the data is small compared to the cost of recomputing the operations. This is a key tradeoff in the design of the solution, and it is dependent on the domain usage of the data.

Rescaling This Solution to Other Levels

This solution can be utilized at other scales, such as the system and enterprise levels, to provide improved performance, reliability, and availability. At the system level, the replicants are complete applications that are replicated in several places in a distributed system. At the enterprise level, the replicants may be entire systems with common data that are replicated at several enterprise locations.

Related Solutions:

> Load Balancing—The technique of spreading the work of a server over many servers that support the same implementation. Replication is most often used to implement a load-balancing policy.
> OMG Concurrency Control Service, OMG Transaction Service—These services can be used to implement coordination between one or more replicated copies of a service.
> Other Examples: IBM SOM Replication Framework, X.500 directory federation.

Agent

Most Applicable Scale: System

Solution Type: Software

Solution Name: Agent

Intent: To simplify client access to disparate information services. To provide uniform, consolidated access to disparate services.

Primal Forces: Management of Complexity

Applicability at This Scale

1. A client needs services from many sources.
2. A client has a need to delegate tasks to other applications.

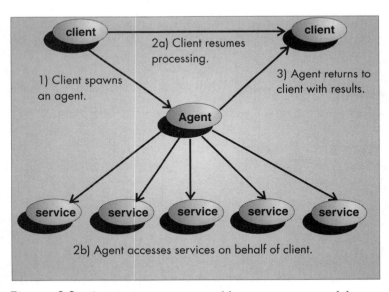

Figure 9.3 The Agent pattern enables a process to delegate actions to other processes.

---

3. A client needs the results of a delegated information-gathering task in order to complete its processing.
4. Coordination between tasks is not a trivial operation.
5. A client potentially needs to be notified after the completion of some task.

Solution Summary

To develop an agent to operate on behalf of a client application, there are at least three key components to be specified.

The first component is deciding exactly what operations will be delegated to the agent application. A good starting point is to identify what tasks are well suited to be performed independently of, and parallel to, the client application. For example, often a client has the task of continuing to monitor a device and would like to delegate the task of obtaining current information about other parts of the system to a software agent. By delegating the information-gathering portion of its execution, the client is able to monitor the device on a more consistent basis.

The second issue is deciding how the agent will be instructed to initially perform the task on behalf of the client application. In the previous example, the client will probably initiate the agent in parallel to its own initialization and have it collect current information on its behalf. Often, an agent will be sent to query one or more services, or some other noncontinuous task, in which case the initialization is on demand.

Finally, a mechanism needs to be specified as to how the agent will communicate its results back to the client application. In the example of a monitoring application, the results are most likely best returned by means of a callback routine. For some data-gathering activities, an event can be sent to the client application, or perhaps the results may be stored in a location accessible by both applications. Additionally, the OMG Event Service may be used to communicate between a task and its designated agents.

Benefits

➤ Provides for a greater degree of parallelism in the system.
➤ A client can perform some other task while the agent is gathering resources.

Other Consequences

➤ An independent process is needed.
➤ May not be able to guarantee an eventual response in the case of a fatal error.

Rescaling This Solution to Other Levels

Increasingly, enterprise-level and global-level agents are becoming common-place. The main obstacles in the development of global agents is the lack of support in global security mechanisms. Often an agent has difficulty negotiating access levels sufficient to perform search and retrieval operations against databases beyond the control of the initiating client application.

Related Solutions

➤ Notification—This pattern is often used to coordinate communication between applications and agents acting on an application's behalf.
➤ OMG Event Service—Provides a standard, generic method of coordinating across applications.
➤ Shopping List and Bag Pattern (Doble 1995)—An agent pattern used to collect items from an arbitrary collection of services.
➤ OMG Mobile Agent Facility—A future OMG CORBAfacility for agent technologies.

Example

The Broadcast Agent will use the Distributed Callback pattern to broadcast a get method to a series of services and provide a sequence of successful responses back to the originating object. This agent assumes that all services share a common interface, and that the names of services are known beforehand.

1. Client invokes function on agent and continues processing, uses the Distributed Callback pattern and passes agent an object reference to its callback object.
2. Agent takes list of names and obtains object references from OMG Naming Service.
3. Agent invokes operation on each of the servers in turn. If operation is successful, it stores the results in a list.
4. After each server has been invoked, the agent invokes the original client's callback routine with the results of the cumulative requests.
5. Client processes the results in the callback routine.

Background

One of the benefits of a distributed system is the ability to perform one or more activities concurrently. For a client application, it is often desirable to have a service perform one or more activities on its behalf. The Partial Processing design pattern is an example of this parallelism, where a server completes an operation initiated by a client. Simple agents of various sorts have been used to maximize the benefits of a distributed architecture for some time. Delegation is an effective tool for processing several requests in parallel. However, more sophisticated uses of agents in the CORBA environment will require more mature CORBA implementations with fully functioning capabilities for browsing interface repositories and robust CORBAservices such as Trader and Query, to allow agents to obtain metadata information about object interfaces.

> Often excess flexibility in an interface is detrimental to interoperability, since additional conventions (in the form of a Profile) must be specified in order for applications to be assured of interoperability.

Architecture Framework

Most Applicable Scale: System

Solution Type: Software

Solution Name: Architecture Framework

Intent: How to establish software interoperability without excessive complexity.

Primal Forces: Management of Complexity

Applicability at This Scale

1. The need to establish interoperability between multiple applications including legacy, commercial, and custom.

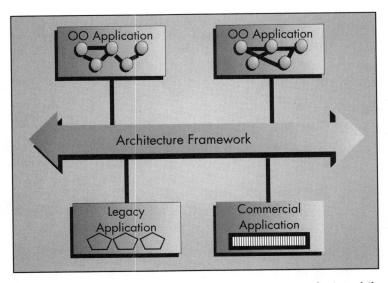

Figure 9.4 An Architecture Framework manages complexity while providing for interoperability and adaptability.

2. The need for system adaptability, to provide an integration solution that can be extended. Adaptability is a key design consideration at the system level, involving about 30% of development cost due to changing requirements, and about 70% of operations and maintenance cost (Horowitz 1993).
3. The need for isolation between subsystems (or loose coupling), to enable localized changes without risk.
4. The need to minimize complexity, to ensure correct understanding of the system by developers and maintainers. About half of programming time involved system discovery (Coplien 1994). An effective architecture framework makes system understanding easy.

Solution Summary

Encapsulate the implementation details of subsystems by defining the system-level interfaces to capture the interoperability needs of the system. Minimize the complexity of the interactions between subsystems through high-level, coarse-grained abstractions in the system-level interfaces. Use reusable, domain-independent designs for the software interfaces, and convey domain-specific details in the data passed through the interfaces.

Benefits

➤ Minimizes system-level complexity, making the system level less expensive to learn, document, develop, and extend.
➤ Isolates subsystems, allowing for localized changes, subsystem replacement, and new subsystems.
➤ Reduces system-level communication traffic, which usually improves performance significantly. Minimizes the number of messages sent between subsystems (i.e., minimizes ORB messaging).

Other Consequences

➤ Limits exposure of domain-specific details inside of subsystem boundaries; system level may not have a natural object-oriented structure.
➤ Requires extra parameter encoding/decoding at subsystem boundaries; involves some extra code and processing compared to a hardwired vertical interface.

Related Solutions

➤ Horizontal-Vertical-Metadata, Metadata—The process of developing fundamentally sound architecture frameworks.

➤ Software Productivity Consortium, Herndon, VA—An industry membership group that provides training, research, and private colloquia devoted to improved software development, with an emphasis on software architecture practices and principles.

➤ Software Engineering Institute, Pittsburgh, PA—SEI has publications and has taught courses in software architecture (Shaw 96).

➤ Architecture-Driven Development—Described by Grady Booch (1995) as the most effective way to develop software.

Example

Suppose there is a set of subsystems to be integrated, as shown in Figure 9.5. Each subsystem has a moderate level of internal complexity, with perhaps 300 to 500 classes each. We can integrate this system by allowing objects in each of the subsystems to communicate directly with objects in other subsystems. It does not take many of these interactions before the subsystems' interactions become quite complex. The system begins to resemble a much larger program with 1200 to 2000 classes. A key consequence of this direct form of integration is that the subsystems have very complex and brittle interrelationships. It is not clear how an additional subsystem could be added to this configuration

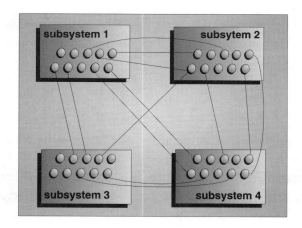

Figure 9.5 Exposed subsystem details lead to brittle interdependencies at the system level.

without substantial additional programming. It is also likely that any changes to individual subsystems will have systemwide impacts.

In an Architecture Framework solution, we define and abstract the interoperability needs for the subsystem interconnections. We choose a simplified interface solution that provides isolation and reusability. Design of this system-level framework involves application of the principles described in the Horizontal-Vertical-Metadata solution. By eliminating close coupling between subsystems, we are better able to adapt the system. Local changes are unlikely to have systemwide impacts.

Background

A key point in this pattern is that there are significant differences between resolving forces at the system level and resolving the corresponding forces at the application level. Understanding these differences is generally not part of the background of software engineers.

We are familiar with many examples of migrations to distributed objects that involve direct translation of subsystem interfaces for use at the system level. This generally has some serious consequences. Consider the following challenges encountered by one such project (Just 1996):

➤ Architectures are domain-specific, hence numerous and varied.
➤ The desire to simplify architecture to more generic forms and looser commitments is strong, but the challenge is great.
➤ Few means exist for interrelating or translating between alternative architectures or views.
➤ Architecture depends on champions, commitments, and long timeframes—all organizationally unnatural.

The resolution of forces at the system level must consider management of complexity and management of change. Projects often disregard these issues for shorter-term objectives, such as demonstration of functionality and optimization of performance. Although these goals are important, they often lead to system-level choices that impact adaptability.

CHAPTER TEN

Using OMG CORBAservices

One of the aims of this work is to increase the awareness of the role of CORBAservices in the CORBA environment. The CORBAservices provide a standard set of services across all CORBA implementations that enhance interoperability across and between application implementations. They are an integral part of the OMA and were designed and developed to work well together. Ideally, source code that was written to a set of object services could be portable across all other ORB environments supporting the same language binding and CORBAservices. Furthermore, as building blocks for applications, the CORBAservices promote code reuse and technological migration as the protocols and implementation details evolve independently from the CORBA and application interfaces.

However, despite these benefits, the purpose of CORBAservices is frequently overlooked, due to a lack of both system profiles and an understanding of their intended usage. In the OMG documentation, there are few, if any, examples and scenarios of the proper use of the interfaces of a particular service. Furthermore, the method of documentation does not promote language-specific examples that could often be beneficial in illustrating the proper preparation of information passed as arguments to operations. By describing many of the early object services as design patterns, any confusion about the use and extension of object services can be minimized and a greater understanding of the intent and motivation of the OMA will be achieved. This is not a criticism of the OMG documents, but rather a recognition of the need to supplement the bare specifications with additional documentation. Such documentation should be customized specifically to either users of the object services, who may extend them through inheritance or composition, or the implementors of CORBAservices.

The examples in the following patterns serve to address the need for specific scenarios in using the various CORBAservices. However, the examples are not tailored to a specific domain. In the development of enterprise- and system-level profiles, additional documentation will be needed to discuss the organizational or team level use of profiles. In many environments, it may be appropriate to only provide documentation for the specific application or system profile, as the learning curve for using the CORBAservices may be considerable higher than a domain-specific set of operations that take advantage of the CORBAservices in their implementation. Furthermore, building a domain-specific set of operations within a profile is a useful technique when there is a lack of vendor implementations for one or more of the CORBAservices. The profile could provide the service transparently to the client using whatever tools are currently available and migrate the CORBAservices transparently to the client, once they have been implemented by the organization or vendor.

Each of the following patterns is based directly on a CORBAservice from the OMA. The CORBAservices comprise the base-level services necessary for software development in a distributed system. They are domain-independent and support either their base-level use or the specialization of their object classes through inheritance. Several important system-level CORBAservices are not discussed, as they have been extensively documented in existing work such as OMG Transaction, Relationship, and the Query Service. Many of the patterns at this level and higher levels could benefit from using these CORBAservices in their implementation, and they should be used whenever appropriate to promote interoperability and to simplify system development.

NAMING

This pattern allows the association of an object reference with a specific name.

TRADER

This pattern allows the association of an object reference with a set of named attributes.

NOTIFICATION

This pattern provides constructs to decouple the communication between objects and to provide a mechanism for defining and coordinating events between applications. This pattern is based on the OMG Event Service.

Implementing Your Own CORBAservices

1. Obtain the standard OMG IDL from the OMG.
2. Run the OMG IDL through vendor's OMG IDL compiler and generate client stubs and server skeleton.
3. Decide on the minimal functionality and implement the interfaces necessary for it.
4. Implement more of the specification as needed by your applications.
5. Share your CORBAservices implementations with others! Trade with friends! Be the first on your block to collect and use them all!

Naming

Most Applicable Scale: System

Solution Type: Technology

Solution Name: Naming

Intent: To find an object, given its name. To organize a name space.

Primal Forces: Management of Change, Management of IT Resources

Applicability at This Scale

1. A means to decouple services from the clients that need their services is required.
2. Service object references change dynamically within a system.
3. It is required to access services by name.

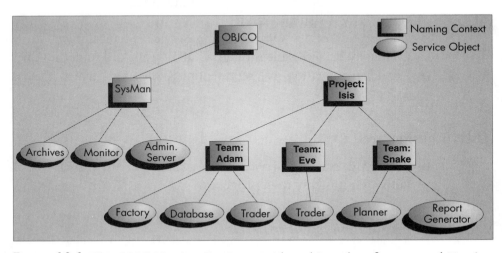

Figure 10.1 The OMG Naming Service provides a hierarchy of names and Naming Contexts, which contain either names or additional Naming Contexts.

4. A well-known repository of services is needed.

5. Separate namespaces are needed to store references for services.

Solution Summary

A naming service is simply a well-known repository that stores named object references. Two basic operations are supported: store(bind) and retrieve(resolve). A key benefit of an OMG Naming Service is that it is distributed, allowing for stored object references to be accessed through a CORBA environment.

Clients use the naming service to locate objects in a CORBA environment. If the name of a service is known, the naming service can be used to obtain an object reference for the service. With the object reference, a client can invoke operations on the service through its interface. Conversely, services advertise themselves with the Naming Service by providing their object reference and associated name. The Naming Service provides multiple namespaces, or Naming Contexts, which provide a scoping capability. A client with access to a Naming Context can navigate through its name hierarchy to locate a service. Alternatively, it can directly access a name through using a compound Naming Component, which specifies the complete path to where the service is located within the naming hierarchy.

Benefits

- ➤ The OMG Naming Service is a distributed facility.
- ➤ It is an OMG standard service.
- ➤ The location of the OMG Naming Service is typically well known and will eventually be accessible through CORBA standard finder routines.
- ➤ Provides a method of representing structured names that is platform-independent.

Other Consequences

- ➤ The OMG Naming Service is not available on all CORBA implementation (although it is easy to implement).

Rescaling This Solution to Other Levels

Definitely scales up to the enterprise level and global levels; however, the larger the scale, the greater the need for the management of various naming services and the contexts they contain.

Related Solutions:

> ➤ OMG Naming Service—Provides the detailed documentation for the OMG standard service.
> ➤ OMG Trader Service—Returns an object reference based on a list of attributes rather than by name.

Example

Following is a piece of source code for using an OMG Naming Service in the C binding:

```
CORBA_Object getReference(char* objectName, NamingContext ctx) {
      CORBA_Environment ev;
      COSNaming_Name name;
      COSNaming_NameComponent name_comp;
      CORBA_Object object;

/*Initialize NameComponent with objectName*/
      name_comp.id=(char*)strdup (objectName);
      name_comp.kind=NULL;
      name._length=1;
      name._maximum=1;
      name._buffer=&name_comp;

/*Retrieve object reference by name (objectName)*/
      object=CosNaming_NamingContext_resolve(ctx, &ev, &name);

/*Check for CORBA exception after resolve() operation*/
      if((ev._major!=CORBA_NO_EXCEPTION) || (CORBA_Object_is_nil(object))){
            return (CORBA_OBJECT_NIL);
      }
      return (object);
}

void storeReference( char* objectName,CORBA_Object objref,NamingContext ctx){
      CORBA_Environment Ev;
      COSNaming_Name name;
      COSNaming_NameComponent name_comp;
      CORBA_Object object;

/*Initialize NameComponent with objectName */
      name_comp.id=(char*)strdup (objectName);
      name_comp.kind=NULL;
      name._length=1;
      name._maximum=1;
      name._buffer=&name_comp;

/*Store object reference (objref) with associated name (objectName) */
      CosNaming_NamingContext_rebind(ctx, &ev, &name, objref);
```

```
/* Check for CORBA exception after rebind() operation */
        if (ev._major !=CORBA_NO_EXCEPTION){
                fprintf(stderr, "Failure adding name to Naming Context.\n");
        }
}
```

Background

In a distributed object system, in order to access a service, a means of obtaining an object reference for that service is necessary. It is also desirable that the services are not forced to choose which clients are allowed to access them and bear the responsibility of explicitly giving each client their object reference. A means to decouple servers in a distributed object environment from the clients that access the service is highly desirable. Also, it is desirable to delay giving a client an object reference to a service until it is ready to make use of it as this allows for the object reference of a service to change independently of the service itself. A well-known repository of object references to services needs to be maintained by the system and should have a mechanism to dynamically provide an object reference in response to the client's requests and should also allow for the run-time alteration of object references in its repository. A simple name lookup is sufficient for many purposes.

The OMG Naming Service is a very simple service that can be used in an identical manner at all levels. The organization of the specific Naming Contexts within an OMG Naming Service is an enterprise issue. Accessing the service is done at the application level in order to locate system-, enterprise-, and potentially global-level services.

Hierarchy of Design Considerations:

1. Use OMG CORBAservices where appropriate.
2. Use existing standard interfaces defined in OMG IDL.
3. Develop new interfaces in OMG IDL with the intention of providing them to others within your enterprise.
4. Develop new, well-designed software components with no intention of ever distributing them as shared components.
5. Develop new, well-designed software components with no intention of ever making them available to others.

Trader

Most Applicable Scale: System

Solution Type: Technology

Solution Name: Trader

Intent: To find and select a service based on desired attributes.

Primal Forces: Management of Change, Management of IT Resources

Applicability at This Scale

1. A means to decouple services from the clients that need their services is required.
2. Service object references change dynamically within a system.
3. It is required to access services by attributes, properties, or service type.
4. A well-known repository of services is needed.

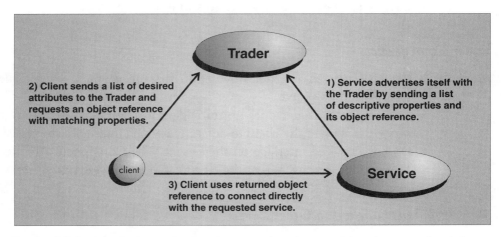

Figure 10.2 The Trader pattern is an essential tool in providing run-time flexibility in a distributed system.

---

5. Applications are interested in Quality of Service information about a service.
6. Services need to advertise themselves to potential clients.

Solution Summary

When a server wishes to advertise itself with the Trader, it invokes a registration function, passing its object reference and a description of the service it provides.

Clients locate services by specifying a search criteria that describes the service desired. The description of services is usually expressed as a sequence of attributes (Named Values), some of which are required and others that express service preferences. The search criteria are matched against the attributes of registered service attributes and if a suitable match is located it is returned to the client.

The Trader allows services to be bound to clients at run-time (like the Naming Service). Since most environments have a substantial number of available services, many traders also support interfaces for federation and linking, which facilitates the cooperation of many traders in servicing a request.

Benefits

➤ It will be an OMG standard service.
➤ Provides for advertising and discovery of services at run-time.
➤ Works with heterogeneous information types.
➤ Supports dynamic properties.
➤ Eases system evolution and aids distribution of services.

Other Consequences

➤ Unlike databases, a Trader provides no guarantees on the completeness of the information provided.
➤ Generally, the Trader does not provide information as to how to access the service. It is up to the client to determine which interfaces are available and to invoke a desired interface on the service. The Component Architecture pattern is useful to ensure that the client can easily access system services.

Rescaling This Solution to Other Levels

Definitely scales up to the enterprise-level and global-level; however, the larger the scale, the greater the need for federation of trader services and the more difficult it is to coordinate activity between traders.

Related Solutions

> ➤ OMG Naming Service—Retrieves object reference by name.
> ➤ OMG Trader Service, ODP Trader Service, ISO Trader—Detailed documentation on the trader services, including the extensive ongoing research by the ODP.

Example

The overall idea of a Trader is simple. Once the OMG Trader specification has been finalized, all traders should conform to its specification. In the meantime, it would be advantageous to keep the functionality of a custom Trader to a minimum, with a plan to migrate to the OMG standard interfaces when they become available. The OMG IDL provided below is sufficient to provide the basic functionality of a Trader.

```
interface Trader {
     exception ALREADY_REGISTERED {};
     exception SERVICE_NOT_REGISTERED;
     exception NO_SUCH_SERVICE {};
     typedef sequence<NamedValue> attrList;

     void Register ( in object, in attrList attributes)
          raises( ALREADY_REGISTERED );
     void Unregister(in object)
          raises( SERVICE_NOT_REGISTERED );

    void Retrieve (in attrList mandatory, in attrList preferences, out object)
          raises ( NO_SUCH_SERVICE );
};
```

The actual implementation of the Trader could be as simple as the above design. The Trader interface could be implemented as a series of extendible columns. Each column could represent an attribute that a server either may or may not support. When a service registers with the Trader, it passes in a list of supported attributes. Each new service is assigned a row in the Trader table. If the object reference being registered is identical to an object reference current in the Trader, an ALREADY_REGISTERED exception is returned. If the service is new, then each attribute is checked to see if it matches a column already in the Trader. If the attribute does match an existing column, then its value is entered into the column for the service row. Otherwise, a new column is added to the Trader for the new attribute and the value of the attribute is placed in the cell for the service row and new attribute column. In this way, new services may be added with unique attributes that can be matched against the needs of clients at run-time.

The Unregister function simply removes a service row from the Trader that matches the object reference of the service passed into the function. If the object reference for the service is not located, then a SERVICE_NOT_REGISTERED exception is returned. Finally, the Retrieve function allows the client to select an object reference based upon a list of mandatory and preferred attributes.

If the Trader does not contain an object reference that has been registered as supporting all of the mandatory attributes, then a NO_SUCH_SERVICE exception is returned by the client. Otherwise, the object reference that matches all of the mandatory and the greatest number of preferred attributes is returned to the client. Obviously, a more discriminating algorithm could be implemented, either by attaching weight to the ordering of preferences or by providing more information in the registration and retrieving routines; however, a simpler scheme is adequate for many small-scale systems.

Notification

Most Applicable Scale: System

Solution Type: Technology

Solution Name: Notification

Intent: To allow an object to notify and receive notification of events. To eliminate direct coupling among groups of objects.

Primal Forces: Management of Change, Management of Complexity

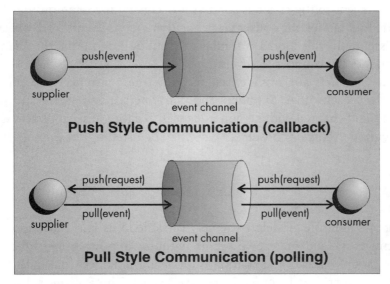

Figure 10.3 The Notification pattern decouples object communication from a specific client-server pair.

Applicability at This Scale

1. An event management capability is needed.
2. Client and services potentially need to be decoupled from each other when managing events.
3. Applications need to be aware of changes in a distributed system.
4. A broadcast capability is desired.
5. Applications are only occasionally interested in events.

Solution Summary

The OMG Event service is used to decouple the communication between objects in a distributed environment. Events can either be directed to or received from a specific client or service or to a shared event channel that can accept listeners and consumers. The OMG Event Service is an example of a service that suffers from the traditional pros and cons of most standards. It is generic enough to be applied to a wide range of applications; however, in its original form it is too generic to be easily understood and tailored to a specific application.

In the Push model, the supplier of events initiates the transfer of events to consumers. Here, the model is similar to a callback, where the event supplier sends the event to the client as soon as it occurs by invoking on the client.

In the Pull model, the consumer explicitly requests events from the event supplier. Essentially, this model is similar to event polling in that the client periodically checks the supplier for events.

Event Channels are provided to decouple the consumers and producers of events from each other. Suppliers and consumers may register and unregister with an event channel with no consequences to either other suppliers who could be providing events or consumers who may be listening for events.

Benefits

➤ It is an OMG standard service.
➤ Supports multiple models, extremely versatile in its implementation.
➤ Clients may send or receive events without supporting any interfaces. The Push model sends events without supporting interfaces, but must implement a set of interfaces in order to receive events. The Pull model may receive events without supporting any interfaces (via polling) but must implement a set of interfaces in order to send events.

Other Consequences

> ➤ The need to specialize the service for specific domains might cause interoperability problems.
> ➤ Other facilities are necessary to meet many of the needs of event handling—methods to locate event channels, classes of event types, and so on.

Rescaling This Solution to Other Levels

This pattern explains the use of the OMG Event Service and is applicable at every level. Within an application, the OMG Event Service is a valuable tool for coordination with other applications. Often, an internal event may be of interest to other applications, in which case an event channel is an ideal mechanism. At the enterprise level, the OMG Event Service may be used to broadcast organizational messages or to allow for coordination between systems. Often, CORBA-based calendar systems are used to coordinate schedules of staff within an organization. Even at the global level, events may be used to send information about expected periods of services being off-line or to request notification of key international events.

Related Solutions

> ➤ Profile—This pattern is often used to tailor the basic OMG Event Service for more specialized purposes.
> ➤ Distributed Callback—This pattern is a custom, lightweight solution to many of the issues addressed by the OMG Event Service.
> ➤ OMG Event Service—The fundamental service for managing events including notification.
> ➤ Resource Exchanger: A Behavioral Pattern for Concurrent Resource Management (Sane & Campbell 1995)—An innovative pattern for resource management that maps well to event management.

Example

This example shows library functions that provide a simple profile to be used to access the generic interfaces of the OMG Event Service and focuses on the use of the Pull Interface.

```
PullSupplier getHighlightService(){
            CORBA_Object objectRef;
            PullSupplier        highlight_service;
/*Retrieve the Event Service object reference from the Naming Service*/
            objectRef=getReference("HighlightSubscriptionService");
            highlight_service=PullSupplier::_narrow(objectRef);
            CORBA_Object_release(objectRef);
            return(highlight_service);


}
void registerForHighlights(){
}
CORBA_any waitForHighlights(){
            CORBA_any    eventAny;
            PullSupplier          highlight_service;
            CORBA_Environment  Ev;


            highlight_service=getHighlightService();
/*Wait for an event to be received from the highlight service */
            eventAny=highlight_service->pull(&Ev); /*Pull Model-blocking*/
            if (Ev._major!=CORBA_NO_EXCEPTION){
                    eventAny._type=TC_Null;
                    eventAny._value=NULL;
                    CORBA_exception_free(Ev);
            }
            CORBA_Object_release(highlight_service);
            return (eventAny);


}
CORBA_any getHighlights(){
            CORBA_boolean       isEventReady=FALSE;
            CORBA_any    eventAny;
            PullSupplier   highlight_service;
            CORBA_Environment  Ev;


            highlight_service=getHighlightService();
/*See if an event is available from the highlight service */
            eventAny=highlight_service->try_pull(&Ev,&isEventReady);/*Pull Model - */
            if (Ev._major !=CORBA_NO_EXCEPTION){                 /*non-blocking */
                    CORBA_exception_free(Ev);
            }
            if (isEventReady == FALSE){ /*If no event available, return a NULL event*/
                    eventAny._type=TC_Null;
                    eventAny._value=NULL;
            }
            CORBA_Object_release(highlight_service);
            return (eventAny);
}
void unRegisterForHighlights(){
            PullSupplier highlight_service;
            CORBA_Environment Ev;
```

```
                highlight_service=getHighlightService();
    /* Disconnect from Event Service */
                highlight_service->disconnect_pull_supplier(&Ev);
                if (Ev._major != CORBA_NO_EXCEPTION){
                        CORBA_exception_free(&Ev);
                }
                CORBA_Object_release(highlight_service);
    }
```

TERM LIST

Most Applicable Scale

Solution Type

Solution Name

Intent

Diagram

References

Applicability at This Scale

Solution Summary

Key Benefits and Consequences

Variations of This Solution

Rescaling This Solution at Other Levels

Related Solutions

Example

Background

Resources

PART FOUR

Enterprise Design Patterns

Enterprise information technology (IT) comprises a system of IT systems. An enterprise may take many forms, from a small commercial services firm to a large government agency, and every size organization in between. The enterprise level is distinct from the global level in that the enterprise exerts guidance, support, and some control over IT systems decision making. This control can be used to centralize a number of important functions, such as IT procurement and technical support. The guidance and control often take the form of policies that are generally followed and occasionally waived by management.

The enterprise level is distinct from the system level in that change is aggregated (from many system-specific changes). At the enterprise level, change appears frequent and continuous. The nature of change itself is different; hence we introduce the new primal force *management of IT resources,* to describe the impacts of large-scale continuous change.

A key issue at the enterprise level is the need for *coordination.* By coordinating system-level IT decisions, the enterprise can enjoy enhanced interoperability, reuse, and graceful transitions as commercial IT evolves and business needs change.

CHAPTER ELEVEN

Building an Organizational Infrastructure

An enterprise is an organizational scope upon which a common set of information technology policies can be imposed. Two key issues at this level are the management of resources and the management of change. In contrast with the system level, the enterprise is a system of systems. Whereas change occurs infrequently at the application level, the cumulative impacts of change are frequent at the system level and occur continuously at the enterprise level. Management of change was a key issue at the system level, and it is also a critical force at the enterprise level. At this level, it is more important than ever to utilize consistent solutions that apply across many resources, such as horizontal and metadata solutions that accommodate change.

Most enterprises are complex; the complexity issues become management of resources issues in that the numerous IT resources must be tracked, inventoried, monitored, supported, and maintained. The enterprise level represents supreme challenges for IT and IT professionals whose responsibilities span enterprise scopes. Much of the experience at this level is negative. In fact, the Chief Information Officer (CIO) job at this level is one of the most highly compensated, but also experiences very high turnover. CIO positions typically turn over every two years, often due to burnout and project failures.

Our solutions at this level are mostly based upon successful practices that have been applied at very large scales, such as government enterprises. Several enterprise patterns contribute to a hierarchy of policy statements (Figure 11.1). These policies guide the organization to manage resources and change in consistent ways.

The Enterprise patterns are summarized as follows:

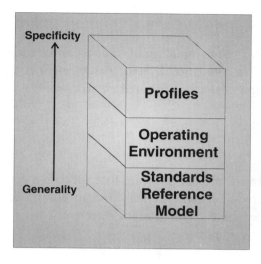

Figure 11.1 The enterprise is controlled through policies designed to manage resources and complexity. The key policies concern the selection of standards (Standards Reference Model), the selection of conventions and products (Operating Environment), and the common usage conventions (Profiles).

STANDARDS REFERENCE MODEL

The Standards Reference Model defines broad policies for software and selection of technology. The IT standards form a guideline that is the basis for commonality and systems migration.

OBJECT REQUEST BROKER

The Object Request Broker is an enterprise infrastructure that provides uniform access to services. This technology simplifies the enterprise infrastructure, and enables management of change and management of IT resources.

OPERATING ENVIRONMENT

The Operating Environment is a common product suite and installation guideline that optimizes the acquisition of technology, training, and support. The Operating Environment is a key solution that makes enterprise management feasible and provides IT for an effective working environment.

SYSTEM MANAGEMENT

System Management comprises the automation of support tasks, such as installation, upgrade, security, and maintenance. System management is a key technology for controlling IT resources in a distributed enterprise.

PROFILE

A profile is value-added software and specification that specialize generic technology and standards to provide specific benefits for an enterprise. Without profiles, all systems undertake these specializations differently, hence a lack of commonality, interoperability, and reuse.

SOFTWARE DEVELOPMENT ROLES

Some of the key enterprise challenges are more people-oriented rather than technology-oriented. The architecture and development roles define some key people-solutions that transfer responsibility where it is needed most.

Standards Reference Model

Most Applicable Scale: Enterprise

Solution Type: Technology

Solution Name: Standards Reference Model

Intent: To manage the evolution of IT resources in a multisystem enterprise.

Primal Forces: Management of IT Resources, Management of Change, Management of Complexity

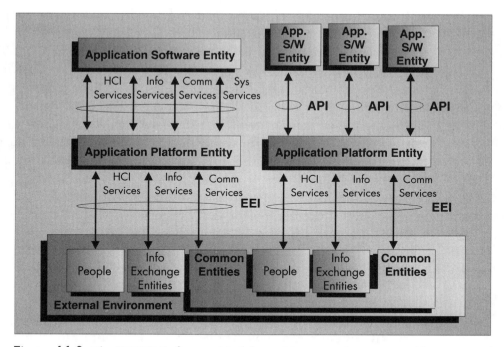

Figure 11.2 The POSIX Reference Model provides general-purpose guidance toward the selection of standards.

Applicability at This Scale

1. An enterprise has highly heterogeneous systems, in particular, the hardware and software diversity in the enterprise is increasing.
2. There is a high risk or cost associated with uncoordinated technology selections in the enterprise. For example, technology selections lead to a lack of compatibility and interoperability. Systems have a mixture of differing incompatible standards, protocols, and data formats.
3. The enterprise cannot immediately migrate, but needs to evolve over time to a common operating environment where systems can interoperate.
4. An enterprise has a lack of coordination in the evolution of IT resources and needs a common technical vision and technology roadmap.

Solution Summary

A Standards Reference Model is a generic architecture for an enterprise's systems. The reference model includes a top-level diagram (or cartoon) that represents the major categories in the model and their relationships. Associated with the reference model is a *standards profile* that lists the recommended standards for each category. Most standards profiles also evaluate the standards with respect to various factors, such as their maturity and market support. The Standards Reference Model can be augmented by a *technology roadmap,* which identifies the evolutionary plan for the support of standards and technologies within an enterprise.

The appropriate starting point for a Standards Reference Model is reuse of an existing reference model. The existing model should apply to a broader domain than required by the enterprise. It is unnecessary to replicate those areas that are covered adequately by the generic reference model. However, it is useful to reduce the number of alternative standards, since most reference models provide multiple alternative standards for each category.

The appropriate steps for generating the model include:

1. Gather information about the needs of the enterprise. In particular, it is important to understand how the enterprise needs extend and specialize the generic reference model.
2. Define areas of functionality that can be addressed by COTS applications versus custom technology. The Standards Reference Model will primarily affect the selection of commercial technology and how custom software will depend on commercial technology.

3. Set enterprise policies, standards, and guidelines. The reference model establishes important standards and guidelines for the acquisition of commercial software. These guidelines are analogous to building codes and zoning laws in the building construction industry. Standards Reference models do not define specific system architectures, but they do provide criteria for acceptability.

4. Encourage the development of explicit profiles demonstrating how the standards are expected to be used. An important area to address is the support for document conversion between formats recommended in the reference model.

5. Provide a mechanism for evaluating architecture compliance of the Standards Reference models and profiles. Provide a plan for the migration to emerging standards, such as a technology roadmap. Important tradeoffs exist between the need for interoperability, the management of risk, and the need to stay current with new technologies.

Benefits

➤ Useful in evolving from diverse standalone systems with closed architectures to an integrated open system based on standards.
➤ Standards provide the enabling commonality for interoperability. Profiles are also needed to assure interoperability.
➤ Enables the use of common architectures and common infrastructure services.
➤ Provides coordination and guidance for procuring new products that work with existing and future systems.

Other Consequences

➤ Standards differ greatly in usefulness and market support.
➤ Reference models can be used to constrain the use of new and experimental technologies.
➤ Application of standards cannot guarantee component reliability, performance, or interoperability.
➤ Standards can be interpreted differently by different vendors. Very few standards are testable: Only about 5% of the standards in a typical reference model can be tested.
➤ Reference models can change frequently as standards and market support evolves. Some current reference models modify as much as 30% of their entries each year.
➤ It can be costly to maintain an accurate reference model.

Related Solutions

Standards are the elements of Standards Reference models. The Standards Reference Model guides the definition of the operating environment; this identifies specific products and technology selections compliant with the model. Profiles identify how the enterprise's systems use standards and the operating environment in order to guarantee interoperability, portability, and other managed benefits.

A number of published Standards Reference models are available for reuse. The POSIX Reference Model is a globally applicable reference model that can be used as a basis for enterprise-specific models. The NIST Application Portability Profile is a guideline for the procurement of systems in the U.S. government.

Object Request Broker

Most Applicable Scale: Enterprise

Solution Type: Technology

Solution Name: Object Request Broker (ORB)

Intent: To simplify distributed computing. To provide transparent client access across a distributed, heterogeneous environment. To separate application software from infrastructure issues such as data marshaling, server location, server selection, and server activation.

Primal Forces: Management of Complexity

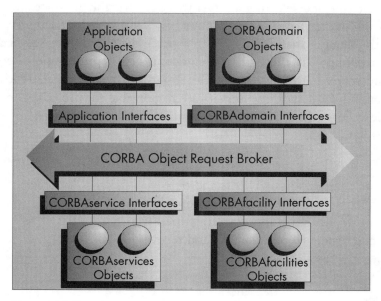

Figure 11.3 Object Request Brokers provide a robust communication infrastructure for an organization using distributed object technology.

Applicability at This Scale

1. A server has a different data representation from the client. A client cannot perform the appropriate translation until after a server is selected.
2. A client is often aware of the service or interface it wants to access but does not know where a server that is capable of servicing the request is located.
3. A client knows the location of a service, but the server is not always active.
4. A server must be initialized in an unusual manner that is unknown to client applications or requires special privileges that are not available to all client applications.
5. A client desires transparency between local and remote operations.
6. The client does not want to explicitly identify the location or implementation that will service its request.

Solution Summary

Provide an intermediate agent between the client and the server, known as an ORB, where client and servers no longer communicate directly with each other. The ORB is responsible for receiving a request from a client, which is made by an interface call, and selecting a server that supports the interface and is capable of servicing the request. If there is not a server available that supports the interface of the request, then the ORB can activate the appropriate server automatically. Furthermore, if there is a difference in data representation between the client and server machines, the ORB translates that data transparently to both the client and the server. The servers are responsible for providing to the ORB instructions concerning server activation commands and policies.

Benefits

➤ Separate compilation of clients and objects.
➤ Reduce complexity of application software.
➤ Separate applications from infrastructure.
➤ Dynamic system reconfiguration and recovery.
➤ Client-side transparency.

Other Consequences

➤ There is some overhead in dynamically binding clients to objects.
➤ Vendor extensions to standards may result in product dependencies.

Rescaling This Solution to Other Levels

The Object Request Broker is not well suited for application-level programming. At the application level, a program is generally in control of its own data and lacks the need for concurrency control and performance benefits resulting from parallelization, which CORBA brings. At the system level, an ORB may be used productively; however, the natural tendency for shared services still results in an Object Request Broker being best used at the enterprise level.

Background

When a client is communicating with a server in a heterogeneous environment, a server might have a different data representation than the client. A client cannot perform the appropriate translation until after a server is selected. Also, a client is often aware of the service or interface it wants to access, but does not know where a server that is capable of servicing the request is located. When a client is aware of the location of a service, the server is not always active. Often, servers must be initialized in a proprietary manner that is unknown to client applications or may require special privileges that are not available to all client applications.

In a traditional client and server environment the client must be acutely aware of the operating conditions of the server. The client must know whether the server is running, and on which machine the server is located. The client needs to know what protocols the server supports and what its internal data formats are so it can send the server data that is meaningful, such as size of integers, representation of strings. Also, if the server is unable, the client needs to know either how to start up the desired server or how to locate another server that can service its request. While a client can be hard-coded to successfully execute only under optimal conditions (a particular server is running on a particular machine under a particular operating system), this is insufficient to meet the needs of a dynamic Inter Process Communications (IPC) environment. Some mechanism is needed to encapsulate the details of client-server communication and provide a transparent interface to client and server implementation details.

Resources

OMG CORBA 2.0, OMG OMA

Stateless versus Stateful Services

Unlike many distributed models, CORBA does not place any constraints on a server as to whether it has to be stateless. CORBA objects may be programmed to behave just like local objects, with the exception that CORBA objects are not limited to the lifetime of a client process. However, CORBA also does not provide any built-in mechanisms to indicate when an object is no longer in use, or when it can be destroyed without affecting other applications. Therefore, an application developer must either provide such mechanisms, or design services such that it has no need of them (stateless).

In general, stateless servers are better suited for the CORBA model. If it appears that a server needs to maintain state, consider a design that decouples the state information from the service being provided. For example, rather than have a client open a session with a server, get and set parameters to set up an operation and close the session to end the transaction, develop a more object-oriented design. For example, have the initial client request to a service return a session object. Let the client perform gets and sets on the session object. Then the client can send the session object to the service in a stateless manner, as all of the data needed by the service is encapsulated in the session object rather than the service itself. When the session is complete the client can destroy the session object, thereby completing the transaction.

If a server is stateless, avoid operations to open/close services as they are traditionally associated with a state. Decouple object implementations from the implementations that created them (in the case of objects created by factories). Configure stateless servers for a limited lifetime if automatic server activation is available.

Operating Environment

Most Applicable Scale: Enterprise

Solution Type: Technology

Solution Name: Operating Environment

Intent: To ensure interoperability and technical support for purchased products throughout an enterprise.

Primal Forces: Management of IT Resources, Management of Technology Transfer

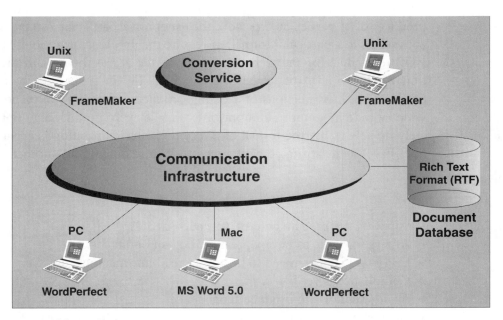

Figure 11.4 A base set of organizational standards is desirable; however, mandating specific products limits system-level flexibility. Often standard formats and services are sufficient to ensure the ability for all platforms to access enterprise data.

Applicability at This Scale

1. An organization is comprised of many fairly autonomous units that have their own unique hardware and software needs.
2. There is a need for document and information transfer between units and even between organizations.
3. Units are using products that are not compatible with products in other parts of the organization, and information transfer is compromised.
4. A single product or collection of products is not sufficient for meeting all of the needs of all of the units throughout an organization.
5. Mandating a single product would freeze the technology level within an organization, ultimately compromising an organization's ability to compete effectively.

Solution Summary

The enterprise level can maximize information transfer without compromising autonomy by only mandating organizational formats that must be supported, rather than particular products. This mandate should take the form of requiring products of a particular type to either support a particular format, support a conversion to a particular format, or require the purchase of a tool that can convert the product format to the format supported across the organization. Traditionally, some level of backwards compatibility is supported by most new products and new versions of existing products, so such a policy provides for wide latitude in a unit's autonomy. Also, while every product may not immediately be able to use the format of every tool, an organization is ensured that it does have the means to convert a data type from one tool to another.

Benefits

> Supports the procurement of specialized tools.
> Allows for units to have a great deal of autonomy.
> Every unit is guaranteed to be able to read information from every other unit.
> Compliance is verifiable.
> Avoids vendor and product dependence.
> Greater productivity could potentially result through the use of specialized tools.

Other Consequences

> ➤ Requires purchase of conversion programs in addition to tools.
> ➤ Greater autonomy limits ability to obtain good volume discounts.
> ➤ Greater learning curves involved in moving between units within same company.
> ➤ Time and resources will be needed to be dedicated toward conversion, either periodically or on demand.

Rescaling This Solution to Other Levels

In a single application, it is reasonable to assume all data will be maintained internally in a single format. If data is received in a format not understood internally, it can either be converted to ensure that particular format, or delegated to an external service to perform the needed conversion.

At the system level, it is necessary to be able to identify the format of received data and to handle data in many formats. A conversion service can simplify this task by allowing applications to send data in an undesired format to the conversion service along with a specified desired format and receive the data in the desired format.

Example

A software development company will typically need to decide on a selection of tools for their organization. The range of applications will include a programming language for prototyping, a programming language for operational development, a word processing package for documentation and office automation, a presentation authoring tool, and a CASE design tool. In considering the tool selection, it is important that the interoperability needs of the tools are deter-

A key architectural constraint is that general facilities do not depend on specialized facilities. Also, while specialized facilities may contain details unique to a domain, the general facilities may not.

mined. For example, will there ever be a need for the diagrams generated from the CASE tool to be importable by the word processing package or the presentation tool? Can the text generated by the word processing package be transferred to the other tools? Will there ever be a need to convert code from the prototyping language to the operational programming language?

System Management

Most Applicable Scale: Enterprise

Solution Type: Technology

Solution Name: System Management

Intent: To reduce operations and maintenance costs through integration of management capabilities with deployed systems and software.

Primal Forces: Management of IT Resources, Management of Change

Applicability at This Scale

1. Complex network of systems and software applications in an enterprise.
2. A system support workload is in need of modification: It requires too many people or is not delivering adequate support.

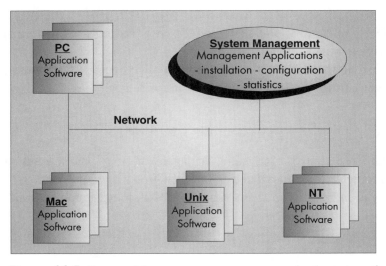

Figure 11.5 System Management can automate the logistics of managing distributed applications and heterogeneous systems.

3. A few majority applications and platforms could leverage automation of System Management tasks.

Solution Summary

System Management comprises the operations and maintenance of software and policies across a distributed enterprise. Some sample System Management operations include: software installation, software upgrade, software license management, file server management, and others.

The solution is to establish a set of common interfaces for the purposes of management of objects. These interfaces should begin with the available standards such as the OMG/X/Open SYSMAN and the Desktop Management Force's Desktop Management Interface. The common interfaces should support all of the System Management capabilities required by the enterprise.

Where available, use applications that support standard management interfaces. Extend these interfaces as needed to support enterprise-specific operations. For other applications, it is necessary to create software wrappers to add the appropriate operations to support management capabilities. A set of management applications is needed that provides a front end for operations and maintenance personnel to perform the management functions.

Benefits

➤ Reduced operations and maintenance costs through automation of System Management.
➤ Consistent application of management policies across distributed systems.
➤ Greater control and monitoring of enterprise resources.

Consequences

➤ Centralized control of System Management functions imposes more severe requirements for homogeneity than locally managed policies.
➤ Integration cost for wrapping commercial and legacy applications to support management interfaces.

Rescaling This Solution to Other Levels

System Management could be applied at the system level. This has the advantage of system-specific management policies. This also has a greater likelihood of higher use of management functions because a single system will have fewer applications and platform types than an enterprise-level installation.

Related Solutions

➤ Common Interfaces—Used as a principle to structure and simplify management interfaces across a wide range of applications.

➤ OMG-X/Open SYSMAN (Specification for Common Management Facilities) is the adopted specification for System Management at OMG. This is a foundational set of interfaces that must be extended for application implementation.

Background

The widespread deployment of personal computers, and more recently the pervasiveness of networking, have created serious management and support problems for enterprises. In a mainframe environment, operations and maintenance took place in a centralized, controlled environment, the cost of which was leveraged across the enterprise. In the PC and networking era, operations and maintenance have been distributed throughout the enterprise. They involve a heterogeneous selection of platforms and user-managed personal software environments.

Initially, enterprises used *self-management,* where individual users would maintain and support their own systems. This led to an ad-hoc environment where many users were unable to obtain desired support, and sharing of information was difficult. The next step was to add shared resources and help desks, where self-managed users could download their own software and had a point-of-contact for support. This was also discovered to be inadequate by many end users. The addition of decentralized, department-level staff for managing systems provided improved support, but was costly. Automated System Management represents the next level of integration and evolution, where many System Management functions can be again centralized.

Profile

Most Applicable Scale: Enterprise

Solution Type: Software

Solution Name: Profile

Intent: To define common usage conventions for general-purpose technologies and standards. To assure that these technologies and standards actually provide the expected and desired benefits.

Primal Forces: Management of Functionality, Management of Complexity, Management of Technology Transfer

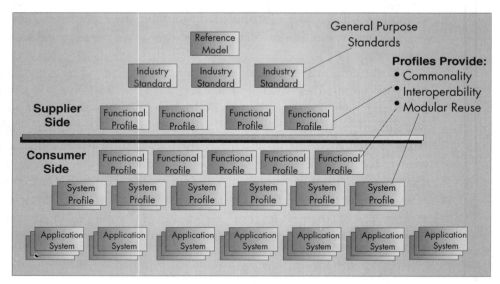

Figure 11.6 General-purpose specifications and technologies are intended to be used in terms of a set of profiles that define common usage conventions across a vertical market (functional profile) and across a set of systems in an enterprise (system profile). General-purpose specifications and technologies are defined by suppliers; profiles are primarily defined by the users of technology.

Applicability at This Scale

1. Using complex standards or technologies.
2. A standard or new technology enters mainstream usage within an enterprise. Often there are groups with different levels of experience (such as research versus operations) and a need to exploit existing knowledge for the benefit of new users and the enterprise.
3. When the needed interoperability or portability of implementations become less than desired or expected from a given standard or technology.
4. When developing software within a domain which is more limited than the target audience for the standard.
5. When there is an emphasis on code reuse and software engineering practices.
6. When the code under development is intended to be reused or maintained for a extended period of time.
7. When consistency of software behavior and implementation is desired across the enterprise or smaller organization.

Solution Summary

A solution to managing the complexity of using standards and general-purpose technologies is to develop a profile. A profile is a set of rules, guidelines, and documentation for using a standard or technology. The profile adds the necessary detail in how to use the standard/technology within an organization to elicit the benefits that the standard/technology enables in a way that is useful in systems.

Specifically, a profile defines a specialized subset of a standard/technology for an enterprise to use. The profile identifies specific protocols, metadata, and usage conventions that guide a developer in using the standard/technology. The profile is established to provide commonality of usage across enterprise systems. Profiles typically involve adding default behavior and usage conventions for how the standard/technology is used. The profile may potentially define a set of metadata schemas and interfaces which define configurations of system parameters at run-time. The profile defines an enterprise-specific design point for controlling the cost and complexity of utilizing a standard or technology.

Benefits

➤ Assures consistent and effective use of standards and general-purpose technologies across multiple systems.

- Maximizes benefits of standards and technologies, such as portability and interoperability.
- Provides essential technology transfer between developers for how to use technologies effectively and uniformly.
- Isolates application software from particular implementations and commercial products, enhancing reuse and system extendibility.
- Manages the complexity of sophisticated standards and complex commercial technologies.

Other Consequences

- Requires planning and coordinated use of standards and technologies between multiple developers or systems projects
- Requires documentation to be generated and maintained
- Requires a detailed understanding of the standard or technology concerned before the profile can be created. In most cases, this knowledge must be based upon prior prototyping experience.

Variations on This Solution

Some profiles can be implemented as a set of language-specific or OMG IDL-defined application programming interfaces (APIs). Such a profile requires an accompanying developer's guide for specifying its usage. The APIs are a set of interfaces that layer on top of, and provide an abstraction for, another set of interfaces that define the standard. Often these APIs are specific to the programming environment, enterprise, or system. The benefit of a well-defined set of APIs in your profile is that they may provide a more convenient method of accessing the underlying interfaces of the standard, and may provide default handling that specializes the use of the more general-purpose APIs of the standard.

It must be noted that profile APIs that are language-specific have limitations in respect to CORBA. By being written in a programming language rather than in the more general interface language of OMG IDL, they may not be portable or reusable across different platforms or other programming languages. Often, this limitation is quite acceptable to an enterprise, and if it satisfies the needs of an enterprise, then this may be a nonissue.

Most generic industry standards could benefit from having one or more enterprises agree upon a profile. When using vendor-proprietary APIs, it is an organizational decision whether to tie software development to the proprietary API or to ease future technological migration by defining a profile and an associated object wrapper (what we call a *profile layer*). Generally, for all but the most short-lived of systems (rapid prototypes, etc.), a profile layer is recommended. If an OMG IDL framework is defined for a system, and an appropriate language binding is available, then a profile layer is not needed as the OMG IDL definitions already provide for technological migration in that new components can be written to the OMG IDL language bindings and seamlessly replace existing components. Since OMG IDL types are self-describing and language-independent, the drawbacks of non-OMG IDL-defined APIs are avoided.

Rescaling This Solution to Other Levels

The notion of a profile is usable at all four of the highest levels of object-oriented architecture. At the global level, a *functional profile* is an industry segment standard; this is designed to meet the needs of some global community (see Figure 11.6). As such, it is designed to be general in order to be usable by as many members in the global community as possible. For example, the medical community has several profiles specifying how medical systems interact with one another. They are currently in the process of formalizing their CORBA-related profiles under the OMG CORBAmed Task Force. The products include profiles of the more generic OMA specifications, as well as vertical market specifications for interoperability among medical information systems. System-level profiles (so-called *system profiles*) are useful in detailing specific characteristics of groups within an enterprise. System profiles can also apply to the trading partners of an enterprise. Finally, *application profiles* detail the specifics of how to interact with a particular system.

Related Solutions

Profiles are used to define common usage conventions for standards that guarantee the standards benefits by constraining implementations. Most general-purpose standards are too flexible to guarantee interoperability or portability without additional constraints. Profiles must be defined for virtually all technologies identified with an operating environment. Profiles are also needed for standards that are actively used from the Standards Reference Model.

Profiles are a vertical element of the Horizontal-Vertical-Metadata pattern. Whereas standards provide risk-reducing horizontal elements to system architecture, the vertical specializations provided by profiles are a necessary part of a balanced architecture that delivers functionality.

Our concept of a profile originates with Cargill (1989), who explained the necessity of profiles in using industry standards.

We have found profiles in widespread use, although they are often called by other names. For example, an *implementation plan* for how to use a particular standard (such as the National Imagery Transmission Format) is an example of a profile.

The creation of profiles usually involves prototyping and implementation experience. Through hands-on experience, one learns enough about a standard or general-purpose technology in order to figure out how to use it effectively. Research projects that are innovators often use technologies years before their mainstream deployment. The participants in these projects gain sufficient knowledge to create meaningful profiles. Unfortunately, this valuable knowledge is often unexploited because technology transfer is inadequately managed.

Example

Suppose we have a number of application systems to buy and we require each to conform to certain IT standards. When using standards, somebody has to make the decisions that comprise the profile. Often, profiles are buried in the application implementation. Whether explicitly acknowledged or not, profiles are required for the use of most standards, to complete the mapping from the enabling specifications to the assured architecture capabilities.

Figure 11.7 below is an example of what happens when standards without profiles are applied to multiple information systems. In the figure, there is a Reference Model that is the conceptual basis for several standards. The Industry Standards define the capabilities provided by the vendors. In this example, the Industry Standards are applied directly to Application System developments. Since the standards are very generic, each application developer must make a large number of decisions about how to use the standard in order to create an application architecture. Much decision making and software are involved in mapping a standard to a particular architecture's needs. Key point: If all these decisions are made independently in each application system, then there will be limited potential for interoperability and reuse between the systems.

Background

The purpose of most standards is to define a very general set of functionality that can be applied to a wide range of applications. A standard enables interop-

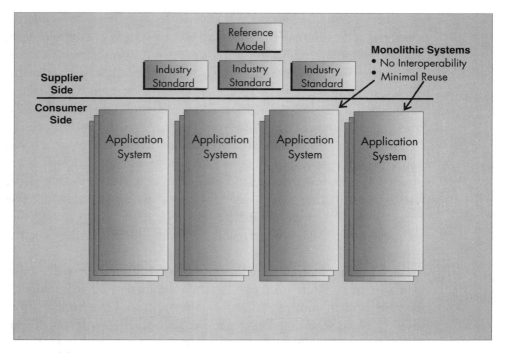

Figure 11.7 When information technology standards are used without common profiles, the application systems make the profile decisions independently and the result is a set of applications that cannot interoperate even though they use the same IT standards.

erability by providing protocols, interfaces, and/or tools that are compatible with other applications that support the particular standard. Within an organization, a standard requires some degree of specialization and customization to determine which portions of a standard are directly applicable to the needs of the organization. Typically, only a subset of a standard is used by most applications, so an organization benefits by clearly agreeing on how the standard is applied within the organization, such as the conventions, defaults, schemas and other details. If these are left undefined, they could potentially undermine the interoperability of the standard. Essentially, a mapping needs to take place between the specification of the standards that enables some set of functionality and the architectural capabilities of the standard that assures long-term interoperability and reuse within an organization.

These comments apply to the selection of proprietary technologies, too. For example, it is not sufficient to say "We support OLE" to really define how you use the technology in your architecture, since OLE is a complex technology with many optional elements. The key difference between standards and proprietary specifications is that open system standards are consensus agreements between multiple vendors. Typically, proprietary specifications are after-the-fact documentation of a single implementation. In contrast, a standard is usually a forward-looking technology agreement that builds upon a long-range reference model, such as the OMG's Object Management Architecture. In general, standards provide a more stable, low-risk basis for system development.

Most open systems standards are defined by a core group of vendors that supply products to a much larger group of consumers, including value-added vendors, systems integrators, and corporate developers. In this sense, the purpose of most standards is to define the *most common* functionality that is useful across the widest range of applications. For vendors supporting the standard, this means that their products will be applicable across the broadest possible customer base.

The purpose of an OO architecture is very different from the purpose of an open system standard. An open system standard *enables* interoperability and other benefits. In contrast, an OO architecture *assures* interoperability and other benefits. There is an important gap between these two levels of support, and that is the whole point: How you use the open system standard in your architectures determines whether you obtain the potential benefits of the standard.

To take a standard from its off-the-shelf form to a form that is directly usable in an application architecture requires some decision making and specialization. Many standards are very complex and broadly applicable. We must determine which parts of the standard provide a useful subset of functionality for our particular application. Then we must define how the useful parts are applied, for example, in terms of a protocol for specific transactions. Then we must supply the details of the schema or metadata as well as the data/parameter syntax. In addition, there may be other important usage conventions that are needed to complete the specialization. Together, these specializations are called an *application standards profile*. We refer to application standards profiles simply as *profiles* in the following discussion.

There is a nontrivial effort involved in applying and abstracting a complex standard to the needs of particular application domains. If we do this independently in each system it becomes a significant duplication of effort. Worse still, we may miss many important benefits because each system uses the standards in different, incompatible ways.

We have seen the importance of profiles in the use of open systems standards. Profiles play an essential role in the overall theory of standards as expressed by

Carl Cargill (1989), the standards guru for Sun and formerly for DEC. There are many levels of profiles between industry standards and the application systems. These profiles capture the common interoperability and reuse conventions.

The first layer of profiles is the functional profiles. Functional profiles are specializations of standards that apply across an entire industry, such as healthcare or financial services. System profiles are specializations of the functional profiles that capture common conventions applied across multiple application systems.

All of the commonality, interoperability, and reuse conventions are embodied in these profiles. Without the profiles, all of these conventions are specific to each application system, as in Figure 11.7.

There are some existing examples of mature sets of profiles. A well-known example is Electronic Data Interchange (EDI). In EDI, there are generic standards (such as X.12), functional profiles for particular industries (subsets of the generic standard), and systems profiles that apply to specific enterprises and their trading partners (which include specific protocols for various EDI transactions).

Note that the majority of the profiles are the responsibility of the consumers of technology. We believe this responsibility is appropriately allocated; only the consumers can truly understand how to specialize generic technologies in ways that provide benefits within their domains. Creation of profiles starts with the consumer of technology and should be part of your normal architecture design approach.

Software Development Roles

Most Applicable Scale: Enterprise

Solution Type: Role

Solution Name: Software Development Roles

Intent: Most problems in human organizations are due to someone not taking responsibility. This solution assures that key software responsibilities are clearly assigned and addressed.

Primal Forces: Management of Technology Transfer, Management of Complexity

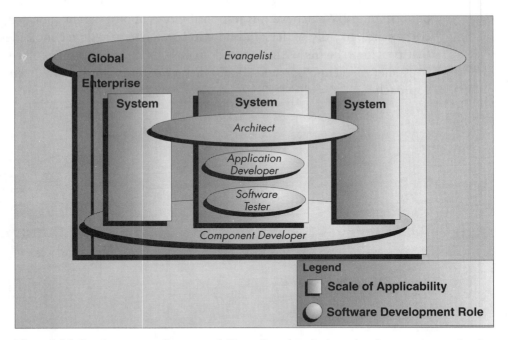

Figure 11.8 The scope of responsibility of each role in a development organization includes knowledge of particular systems and may include other systems inside and outside the enterprise.

Applicability at This Scale

1. Software development repeatedly fails to meet schedule, budget, and system functionality objectives, including project cancellation and failure.
2. Systems are unable to adapt to changing business needs. For example, software operations and maintenance are not able to make desired system extensions.
3. Despite sufficient technical training and solutions, the software development organization is unable to produce consistent project results and manageable systems.
4. Many software organizations are organized according to egalitarian principles; all software developers have the same job description. In such organizations, no particular individual, other than a manager, has responsibility or authority for resolving problems. Problems may be technical or organizational; there is often high overlap between the two categories. For example, reuse and collaboration between developers is highly related to proximity of developers. Managers are unlikely to have sufficient knowledge of project-specific details to resolve technical problems.

Solution Summary

Assign key roles within the enterprise software development organization. Each role is defined to resolve key responsibility issues. Management backing of these roles and responsibilities is critical for their successful implementation.

ARCHITECT

The architect role addresses two key issues: 1) making sure that the system-level architecture supports system adaptability, and 2) minimizing the need for developer guesswork, that is, system discovery. The responsibilities of the architect include coordination, definition, and communication of system-level interfaces. This scope extends the usual role of architects by making them responsible for detailed interface designs. If the architecture is to be realized consistently with the system vision, we see this responsibility as a critical one, which cannot be delegated to developers.

Only a small percentage of developers have the appropriate abstraction skills to perform the architecture role. The principal difference between an architect and a developer is the consideration of the cost impacts of particular design decisions. Cost impacts are often minimized when abstraction is used appropriately (See "Common Interface Solution").

APPLICATION DEVELOPER

Most developers would probably fit in either this category or that of Component Developer. An application developer is responsible for the design and development of a particular application software module. In addition, he or she is responsible for making the system work through the integration of preexisting components and the development of new code. Typically this software module would reside within the scope of one system, although modules may be reusable between systems. Application developers are responsible for implementing the functionality of a system. This includes the mappings to the user interface and the system-level interfaces. Application developers may reuse software components provided by Component Developers.

COMPONENT DEVELOPER

Whereas most application developers are usually vertically oriented to the development of a particular system, component developers are concerned with lower-level general-purpose capabilities that can be reused across multiple systems. Application developers are coding to system-level interfaces; component developers may be coding to finer-grained interfaces, such as libraries or frameworks (see "Relevant Solutions"). The component developer takes responsibility for complex reusability capabilities, so that application developers do not have to reinvent all functionality vertically.

SOFTWARE TESTER

Assurance of software quality is critical to the successful delivery of software. Developers alone cannot be held responsible for objective testing of their own work. A separate role of software tester is needed in order to assure component, application, and system functionality in an objective manner. The software tester is responsible for validating specifications and certifying implementations. Regression testing is an important part of the testing; every time a software module is modified, it is necessary to retest the module and its larger-scale usage.

EVANGELIST

The evangelist is responsible for technology transfer and promoting reuse. The evangelist creates developer awareness and delivers developer education that leads to reuse. This role may have a broad scope across several scales, including global. Evangelism at the global scale is a key aspect of commercial software sales and marketing. Evangelism has an analogous role at the enterprise level to encourage awareness, coordination, and a critical mass of knowledge and advocacy necessary for reuse.

MANAGEMENT

Management roles and responsibilities are manifold; we do not attempt to enumerate them here. Some key responsibilities of management in support of software development include project marketing and role support. By project marketing we mean the internal or external communication necessary to create (or sell) the project and assure project continuation. Project marketing is a continuous responsibility; it is absolutely critical to maintaining the organizational stability necessary to foster a productive working environment. Role support is the reenforcement of the technical roles through appropriate delegation of authority. When problems arise in the project, management can support the roles by delegating the technical decision making to the person with the appropriate role. If management delegates inconsistently with the roles, it undermines the authority of the technical roles.

Organizations have both formal and informal instantiations. The formal organization comprises the formal job titles and job descriptions. The informal organization is based upon individuals' actual contributions to the productivity and functioning of the enterprise. The two organizations may vary significantly in practice. Ideally, the roles defined above recognize and support the contributions of the informal organization, and make it more effective.

Benefits

> ➤ Clarifies responsibilities of technical staff.
> ➤ Assures that someone is responsible for each key software project issue.

Other Consequences

> ➤ Requires guidance and training for technical personnel and management.
> ➤ Requires new patterns of coordination and technical decision making.

Variations of This Solution

There are unlimited variations of this solution. A well-known variation is the IBM Chief Programmer Team. In this solution, a single experienced programmer produces all of the code and is supported by a team of professionals, such as a librarian, tester, and others.

Rescaling This Solution to Other Levels

This solution is presented at the enterprise level because to be implemented effectively, the scope of these roles should probably be implemented on an enterprise scale.

The individual roles vary in their scale of applicability and scope of responsibility. The evangelist role is enterprise and global in scope. Several of the roles apply to system-level scale: application developer, architect, and tester. More detailed descriptions of these roles would best be discussed in the context of these other levels.

Related Solutions

The Architect and Component Developer would be responsible for the specification of Common Interfaces. They could also use the Architecture Mining process as part of their analysis to define these interfaces. The system-level patterns are primarily intended for the Architect. The application-level solutions are directed primarily at the Application Developer and Component Developer. Coplien's Organizational Patterns is another pattern language addressing organizations (Coplien 1994).

Example

The following are some project scenarios that we have encountered.

PROJECT A

Project A is a large development project that has a rigorously managed development process. The development staff (programmers) comprises about 10% of the people. The other people are managers and other functionaries that handle support functions and management information. There is an architecture group that defines the system at high levels of abstraction, suitable for management audiences. The technical details of the interfaces and design are left to the developers.

The project conducted frequent status meetings that consumed more than 20% of managers' time. The formal organization of the project required an endless stream of documentation and status reporting, which indicated orderly progress toward the system objectives.

The development staff comprised the informal organization of the project. There was a disparity between the management information and the actual software progress. This disparity extended to the system architectures that management closely reviewed for the system. The development staff, unable make progress through the formal organization's process, began to develop capabilities in spite of the formal processes. When deadlines were missed, these initiatives were able to deliver capabilities that satisfied short-term goals.

The project was chronically over budget and behind schedule. The funding source began a series of budget cuts, which had the effect of reducing the size of the nondevelopment staff on the project. Each time the budget was cut about 10%, management reported a corresponding productivity increase of about the same amount.

The delivered system lacked the desired flexibility. The end users experienced performance and reliability problems. They were forced to work around system weaknesses rather than risk system extensions.

Key points from Project A: Management's role and the formal organization greatly overshadowed the role of the development staff. This created a strong disparity between the formal and informal organizations. The designated architects were not involved in the actual design of system-level interfaces; this led to a lack of extendibility.

PROJECT B

A moderately sized project team consisted of highly motivated and talented individuals constructing an advanced testbed. The team had well-defined roles including an infrastructure team in charge of the system-level interfaces. The infrastructure team conducted the interface designs, the infrastructure software designs, as well as the programming. Despite high risks in the research software, they completed the system on time, on schedule, and exceeded the performance objectives. This architectural success was achieved despite the fact that much of the programming was done in assembly language by a handful of people who had to deliver their software on multiple operating systems.

Key points from Project B: The project had well-defined roles that corresponded to the informal organization. The infrastructure team took responsibility for the architecture, interfaces, and implementation.

Global Impacts of Local Decisions

Suppose we have a system-level architecture specified in OMG IDL. For the developer it is easy to consider adding an OMG IDL operation for a newly perceived need. For example, an operation get_TIFF_header(), could be added to the OMG IDL if we need to retrieve a file header. Later if we need a GIF header, we can add the OMG IDL operation, get_GIF_header(), an operation get_PICT_header(), and so on.

A well-trained architect may strongly object to such additions. Every time we add new OMG IDL operations we increase the complexity of the system-level architecture. Every subsystem developer is exposed to the complexity contained in this OMG IDL. Every new operation requires implementation code to support it. For each client using the operation, there is also software required. If a new format is introduced, many programs will have to be modified. The architect, responding to the combined forces of managing change and complexity, can design a superior solution, for example, a get_file_header(), where the file format is contained in metadata instead of hardwired into the software of all clients and servers. In addition, some common header information, independent of format, may be useful to include in the metadata.

The forces affecting software decisions can be visualized in the following table. For this discussion, we borrow the popular environmental slogan *think globally, act locally* to refer to the differences between decisions that affect a small software scope and decisions that affect a large scope, such as an entire system or an enterprise.

Table 11.1   Software Decision Forces

	Act Locally	*Act Globally*
Think Locally	Who: Application Developer Force: Management of Functionality	Who: Component Developer Forces: Management of Functionality and IT Resources
Think Globally	Who: System-Level Architect Forces: Managing Complexity and Change	Who: Management (CIO, CEO) Forces: Management of IT Resources and Technology Transfer

(Continued)

In Table 11.1, the management determines the allocation of IT Resources and how the organization relates to the external market. The architect is concerned with the systemwide impacts of design decisions. The software architecture divides the system into subsystems that define local scopes. Each application developer can make independent decisions within his or her scope. Finally, the component developer, who develops software for enterprisewide reuse, manages the detailed functionality of the reusable components. The component developer also conserves IT resources by consolidating development, documentation, support, and testing for the reusable software.

TERM LIST

Most Applicable Scale

Solution Type

Solution Name

Intent

Diagram

References

Applicability at This Scale

Solution Summary

Key Benefits and Consequences

Variations of This Solution

Rescaling This Solution at Other Levels

Related Solutions

Example

Background

Resources

PART FIVE

Global Design Patterns

The global level consists of numerous enterprises and individuals. At the enterprise level it was possible to control technology direction through roles and policies. There are enterprise analogies at the global level, such as governments and laws, but these are usually in place to enforce extreme limits as opposed to controlling direction. At the global level, relationships do not involve direct control of people and technologies; instead they involve alliances, agreements, and collaborations. The latter option is sometimes called virtual enterprises.

A key enabler of global information technology is the Internet. Although there are too few examples of Internet solutions to call them true design patterns, there are nevertheless many useful technologies that have global scope. These technologies are also highly applicable within enterprises; hence the popular practice of enterprise-specific Internets, or so-called *intranets*.

The Internet has had a profound impact upon society. This changes everyone's relationship to the global level. Through the Internet, the global level has become much more accessible. It is possible to access information easily and disseminate information easily. For example, through electronic mail and the World Wide Web virtually anyone can advertise and communicate globally. Through these technologies, we all have a very immediate participation in the global level. Paradoxically, we have also found that some results are easier to achieve at the global level than at the enterprise level.

In Part V, we define solutions relating to two key aspects of the global level.

ROLE OF OPEN SYSTEMS

In Chapter 12 we introduce a few key solutions that define fundamental principles of open systems. Through an understanding of these basic principles, there are potential benefits for management of technology transfer and IT resources.

INTERNET DESIGN PATTERNS

In Chapter 13 we introduce various Internet technology patterns, which have applicability at both global and enterprise levels for information sharing and dissemination. The discussion includes the Java technology.

CHAPTER TWELVE

Role of Open Systems

Open systems is at once a technology vision and an emerging market representing a loose alliance of consortia and vendors. The vision of open systems is one of universal interoperability and portability across multivendor product offerings. With open systems, technology risks and obsolescence are reduced or eliminated. Of course, this vision is far from reality.

The open systems market is a very active arena involving standards generation and product delivery. Vendors, integrators, and end users are involved in the standards activities which lend substance and credibility to this market.

The open systems patterns are summarized as follows.

STANDARDS

Until recently, standards were either the product of years of committee work (formal standards) or the result of popular market forces (de facto standards). Today, standards activities are practiced across a much broader range of organizations and alliances. The introduction of CORBA technology has provided a new tool for standards writers in all organizations.

REFERENCE TECHNOLOGY

Reference technology is distributed to promote rapid adoption and consistent implementation.

COMMON INTERFACE

The common interface is the fundamental structure behind many other patterns. The common interface is the overall structure of standards, horizontal interfaces, and many microarchitecture patterns (Gamma 1994).

Standards

Most Applicable Scale: Global

Solution Type: Process

Solution Name: Standards

Intent: To reduce risks for suppliers and consumers (or clients and servers) of technology through specifications that are multilateral technology agreements.

Primal Forces: Management of Technology Transfer

Applicability at This Scale

1. There are numerous suppliers of similar technology with proprietary, competing software interfaces.

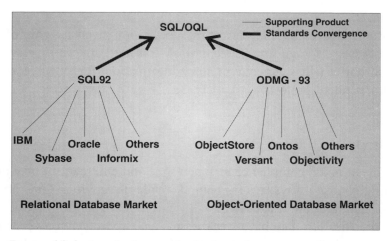

Figure 12.1 Standards provide the basis for commonality among suppliers that reduces risks for suppliers and consumers. The database market has benefited from several key standards such as SQL and ODMG, and the markets are planning to merge in a future SQL/OQL joint standard.

2. Vendors' products do not interoperate adequately for consumer's needs.
3. The size of the market is constrained by the lack of compatibility among vendors.
4. Consumers are wary of proprietary solutions and interfaces.
5. The market is viewed as immature (or nascent).
6. The market has low overall visibility.

Solution Summary

A group of suppliers collaborate to create a technology agreement. The agreement is a joint specification of the technology. The suppliers publicly announce the availability of the standard and their commitment to provide compliant products.

Benefits

> ➤ The standard lends credibility to the market and the suppliers' products.
> ➤ The standard and the standards activity gives visibility to the market and the suppliers' products.
> ➤ Consumers have a consistent specification that applies to many suppliers' products.
> ➤ Consumers have multiple sources of supply for a given category of products.
> ➤ Standards are a key form of technology transfer between organizations that would not usually cooperate or share information, for example, competitors or independent projects.

Other Consequences

> ➤ The meaning of compliance may be vague and enforcement may be lacking. Testing almost always lags far behind standards activities. Only about 6% of all IT standards are testable.
> ➤ The specification may have weaknesses that expose vendor dependencies to consumers. This may reduce the portability benefits and risk reduction of the standard.
> ➤ The technology may be so flexible that there are many layers of profiles that need to be defined in order to realize the benefits of the standard. (See the ENTERPRISE::Profile Solution.)

Variations of This Solution

➤ Formal Standard—An accredited standards group pursues a formal process for the definition, issuance, and approval of a standards document. Accrediting authority for information technology standards is derived from the International Standards Organization (ISO). This authority is delegated to national standards bodies (ANSI, DIN, etc.), and to other organizations (ECMA, IEEE, etc.). An accredited standards group must follow certain types of formal procedures that often make for slow progress. A typical formal standard takes four to seven years to complete; many formal standards are obsolete before they have completed the process.

➤ Public Consortium Standard—A membership organization of suppliers and consumers is formed in order to generate public specifications, that is, consensus standards from their membership. Examples include: X/Open, OMG, and Open GIS Consortium.

➤ Research Consortium Standard—A group of vendors form a corporation to perform joint research and generate consensus specifications. This often occurs in profitable vertical markets: oil, semiconductors, and so on. In addition, some of these consortia may be created through government funding or private initiative. Examples include: Petroleum Open Systems Corporation (vertical market), SEMATECH (vertical market), National Information Infrastructure Interoperability Project (US—government), Architecture Projects Management (UK), and Distributed Systems Technology Centre (Australia—government).

➤ Alliance Standard—A group of vendors form a permanent or temporary alliance in order to generate standards as technology agreements. This form is sometimes chosen in order to create a more efficient or responsive standards generation process, since a new alliance organization can operate under unique rules and procedures. Examples include: Common Open Software Environment (COSE), Objective Technology Group, and Object Definition Alliance.

➤ Unilateral De Facto Standard—One dominant vendor unilaterally issues a specification and technology and declares that it is the new industry standard. The vendor may disseminate this version of reality through public relations and marketing media. In this case, the standard is an implicit agreement between a vendor and the consumer market that it controls.

➤ Popular De Facto Standard—Popular usage of a technology leads to its de facto acceptance as a standard, for example, TCP/IP and the World Wide Web. In this case, the standard is an agreement among users of the technology.

It is always a good strategy to obtain backing for the standard from a dominant, high-credibility vendor. In the SQL example, IBM was the key vendor that provided credibility to the nascent relational database market by being a visible backer of SQL89.

Rescaling This Solution to Other Levels

Consortia within vertical or specialty markets are commonplace. While still at the global level, these consortia may have a very narrow scope compared to the public consortia.

The consortium concept can be applied at the enterprise level. In this case a group of projects and/or suppliers could be formed to resolve technical issues through the creation of specifications.

For example, enterprise consortia are used in the government market, where it is necessary to resolve interoperability issues between disparate information systems. These consortia can be formal government working groups or less formal vendor coalitions facilitated by interested government organizations.

Related Solutions

- ➤ The Common Interface pattern is a higher-level pattern that is the basis for the Standard solution.
- ➤ OMG Standards: CORBA, CORBAservices, CORBAfacilities, and CORBA-domains Information Technology Standard (Cargill 1989), OMG IDL Specification (Soley 1995).

Example

CORBA is the result of a public consortium standards process from vendors involved in the object technology and distributed computing markets. In order to provide visibility and acceptance of the market, a number of suppliers of distributed computing toolkits proposed alternative solutions for defining the foundational technology in this market. The two joint submissions included the Dynamic Invocation Interface (DII) and the OMG IDL-based static interfaces. By merging the submissions, the technology provided both solutions. The initial products implemented parts of the specification, but the market has come to support the full specification, which by chance or circumstance included two key capabilities for building distributed systems, one highly flexible, the other very convenient and natural.

Other examples of the different types of standards are contained in Table 12.1. Note that some standards are appropriately listed in multiple categories.

Table 12.1   Categories of Software Standards

Formal Standards	De Jure Standards	De Facto Standards	Consortium Standards
Ada95	Ada95	Microsoft Windows	CORBA
SQL92	MIL STD 498	Microsoft Office	COSE Spec 1170
PCTE	NIST APP	TCP/IP	X/Open SYSMAN
ODP	FIPS	WWW HTTP	WWW HTTP
POSIX	GOSIP	WAIS	OpenDoc

The acronyms in the table are defined in the appendix.

Resources

Most standards groups have WWW home pages and information about their standards on the Internet. Many groups also have standards available on-line.

Reference Technology

Most Applicable Scale: Global

Solution Type: Technology

Solution Name: Reference Technology

Intent: To facilitate rapid adoption of new technology and common profile conventions.

Primal Forces: Management of Technology Transfer

Applicability at This Scale

1. There is a technology that must rapidly gain market acceptance to become successful. For example: Java's success is due in part to the ready availability of Java System Development Kits on the Internet.
2. There is an enabling technology that must gain market support in order to facilitate the adoption of related technologies. For example: Market acceptance of OMG IDL is essential to the acceptance of CORBAservices and CORBAfacilities.
3. There is a technology that a number of implementors must support consistently in order for the technology to become successful. For example: The CORBA IIOP interoperability protocol must be supported consistently by multiple ORB vendors.
4. There is a need to encourage reuse and rapid adoption of a technology.
5. The market is viewed as immature (or nascent).
6. The market has low overall visibility.

Solution Summary

A development organization creates an example implementation of the new technology. The technology is made widely available in source code or development kit form, called a reference technology. The reference technology is either free or available at nominal cost. The Internet is usually the most suitable distribution medium.

The development organization can take many forms. If the development organization is a consortium, the consortium makes the technology available at some advantage to its membership, perhaps with respect to time availability or technical support. Examples include: SEMATECH, the Microelectronics and Computer Technology Corporation (MCC), the Open Software Foundation (now OSF), and the Component Integration Laboratories (CI Labs). CI Labs provides testing services to its membership and makes source code of its technologies available on the Internet to any interested parties.

The development organization may be a major supplier or related technologies attempting to get a new product market started. Examples include: Sun Microsystems in its release of the Open Networking Computing RPC freeware, the OMG IDL compiler development kit, the CORBA IIOP interoperability kit, and the Java System Development Kits. Microsoft has had a number of freeware beta-test technology releases such as early releases of Windows NT. In addition, major suppliers can promote their technologies by bundling them with their platforms. For example, IBM bundles its CORBA implementation SOM with OS/2 and an increasing number of platforms.

The development organization may be a public or private sector organization interested in free dissemination of its research to like-minded individuals or organizations. For example, The MITRE Corporation made available its DIS-CUS Technology Transfer Kit to other government contractors in order to shorten contractor learning curves for distributed object technology and to coordinate government organizations.

Finally, the reference technology approach can be used within an organization to encourage consistency of usage and implementations, as well as rapid adoption and reuse of technology.

Benefits

> The reference technology eliminates barriers to technology adoption by external organization.
> The reference technology gives market visibility to the technology and the supplier.
> Users of a reference technology adopt a consistent and compatible approach.
> The reference technology maximizes the potential for interoperability and portability of implementations. The level of consistency between implementors is much greater than if only a standard exists to define the common technology.

> A standard and a reference technology can work together to maximize credibility and adoption of a new technology. The reference technology accelerates adoption of the standard.

Other Consequences

> The developing organization may be giving away its competitive advantage by disseminating the reference technology, unless it has an associated strategy for exploiting the widespread adoption of the reference technology. This is not a factor for public sector organizations.

> The recipients of the reference technology will modify the technology for their own platforms and environments. This may create inconsistencies and incompatibilities that mitigate the technical benefits of a common implementation. For example, the Microsoft implementations of OSF DCE (as in Microsoft RPC and DCOM) no longer support interoperability and portability with other implementations of DCE.

Variations of This Solution

Freeware—Freeware is license-free software. It may be copyrighted with restrictions, for example, that it not be incorporated into some commercial product. Some freeware is not a reference technology, but a finished implementation intended for immediate usage. For example, the Free Software Foundation distributes a diverse set of software packages that provide a license free of charge.

Shareware—Shareware is software that has a voluntary licensing agreement. Users may copy the software and use it free of charge. Optionally, users may elect to pay the license fee, presumably out of gratitude for receiving quality software. Shareware is a lucrative market. It is said that even the most ethical of organizations have software piracy rates exceeding 50 percent. Overall, software piracy accounts for about 70 percent of all software licenses in use. Interestingly, shareware vendors receive about a 30 percent voluntary license registration rate. One might conclude that shareware vendors are receiving nearly the same licensing compliance as other forms of software vending. The advantage of shareware is that vendors can distribute their software to a much wider audience because distribution is free and ubiquitous on the Internet.

Related Solutions

A standard can define the specification of a reference technology. Standards and reference technologies are particularly effective when combined for a technology intended for widespread adoption.

Many forms of software reuse are closely related to the reference technology pattern. Whereas software reuse is a general approach to the reuse of a large number of modules, reference technologies are focused on unique technologies and capabilities where the goal is widespread adoption and market convergence.

Uses of Terminology

In software engineering there is much confusion about terminology. Terms such as *architecture* mean many different things to different people. A glossary is a useful tool for software projects, and we have included a glossary for our terminology in this book. We also intend to use our definitions to allocate responsibilities appropriately. For example, in our definition, the term *architecture* includes the interface definitions because we believe that coordination of interfaces is essential for successful architectures.

Another important terminology problem is the use of different names for the same idea or for related concepts. An important distinction is between terminology that refers to horizontal architecture concepts and terminology that is vertically oriented. Table 12.2 shows two sets of terminology. The vertical terminology refers to domain specifics and custom solutions. The horizontal terminology refers to common solutions applied across multiple implementations. For example, terms such as *design reuse* and *common interfaces* are very closely related and in some cases interchangeable. The structure of most design patterns (or variation-centered designs) is a common interface, and so forth (Gamma 1994).

Table 12.2   Software Terminology: Horizontal vs. Vertical Concepts

Horizontal Terminology	Vertical Terminology
Common Interface	Domain Object Model
Standard Interface	Domain Analysis
Design and Software Reuse	Object-Oriented Analysis
Frameworks	Requirements Analysis
Component Software	External Model
Variation-Centered Design	User Interface Prototype/Mockup

(Continued)

Terminology is sometimes used for destructive purposes. *Intellectual violence* is the intentional use of terminology unfamiliar to an individual or a group. For example, the term *lambda calculus* is familiar to computer science undergraduates of MIT because it is included in the required coursework, but it is unfamiliar to computer science graduates of many other institutions. Intellectual violence can be used to intimidate individuals or groups.

We have also seen terminology used for political purposes, by associating adjectives with negative connotations for competing ideas. For example, one could characterize alternative designs as *shallow* or *deep,* depending on which design one views more favorably.

Terminology can be exploited for marketing purposes. Marketers sometimes use vague phrases such as *CORBA conformant* or *logical superset of OMG IDL* to imply product attributes that may actually be absent. Some marketers also change terminology with each minor product upgrade. Name changes can cause great confusion and are often the subject of much discussion, which may be the marketers' intended purpose.

Common Interface

Most Applicable Scale: Global

Solution Type: Software

Solution Name: Common Interface

Intent: To provide interoperability, replaceability, and reuse between multiple software modules that may be independently developed.

Primal Forces: Management of Change, Management of Complexity, Management of Technology Transfer

Applicability at This Scale

1. There are several software modules to integrate. It is possible to define a common abstraction to support interoperability between these modules.

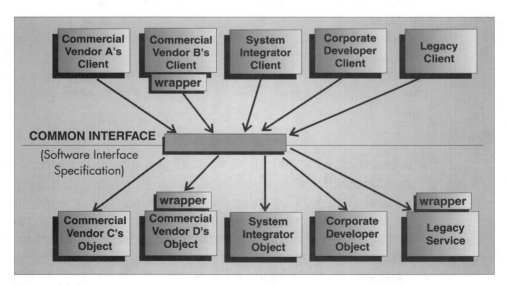

Figure 12.2 A Common Interface enables multiple clients and object implementations to interoperate seamlessly.

2. There is a need to extend the system, once integrated.
3. There is a need to replace or substitute one or more modules, either statically or dynamically.
4. Interoperability is needed, but most software packages have unique or proprietary interfaces and data formats that constrain interoperability.
5. Dependence of consumer-generated software on proprietary interfaces is risky. A single supplier can change the interfaces unilaterally. Support of one vendor's interfaces does not allow interoperability with other vendors' interfaces, as well as other pre-existing software. Risk is a primary consideration in software development, with about a third of all software projects leading to failure and only a handful of projects that are considered successful.
6. The cost of integration increases dramatically with system size, due to complexity and the lack of common interfaces or effective standards.

Solution Summary

There are several software modules that should interoperate. At the global scale, our intention may be to just define a common way for these modules to interoperate that other people will implement. Alternatively, suppose we are building an integrated system from these modules. Define a common abstraction for these modules that captures the common interoperability needs and hides the implementation differences. Specify this interoperability solution as a set of software interfaces.

Implement these common interfaces as either a direct interface or a wrapper to the software modules. The complete set of software modules will then interoperate through the Common Interface, without having direct dependence upon the implementation details of the other software modules.

Benefits

➤ Interoperability—Software modules can interoperate with each other through the Common Interface.
➤ Extensibility—By supporting the Common Interface, new software modules can be added to the system to interoperate with existing software.
➤ Abstraction—The Common Interface simplifies and generalizes the interfaces of the individual software modules.
➤ Isolation—Individual software modules can change without impacting the rest of the system.

- Interchangeability—Individual software modules can be upgraded or replaced without impacting the rest of the system.
- In our experience, Common Interfaces provide direct cost savings compared to custom interfaces, probably due to the shared learning curve and design reuse.
- Parallel software development is enabled once a common interface is defined and stabilized.

Other Consequences

- The Common Interface does not expose all of the specialized functionality of each software module. This may be exposed as a vertical extension (See "Horizontal-Vertical-Metadata" pattern).
- Establishing agreement for Common Interfaces requires coordination.

Variations of This Solution

Common Interfaces can represent the lowest common denominator of interface functionality or they can represent a best-of-breed solution. Often the lowest common denominator solution does not provide sufficient functionality. Using the Architecture Mining Solution, one can devise best-of-breed solutions efficiently.

Rescaling This Solution to Other Levels

This solution has applicability at all scales: global, enterprise, system, application, and smaller scales. As a microarchitecture design pattern, common interfaces are used as the structural approach behind most of the key design patterns in Gamma (1994), such as Observer, Strategy, Facade, and so on. It is important to note that the microarchitecture patterns differ in intent, even though the structures are similar.

Related Solutions

For standards defining APIs, the common interface is the concept underlying the standard's benefits. Common interfaces can be derived for sets of overlapping legacy systems, standards, and commercial technologies by using the architecture mining process. The horizontal element of the Horizontal-Vertical-Metadata pattern comprises a set of common interfaces.

The Common Interface pattern is utilized repeatedly in Gamma (1994) as a common structural element in microarchitecture patterns. For example, the patterns for strategy, observer, and facade use common interfaces to provide for management of change. As John Vlissides states, "The structure of most patterns is similar." One might conclude that the common interface is the structural abstraction behind variation centered design.

The horizontal architecture pattern in Mowbray & Zahari (1995) is an example of a Common Interface. In that discussion, the quantitative benefits of common interfaces are analyzed and compared with other typical architecture patterns.

Example

Suppose there are four applications with unique software interfaces:

```
interface A {//PIDL for application A
        void load(in string s);
        void save();
        void histogram(in Region r);
        void annotate(in string t, in Location l);
        ...
};

interface B {// PIDL for application B
        void store(in FilePointer f);
        void restore(in FilePointer f);
        void overlay(in Image A, in Image B);
        void select(out long x, y, z);
        boolean line_of_sight(in Point p1, p2);
        ...
};

interface C {//PIDL for application C
        Font current_font();
        void change_font(in Font f);
        void spell_check(in TextPoint t);
        void set_style(in Style s);
        ...
};

interface D {//PIDL for application D
        void commit();
        void rollback();
        void update(in Data d);
        void insert(in Data d);
        void delete(in Reference r);
        ...
};
```

In this example, our goal is to provide interoperability between the three applications. We want data from any application to be exchangeable with data from any other application. One way to solve the problem would be to define a custom integration between each pair of applications. To make interoperability bidirectional, we need to write integration software for transfers in each direction. This includes software that supports transfers from between each pair of applications: A to B, A to C, A to D, D to A, C to A, B to A, B to C, C to B, B to D, D to B, C to D, and C to D.

System extension is a very frequent occurrence during both development and system operation and maintenance, accounting for about half of all software cost (Horowitz 1993). In this example, system extension would take the form of adding a fifth application, E. In the custom integration case, this means that we need to provide additional integration software from A to E, E to A, B to E, E to B, C to E, E to C, E to D, and D to E. In other words, system extension is nearly as costly as developing the original integration solution, and the cost increases with the scale of the system.

Alternatively, we could use a Common Interface solution. To achieve interoperability, we could define a Common Interface that all three applications would support. For example, the following interface might suffice:

```
interface X {
        void load(in PathName p);
        void store(in PathName p);
        Data exchange(in Data d);
};
```

To implement the Common Interface solution, we would need to wrapper each application to map the unique interfaces to the common interface. In other words, we need software for A to/from X, B to/from X, C to/from X, D to/from X. Then to extend the system all we need is software from E to/From X. With common interfaces, system extension becomes inexpensive and it is independent of system size.

CHAPTER THIRTEEN

Internet Design Patterns

Of all the distributed computing models in active use today, none is more influential than the Internet. Any other distributed computing model must be aware of the existing scope of the various technologies that make up the Internet, and be capable of integrating within the overall mosaic. CORBA has the potential to add a lot to the Internet in the development of object-oriented applications and in providing an architecture for the access and use of distributed information resources. It is rather early in the symbiosis of the Internet and CORBA to establish detailed reusable solutions, especially given the rapid evolution of both technologies. The Internet is already expanding to incorporate more robust and object-based technologies and, at the same time, CORBA implementations are improving their performance to match the needs of the Internet and new specifications are being proposed to handle the new multimedia content that the Internet is being depended on to provide its clients.

Using the Internet as the basis for application development provides many benefits to the intelligent systems integrator. With Java and other emerging technologies, the Internet provides unparalleled access to text, graphics, and application programs. Developing new content is easy, and with the tremendous growth in Internet software development tools and environments, it is becoming even simpler every day. The inherent hyperlink capabilities of HTML and other content standards provide a means to associate related information and navigate through the tremendous content. The Internet technologies have become the world's most widely used standards, with an assortment of browsers, servers, and tools providing an extensive information framework (Figure 13.1). While the level of Internet security is still less than desired for many government and finan-

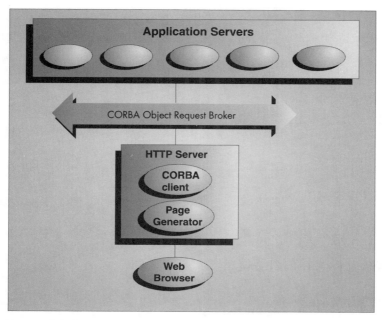

Figure 13.1 Example of how CORBA may supply services to Web-based applications.

cial purposes, it is perfectly sufficient for many less critical tasks. Additionally, strides are being made that should result in one or more security standards that are robust enough to support electronic currency.

Use of the Internet as a dynamic applet distributor has increased the overall robustness of the Web, although transient sites and stale URLs are still an all too frequent occurrence. Web-based tools in many key areas, such as configuration management and dynamic page construction, are fairly numerous and growing at an exciting rate. Any enterprise that desires to compete in global markets must strongly consider the use of Internet technologies as a powerful tool in accomplishing business objectives.

CORBA-CGI Gateway

Most Applicable Scale: Global

Solution Type: Software

Solution Name: CORBA-CGI Gateway

Intent: To use CORBA as a data source for the generation of HTML pages.

Primal Forces: Management of Change

Applicability at This Scale

1. Need to integrate existing applications with an intranet or the Web.
2. Need or desire to access legacy system data from Web browsers.
3. Use of CORBA as an infrastructure mechanism for application integration.

Solution Summary

A URL is a preprogrammed information request. In the Web model, selecting a URL sends an information request to a server. The Common Gateway Interface

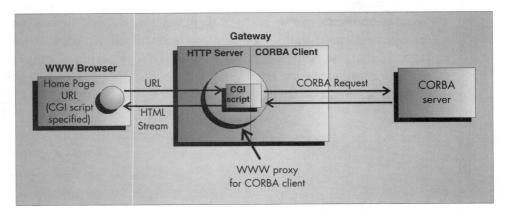

Figure 13.2 The HTTP CGI interface can be used to invoke CORBA clients, which respond by using CORBAservices in the dynamic construction of an HTML page.

(CGI) is part of the HTTP protocols and permits the running of external programs and scripts on a server.

First, create a mapping from a URL on an existing, static HTML page to a CGI script to be executed on the HTTP server. This CGI script should be a CORBA client, with a supporting ORB existing on the same machine as the HTTP server.

By specifying a CORBA client to be invoked through the CGI interfaces, the CGI script/CORBA client can process the request by accessing CORBAservices. This client can receive the full benefit of CORBA location transparency, dynamic binding to service implementations, automatic server activation, and so on. This is important: While the client application must be located on the same machine as the HTTP, the CORBAservices used by the client can be distributed.

After the CORBA requests are processed, the CORBA client assembles the data on the HTTP server. Since the output of a CGI script must be an HTML page, the CORBA client is responsible for generating a page dynamically or providing the location of a page as output to the HTTP server.

The client dynamically generates an HTML document, or potentially a Java applet, for transport back to the client. The HTTP server sends the generated HTML document to the client as a response to the initial request.

Benefits

➤ Using CORBA in this way cooperates with the Web object model.
➤ Browser user is not exposed to CORBA or object references
➤ Works with, rather than against, the Web object model. Maintains clear separation of Web and CORBA environments with the boundaries encapsulated within the CGI/CORBA clients.

Other Consequences

➤ There is no real direct access to CORBA objects.
➤ The CORBA client has to run on the same machine as the HTTP server (although a script could access other machines through another mechanism, i.e., rsh, ftp, etc.).
➤ Either the CORBA client or a specialized HTTP server (Web) needs to dynamically construct an HTML page using the CORBA data.

Rescaling This Solution to Other Levels

This pattern is an interesting variant of the Gateway solution and has an equivalent scalability. Specifically, this pattern could be used to either to provide a gateway with the Internet and some other technology, or as a template for wrapping the CORBA client functionality with an existing technology.

Related Solutions

➤ Gateway—The gateway is a more general solution for interoperability among disparate object models. The example provided in the gateway pattern illustrates how the CORBA-CGI Gateway solution can be reversed to allow the Internet to become a data source for CORBA applications.

Background

Typically in Web-based information discovery, a user enters or selects a link in a browser or enters data into an HTML form and activates an HTTP URL. The browser assembles the information into a series of named-value pairs and sends it to the HTTP server indicated in the URL string. The URL may identify an HTML document on the server, a file, or a script to be executed. The HTTP packages the data in the HTML file, or the output of the program in the case of a script, and transports the data back to the browser. The mechanism is both simple and powerful; however, for the most part, the interface is used for displaying static information stored in previously authored HTML files. Some scripts for constructing dynamic pages are available, but they generally are hard-coded scripts that either are located on the HTTP machine or provide references to specific data sources, limiting the flexibility of the system. By incorporating CORBA clients as the enabling mechanism for constructing dynamic pages, the pages can be bound to a specific implementation at run-time and can access services through a more flexible, migratable, and maintainable OMG IDL interface.

> A naming service is a must for CORBA-Web integration. Use it to associate an object reference with a meaningful name or label you can embed in an HTML document. Later, when your CORBA client receives the label, it can go to a naming service to retrieve the associated object reference at run-time.

CORBA-Web Server

Most Applicable Scale: Global

Solution Type: Software

Solution Name: CORBA-Web Server

Intent: Extending the capabilities of Intranet or WWW applications, in particular the statelessness of Web pages. Using CORBA to maintain state of Web objects.

Primal Forces: Management of Functionality

Applicability at This Scale

1. Need to retain state information on the server application.
2. Need to optimize performance by limiting the size of URL handles.

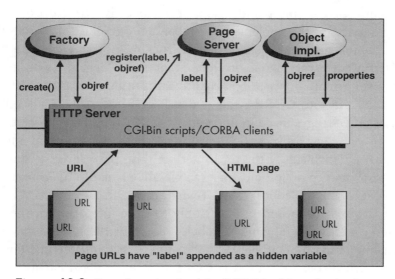

Figure 13.3 State is maintained in CORBA objects by having a page service map a displayable "label" to a CORBA object reference.

3. Need to implement more powerful Web pages.
4. CORBA does not need to be available in the client environment.

Solution Summary

First, on the initial call to a CORBA client through the CGI interface, a token must be created to identify the current object in use in the CORBA environment. The token can be either a name, a label, or a stringified reference. Since a big advantage of using this pattern is to limit the amount of information passed to and from the browser, the stringified object reference, which can be as long as 1K bytes, is not recommended as a token. This token value will be passed as a variable and attached to the URL with each page, using the CGI interface. The token is passed as a hidden variable at the end of the URL. Depending on the application, the name may either be entered by the user via the Forms interface or automatically generated each time the page is accessed.

When a CORBA client is invoked, it can modify the state of the object as a standard CORBA client. However, there is no need to send an entire collection of variables to represent the current state of the object back to the Internet browser. Instead of storing a list of hidden variables at the end of the URL to represent the state of the current object, simply send the token for the object.

When a CORBA client is subsequently invoked, the token is used to identify the current CORBA object, and its object reference is retrieved from the OMG Naming Service, or the implementation that is responsible for storing the mapping of the token to the object reference. Once the object reference is obtained, the CORBA client can invoke on the current object, regardless of its location, and retrieve current information, including any attributes or properties that were modified by previous CORBA clients that had access to the same object. Furthermore, any changes made by the initial CORBA client are preserved and can be used by subsequent invocations of CORBA clients. Furthermore, any CORBA clients that are invoked by the CGI interfaces also have access to any CORBA objects known at compile-time, for example, the name of CORBAservices such as the OMG Naming Service, OMG Trader Service, or a factory.

Now, the Web environment needs only to store the token for the object. If the token is a meaningful name or label, it could be displayed either as part of the dynamic creation of an HTML page or as a default value in a Forms interface. On each invocation from the CGI interface, CORBA clients can use the name to retrieve the object and can use the object interface to store and retrieve state information about the object.

If the OMG Naming Service is used to associate the token with the CORBA object reference, then there is little additional overhead; however, the OMG Naming Service can become populated with object references with no means to determine the end of their lifecycle. Therefore, it is often desirable to create a separate service to store object references used to maintain the state of objects used to service browsers so their lifecycle can be managed by separate policies (specifically, removed if not accessed by a specified time frame). The Dynamic Attributes Pattern is a useful method of storing object attributes associated with an object reference, as is the OMG Property Service.

Benefits

- State information can be transferred within the stateless Web environment.
- Services can be accessed dynamically using the OMG Naming and Trader Services.
- A CORBA ORB is not required on the client side.
- By providing only a minimal extension to the URL (object name) it increases the portability of the URL.

Consequences

- Lifecycle issues are more difficult. For example, when is it all right to delete an object?
- The client needs to know how to create an HTML page.
- The name of the object is passed from page to page.

Related Solutions

- CORBA-CGI Gateway—This pattern is used in order to invoke CORBA clients that need access to the state information that services the Web pages.
- Gateway—This pattern can be substituted as a more general means of accessing information from a disparate environment.

Background

The HTTP model uses a stateless protocol to implement a point-to-point client-server model. The information provided by transversing URL links is not dynamically related and browsers employing this protocol generally do not engage in continuing interactivity with stateful servers. Again, this model is powerful and sufficient for most purposes; however, there are times when it is desirable to maintain an ongoing conversation with referenced objects and services in the Web environment. Typically, when state is maintained in the Web environment, a collection of named values representing the state is passed along back and forth from the client to the server and back again whenever information is exchanged. Often, this collection of named values becomes quite long and instances where interoperability is comprised by exceeding the maximum length of URLs on some browsers are not unheard of. Also, the continual creation, extraction, and modification of the URL string to include the current state is unwieldy and imposes a large burden upon the developers responsible for creating the pages and supporting programs and scripts. Ideally, the state of the object could be maintained separately from the URL, and a mechanism created so that the information relevant to a particular client could be extracted on demand.

Java

Most Applicable Scale: Global

Solution Type: Technology

Solution Name: Java

Intent: To provide an object-oriented language and architecture that allows an application to execute on heterogeneous platforms and environments. To extend Web applications and browsers with animation and migrating functionality.

Primal Forces: Management of Technology Transfer, Management of IT Resources, Management of Functionality, Management of Complexity

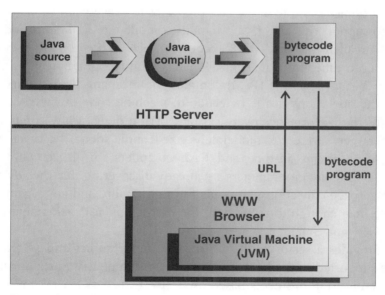

Figure 13.4 The Java Virtual Machine (JVM) executes portable bytecode programs within a Web browser.

Applicability at This Scale

1. The need to add new capabilities to Web browsers and network computers.
2. The need to overcome the complexity of legacy programming languages, such as C++.
3. The need to migrate software to networked client platforms.
4. The need for portable software across multiple platforms.

Solution Summary

Java is an excellent general-purpose programming language for applications. It is completely object-oriented and provides many constructs for distributed computing that are not available in the more widely available programming languages. In particular, Java provides for the explicit declaration of interfaces and can assign implementations for a given interface at run-time. While there is currently no official OMG IDL binding for Java, there are many proprietary bindings and a standard specification from OMG should enter the OMG process soon. It is quite possible that Java will have one of the cleanest language mappings thus far, as Java is already geared for cross-platform development.

Design goals of Java are to support applications in a heterogeneous distributed environment, and to allow Java programs to execute anywhere on the network. To support this aim, Java programs compile into a platform-independent file format called *bytecode*. This bytecode can be executed on any platform that has a Java run-time virtual machine, which is a lightweight, bytecode interpreter. The Java Virtual Machine (JVM) contains the mechanisms necessary for converting the operations in the bytecode to machine code executed at run-time. Currently, the performance overhead of JVMs in dynamically compiling bytecode is rather severe for moderately sized applications; however, with the advancement of just-in-time and flash compilers this is certain to change rapidly. As is, many programmers are already discovering that the advantages of built-in garbage collections, cross-platform portability and an elegant language are more than enough to move from the more popular development languages such as C++ and Smalltalk.

Java provides a set of built-in libraries from graphics and system services that are supported in the JVM. Furthermore, its emphasis on supporting popular communication protocols based on TCP/IP such as HTTP and FTP make it an excellent mechanism for many types of distributed communication. However, it lacks a method of specifying standard interfaces that can be used by a number of application clients. This is where Java benefits from integrating with CORBA and taking advantage of its OMG IDL specification, which allows clients to access services across language, application, and platform boundaries. While Java can take advantage of many of the design patterns discussed as pertaining to CORBA, two of the most important CORBA-Java integration techniques are discussed separately as applet and ORBlet technology patterns.

Perhaps Java's greatest strength and its biggest weakness is that it is a rapidly growing and emerging standard. It is a strength because of the great innovation and experimentation, which is already leading to great strides in distributed application development. However, it is also a standard that is expanding rapidly in the development of add-ons and extensions, which compromises its interoperability and portability. It has security issues that are still growing much more rapidly than corresponding security solutions, and its longevity is still the subject of speculation. Certainly, the ideas and technology within Java are strong enough to stand the test of time; however, whether or not Java will continue to be the means by which they are brought to the mass market remains to be seen.

Benefits

➤ Implementations are portable across platforms.
➤ Entirely object-oriented.
➤ Support for distributed constructs such as threads.
➤ Browsers are standardizing on a bytecode interpreter.
➤ Built-in garbage collection, multithreading capabilities, and synchronization methods.
➤ Support for interface and implementation separation.
➤ Standard cross-platform application development libraries.

Other Consequences

➤ Currently, there is a significant performance problem for large applications.
➤ With applets, can only communicate with the host machine.
➤ Many security problems plague current implementation.

Rescaling This Solution to Other Levels

As a programming language, Java is useful at all architectural levels. Its benefits are particularly well suited for the development of client applications that are faced with rapidly changing requirements or changes to their operating environment. The ability to dynamically distribute applets on demand can simplify many of the enterprise-level system management concerns.

Related Solutions

> ➤ CORBA—While Java is an excellent implementation language for distributed development, it is an ideal complement to, and not a replacement for, OMG IDL specifications.
> ➤ *Java Report* is a magazine for the Java developers' community. The March/April 1996 issue was a valuable resource in preparing this pattern.

Background

Java is a programming language released by Sun Microsystems in May 1995. Since its release it has become an important emerging standard for the development and distribution of small applications. As the technology matures, it may quickly expand into the preferred general-purpose development language of object applications. Regardless of its future, its overall capabilities and focus on platform and operating environment independence will be a part of future distributed environments.

Developers are creating objects and systems in a multitude of languages and environments. It is difficult, or often impossible, to share objects across language and environment boundaries without developing in a CORBA environment and defining interfaces for sharable objects in OMG IDL. Many objects are not meant to be shareable among applications; however, it is desirable to reuse the object implementations in multiple applications regardless of their implementation language or platform. Many languages require a developer to completely manage the lifecycle of dynamically created objects in an application. Managing object lifecycles can be complex and is the source of many implementation errors or misuse of application resources.

Applet

Most Applicable Scale: Global

Solution Type: Software

Solution Name: Applet

Intent: To allow access to executable content in a Web-based environment. To migrate functionality to client platforms.

Primal Forces: Management of Technology Transfer, Management of IT Resources

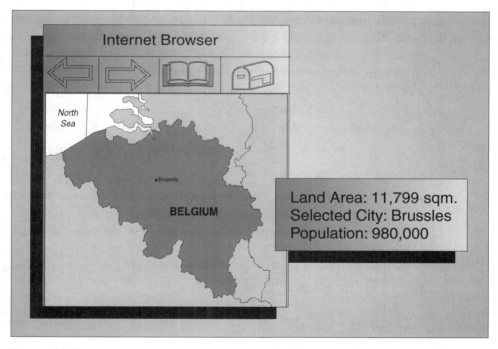

Figure 13.5 An applet is a small program which executes with the Web browser and can provide exciting new functionality to Web-based applications.

Applicability at This Scale

1. Need more powerful Web capabilities than offered by universal clients and browsers. For example, need animation, statefulness, or application-specific functionality.
2. Need to migrate application functionality to the Web client, including on-demand transfers.
3. Need to provide an application on a wide variety of platforms.
4. Need to optimize performance: limiting network communication through client-side processing.
5. Need to minimize maintenance costs due to updating client software.

Solution Summary

A Java applet is a specialized application capable of being executed in a Web browser containing a JVM. Java applets are typically small and lightweight, and perform a specialized task. Most Java applets are written to enhance the Web experience by providing greater interaction or functionality to the user. In particular, many of the existing applets add various multimedia enhancements to HTML pages that are not otherwise supported by the current generation of Web browsers. Some applications use Java to distribute applications, gather client data, or perform other system management tasks. However, since applets are developed with a fully functional programming language with a growing set of standard class libraries (also known as *packages*), the ultimate utility of applets is that their functionality is limited only by the creativity and skills of applet developers.

Benefits

➤ Programs can be interpreted or compiled on all platforms (portable).
➤ Local program execution avoids server-side bottlenecks of remote execution.
➤ Applets can be distributed on demand, using the Internet as a distribution channel.
➤ Standard, extensive set of class libraries is available on all platforms.
➤ A rapidly growing and emerging standard.

Other Consequences

➤ Server latency is a concern on the Internet.
➤ A rapidly growing and emerging method of displaying and interacting with information.

Rescaling This Solution to Other Levels

Java applet technology is geared for running small applications, and taking advantage of several of the standard Java libraries that are part of the Internet browser environment. It is not currently intended for large, computationally intensive applications, or for managing applications that are not part of the client environment. As such, applets are not currently scalable to system and enterprise levels, although the technology is still new and future developments may bring about a change in how applets are currently viewed.

Related Solutions

➤ ORBlets—Java applets containing a Java binding to OMG IDL that allows direct communication with a CORBA ORB. ORBlets can directly access CORBA applications and services through their OMG IDL interfaces.

Background

With the rapid growth of the Internet, technology that increases the functionality of the Internet, especially the Web environment, is highly desirable and sought after. The ability to develop applications that can be executed on any of the diverse platforms that communicate using the Internet eliminates many of the concerns of sharing applications. Automatically delivering and installing applications to machines in an enterprise eliminates many system management concerns. Much of the functionality desired from Web browsers can be delivered in relatively small programs.

ORBlet

Most Applicable Scale: Global

Solution Type: Technology

Solution Name: ORBlet

Intent: To access CORBA-based applications and services from a Web browser.

Primal Forces: Management of Functionality

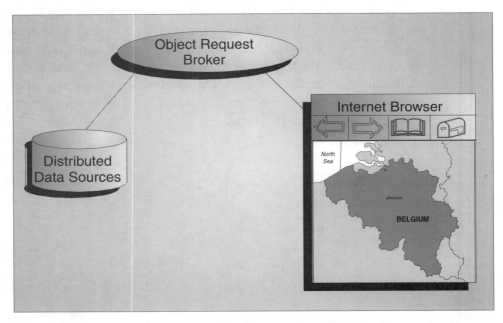

Figure 13.6 An ORBlet is an applet that contains CORBA client stubs that can remotely access CORBA applications.

Applicability at This Scale

1. Need more powerful applets, including expanded communications capability.
2. Need applets to communicate with other applications and non-Web-based software.
3. Need applets to communicate with non-Java software.
4. Need applets to interoperate with multiple hosts.
5. Need applets to interoperate with CORBA applications.

Solution Summary

ORBlets are based upon the existence of a language binding between OMG IDL and Java, and an OMG IDL compiler that generates Java code that supports OMG IDL-defined interfaces. OMG IDL allows for the definition of interfaces which can be compiled into client and server stubs. Using the client stubs, a client can transparently invoke an OMG IDL object without regard for its current location or implementation language. Similarly, a Java server will be able to handle requests from other clients that invoke operations through its OMG IDL interface.

Benefits

➤ Best of both worlds—standard OMG IDL interfaces and portable implementations.
➤ Does not have the limitations of an applet (i.e., can communicate with multiple hosts, direct access to ORB interfaces, etc.).
➤ Benefits from having a direct CORBA binding (location transparency, direct calls to CORBAservices regardless of underlying programming language or platform, etc.).

Other Consequences

➤ Requires ORB capabilities on the client machine. As advances in CORBA and Java occur, lightweight CORBA clients with Internet Interoperability Protocol (IIOP) capabilities will be cheap enough that this consequence will become irrelevant.
➤ Server latency is a major issue—may need to rely more on truly asynchronous calls instead of deferred synchronous calls.

Rescaling This Solution to Other Levels

Initially, ORBlet appears to be limited to the application level, much like applets. However, by communicating via the IIOP protocols, large-scale coordination among ORBlets and CORBAservices is possible. Even more so than applets, ORBlets' ultimate scalability may be radically altered by future developments in Java and CORBA technology.

Related Solutions:

➤ Applet—A direct precursor to ORBlet. They are both small Java programs that use the protocols in the standard Java libraries to interact with the HTTP server and do not contain a direct interface to a CORBA ORB. The SunSoft Java Web Page is an important information resource for information about applets, ORBlets, and Java.

Background

There is currently some degree of confusion concerning the relationship of ORBlets and standard Java applets. ORBlets are simply applets that have been constructed using the client stubs generated from a Java OMG IDL compiler. As in other languages, the emphasis of a CORBA Java binding will be to maintain transparency with how other objects in the environment are accessed. That is, a client should access OMG IDL-defined remote objects in a manner that is identical to how local objects are accessed.

Clients may want to communicate with distributed objects that may be bound at run-time to one of a number of different implementations. Applications may want to access objects across language and protocol boundaries. Servers sometimes need to provide operations to a variety of different clients simultaneously, rather than distribute a new applet or application to the client at run-time. Client and services may desire direct access to CORBA objects, CORBAservices, and CORBAfacilities. Applications may want to access distributed objects in other ORB environments.

DII-Web Server

Most Applicable Scale: Global

Solution Type: Software

Solution Name: DII-Web Server

Intent: To utilize the CORBA DII facilities from a Web browser.

Primal Forces: Management of Functionality

Applicability at This Scale

1. Need to invoke arbitrary CORBA operations from the Web.
2. Need to invoke dynamically discovered interfaces from the Web.

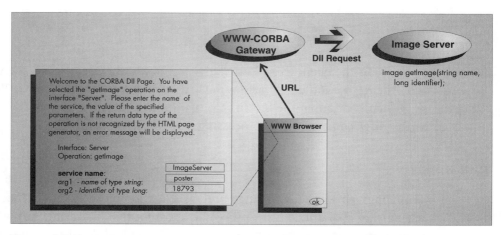

Figure 13.7 While it is possible to invoke CORBA's DII based on information entered from the HTTP forms interface, unless provisions are made to intelligently incorporate the CORBA return types into an HTML page, it has limited practical value.

Solution Summary

First, a Web interface must be presented that allows the client to browse the interface repository of the CORBA environment. Ideally, the real-time contents of the interface repository will be displayed, although static Web pages maintained in conjunction with the interface repository can be used. This interface needs to allow the client to select the interface through which it wants to communication with CORBA applications.

Next, a trader is needed to allow the selection of implementations capable of supporting the desired interface. This selection will have to be a dynamically generated HTML form for the client to enter in the parameters for the interface. Most parameters will also need a type specified in order to convert from the simple types of HTML to the more complex types in the CORBA environment. The HTTP server will have to construct a DII request on behalf of the client.

A DII client will need to serve as the gateway between CORBA and Web. It will have to take the parameters from the Web client via the HTTP server, construct and invoke the DII request, and then intelligently convert the results into an HTML page for transport back to the browser client.

Benefits

➤ Allows access to CORBA services and their interfaces dynamically at runtime.

Other Consequences

➤ Requires the client to be knowledgeable about the specifics of the DII.
➤ Difficult to handle the various data types and data formats from a Web page.
➤ Difficult to format the return information in a meaningful way.
➤ Requires complex client processing.

Background

This approach was experimented with as a method of CORBA-Web integration, but quickly abandoned once it became apparent that authoring was a key component of publishing information on the Internet and that just getting at remote data sources alone was insufficient and somewhat misguided. This method of integration might one day be useful for browsing interface repositories to see what classes of object are available; however, the actual invocation should be tied into existing authoring processes where an HTML page developer could specify which methods of object implementations to invoke to gather data and populate areas of a dynamically generated document.

If a CORBA-Web integration solution is to be totally generic and usable in any environment, then it cannot rely on a specific set of OMG IDL interfaces existing in the CORBA environment. A method of dynamically discovering the contents of the interface repository is needed in order to allow the selection of CORBA interface types. The CORBA DII is capable of dynamically invoking on any CORBA interface type, so a generic solution should be based on the DII. In some environments, obtaining the data from a source is more important than the presentation of the data. Most OMG IDL interfaces do not specify complex data types and, therefore, having a user enter in values for CORBA types is usually not a big deal.

Acronyms

3T	Three tier
ACAS	Application Control Architecture Services (AKA DEC ObjectBroker)
ANSI	American National Standards Institute
API	Application Programming Interface
APP	Application Portability Profile
BOA	Basic Object Adapter
BPL	Buschmann Pattern Language
Cd	CORBAdomain
CD-ROM	Compact Disk Read Only Memory
Cf	CORBAfacility
CGI	Common Gateway Interface
CIO	Chief Information Officer
COM	Microsoft Component Object Model
CORBA	Common Object Request Broker Architecture
COSE	Common Open Software Environment
COTS	Commercial off-the-shelf
Cs	CORBAservice
DDE	Dynamic Data Exchange
DEC	Digital Equipment Corporation
DCE	Distributed Computing Environment

DDL	Data Definition Language
DII	CORBA Dynamic Invocation Interface
DIN	German National Standards Organization
DISCUS	Data Interchange and Synergistic Collateral Usage Study
ECMA	European Computer Manufacturers Association
EDI	Electronic Data Interchange
ESIOP	Environment Specific Interoperability Protocol
FIPS	Federal Information Processing Standard
GIOP	General Interoperability Protocol
GPL	Gamma Pattern Language
GUI	Graphical User Interface
HTML	Hypertext Markup Language
HTTP	Hypertext Transfer Protocol
HVM	Horizontal-Vertical-Metadata Pattern
IDL	CORBA Interface Definition Language
IEEE	Intitute of Electrical and Electronics Engineers
IIOP	Internet Interoperability Protocol
IPC	Interprocess Communication
IR	Interface Repository
ISO	International Standard Organization
IT	Information Technology
JVM	Java Virtual Machine
NIST	National Institute of Standards and Technology
NOP	No Operation
ODP	Open Distributed Processing
OLE	Microsoft Object Linking and Embedding
OMA	Object Management Architecture
OMG	Object Management Group
ONC	Open Network Computing
OO	Object-orientation, Object-oriented
OOAD	Object-Oriented Analysis and Design
ORB	Object Request Broker
OSF	Open Software Foundation

POSIX	Portable Operating System Interface for Computer Environments
RPC	Remote Procedure Call
SQL	Structured Query Language
SYSMAN	X/Open System Management
TCP/IP	Transmission Control Protocol/Internet Protocol
UIMS	User Interface Management System
URL	Universal Resource Locator
WAIS	Wide Area Information Search
WWW	World Wide Web

Glossary

Action lever—An action lever is the most effective mechanism for effecting change or problem solving. For example, in performance optimization, an action lever is a small code segment causing a performance bottleneck, discovered through measurement.

Architectural benefits—Architectural benefits are the positive outcomes that result from the design and utilization of good architecture and associated software interfaces. Typical benefits include adaptability, cost reduction, risk reduction, and so forth.

Architectural characteristics—These are the characteristics associated with a design artifact that affect its usage and placement within architectural partitions. For example, architectural characteristics include maturity, domain specificity, flexibility, constraint, implementation-dependence, complexity, stability, and so forth.

Architectural partition—One important way to look at architecture is that it defines boundaries between categories of design artifacts. These partitions provide an isolation between categories of entities with different characteristics. Partitions help to separate concerns, reducing the number of conflicting forces, and making problem solving easier. Partitions also provide isolation between entities that are likely to change independently. For example, provide an architectural partition between a generic reusable object and domain-specific one.

Architecture—An architecture is an easy-to-understand explanation that answers the question: "How is the system put together?" Architectures explain how the internal model of the system works. Architecture also applies at other levels such as the application level and the enterprise level. An architecture is an abstract description of a set of software components. The elements of architecture include identification of the fundamental components (entity categories), descriptions of component interoperation (IDL, transaction sequencing, and messaging scenarios), and identification of strategic partitions between design elements with different architectural characteristics.

Architectural placement criteria—Design patterns reside at a level where the problem statement is most applicable and where the boundaries of the solution are within the scope of the level. Since this definition has two criteria, problem applicability takes precedence over solution scope. Some design patterns could potentially be placed at more than one level; the scalability section of the pattern template addresses the use of the pattern at alternative levels.

Bytecode—An intermediate representation between a high-level programming language, such as Java, and machine code.

Component or *software component*—A software component is a small-scale software module, at application-level or smaller scales. In a component architecture, a component shares a common interface with other components to support interoperability, component substitution, and system extension.

Data Definition Language (DDL)—A language used to create a persistent version of an IDL object, providing that its state is defined by the current values of its IDL attributes. See OMG Persistence Service for more detail.

Data Interchange and Synergistic Collateral Usage Study (DISCUS)—A U.S. government–developed reference CORBA architecture for creating data interoperability between COTS, GOTS, and legacy custom applications.

Design—In this guide, we choose to use design as a verb (as in "to design"), or as an adjective, in a phrase defined below. When used as a noun, *design* is an ambiguous and anachronistic term from the structured programming era or the first-generation OO era.

Design artifact—A particular instance of a design choice.

Design pattern—A problem statement and solution that details a predefined common sense approach to solving a design problem. The pattern is described in a fixed outline (or template), which guarantees conciseness and comprehensive coverage of the details, issues, and tradeoffs.

Design point—A specific tradeoff within an allowable range of options within a design pattern. When we consider the full range of design options for a given problem, it forms a continuum of alternative choices. A design point is one of these choices, which resolves the forces and provides the right balance of benefits and consequences, for example, choosing a string datatype as opposed to an enumeration in an IDL parameter specification. Whereas the enumeration has a fixed set of alternatives that is not extensible without change to the IDL, a string type could support a wide range of usages and extensions.

Horizontal forces—Horizontal forces are applicable across multiple domains or problems. These are forces that influence design choices across several software modules or components. With horizontal forces, design choices made elsewhere may have a direct or indirect impact on design choices made locally.

Forces—The contextual motivating factors that influence design choices. The forces are identified in the applicability section of the design pattern template. They are resolved in the solution section of the template. See the Glossary definitions for *horizontal forces, vertical forces,* and *primal forces.*

Implementation—The code (or software) comprising the mechanism that provides services conforming to an interface. Also called an *object implementation.*

Interface—A software boundary between the consumers of a service and the providers of a service (clients and implementations).

Java Virtual Machine—A run-time system used by the Java language to dynamically interpret Java bytecode. It is also responsible for the management of other Java capabilities such as garbage collection and object creation.

Mining—The study of preexisting solutions and legacy systems in order to rapidly gain a robust understanding from previous experts for the purposes of solving a new problem. Mining leads to potential reuse of previous solutions, horizontal generalization of multiple solutions, or an understanding of the wrapping requirements for legacy systems.

Module or software module—A software module is a generic term referring to a piece of software. The term *module* is used to refer to software at various scales. An application-level module is a subsystem, a system-level module is an entire software system, and so forth. A module is separable from other modules at the same scale.

Primal forces—A certain class of horizontal forces are pervasive in software architecture and development. These are the *primal forces.* The primal forces are present in most design situations, and should be considered part of the contextual forces driving most solutions.

Template—The outline used to define the explanatory sections of a design pattern.

Vertical forces—Vertical forces are situation-specific forces that exist within some particular domain or problem context. Domain-specific forces are unique to a particular situation due to the domain addressed. Because vertical forces are unique (or local) to one software situation, resolution of vertical forces usually results in unique solutions for each software problem. Interfaces generated that are solely based upon vertical forces are *vertical interfaces.*

Bibliography

Alexander, Christopher. *A Pattern Language.* Oxford, England: Oxford University Press, 1977.

————. *The Timeless Way of Being.* Oxford, England: Oxford University Press, 1979.

Beck, K. "Guest Editor's Inroduction to Special Issue on Design Patterns." *OBJECT Magazine,* January 1996.

Bennet, L. (ed.) *CORBA Products Directory.* Framingham, MA: Object Management Group, 1996.

Booch, G. *Object Oriented Analysis and Design.* Reading, MA: Addison-Wesley, 1994.

————. *Object Solutions.* Reading, MA: Addison-Wesley, 1995.

Brodie, M.L. and M. Stonebraker. *Migratory Legacy Systems.* Morgan Kaufmann Publishers, 1995.

Buschmann, T., R. Meunier, H. Rohnert, P. Sommerlad, and M.Stal. *Pattern Oriented Software Architecture: A System of Patterns.* New York: John Wiley & Sons, 1996.

Cargill, C.F. *Information Technology Standardization: Theory, Process, and Organizations.* Digital Press, 1989.

Connell, J., et al. *Rapid Structured Prototyping.* Reading, MA: Addison-Wesley, 1987.

Coplien, J. *Object World Briefing on Design Patterns.* Hillside Group, 1994.

Cornwell, D., M. Katz, T. Mowbray, and R. Zahavi. "DISCUS Technology Transfer Package." *MITRE Technical Report,* 1994.

Dolberg, S.H. "Integrating Applications in the Real World." *Open Information Systems: Guide to Unix and Other Open Systems.* Boston: Patricia Seybold Group, July 1992.

Faithorne, B. (ed.), et al. "Security White Paper." *OMG TC Document.* Framingham, MA, OMG, 1994.

Fowler, M. "A Comparison of Object–Oriented Analysis and Design Methods." *Quoin Technical Report TR-MI.* Boston, MA, 1995.

Gamma, E., R. Helm, R. Johnson, and J. Vlissides. *Design Patterns.* Reading, MA: Addison-Wesley, 1994.

Goldberg, A. *Smalltalk-80: The Interactive Programming Environment.* Reading, MA: Addison-Wesley, 1984.

Goldberg, A. and D. Robinson. *Smalltalk-80: The Language and its Implementation.* Reading, MA: Addison-Wesley, 1983.

Hagman, R. "Concurrency Within DOE Object Implementations." May 27, 1993. SunSoft Microsystems.

Halliwell, C. "Camp Development and the Art of Building a Market Through Standards." *IEEE Micro.* 13(6):10-18.

Helm, R. "Design Patterns Keynote Address." *OOPSCA95.* 1995. ACM.

Horowitz, B. *Strategic Buying for the Future.* Washington D.C.: Libey Publishing, 1993.

Horowitz, B. Written Presentation to the President's Forum and MITRE Paper. New York, 1995.

Hutt, A. (ed.). *Object Oriented Analysis and Design.* New York: John Wiley & Sons, 1994.

IEEE. *Draft Guide to the POSIX Open System Environment P1003.0.* New York: Institute of Electrical and Electronics Engineers, 1993.

IEEE. *The Portable Open Systems Reference Model.* New York. Institute of Electrical and Electronics Engineers, 1994.

IEEE. *Threads Extension for Portable Operating System.* POSIX Working Group P1003.4a/D6. New York: Institute of Electrical and Electronics Engineers, 1993.

Jacobson, I., M. Christerson, P. Jonsson, and G. Övergaard. *Object-Oriented Software Engineering.* Reading, MA: Addison-Wesley, 1992.

Jacobson, I. and F. Lindström. "Reengineering of Old Systems to an Object-Oriented Architecture." *Proceedings of OOPSLA '91.* 340-350.

Just, J. "Joint Task Force Advanced Technology Demonstration—Status Briefing." Technology Corporation, February 1996.

Katz, M., D. Cornwell, and T.J. Mowbray. "Systems Integration with Minimal Object Wrappers." *Proceedings of TOOLS 93*, August 1993.

Kreindler, R. Jordan, and John Vlissides. *Object-Oriented Patterns and Frameworks.* Stanford University, August 1995.

Linn, J. "Generic Security Service Application Program Interface." (Internet Draft). IETF Common Authentication Technology WG, April 1993.

Linton, M. "An Introduction to Fresco." *Tutorial W7, XWorld Conference.* June 1994. New York.

Mattison, Rob, and Michael J. Sipolt. *The Object-Oriented Enterprise.* McGraw-Hill, 1994.

Mowbray, T.J. "Distributed Objects Everywhere: An Early Assessment." *OBJECT Magazine.* January 1994.

——— and R. Zahavi. "Distributed Processing with Object Management." *ConneXions—The Interoperability Report.* February 1994.

———. *The Essential CORBA.* New York: John Wiley & Sons, 1995.

——— and T. Brando. "Interoperability and CORBA-Based Open Systems." *OBJECT Magazine.* September 1993.

———. "Managing Complexity in OO Architectures." *OBJECT Magazine.* December 1996.

——— and R.C. Malveau. "The Relationship Between Design Patterns and CORBA." *First Class.* February/March 1995.

Object Management Group. *Common Facilities Architecture.* Framingham, MA: OMG, November 1995.

———. *The Common Object Request Broker: Architecture and Specification.* New York: John Wiley & Sons, 1995.

———. *Common Object Services Specifications.* New York: John Wiley & Sons, 1995.

———. *Object Management Architecture Guide.* New York: John Wiley & Sons, 1993.

———. *Object Services Architecture.* Framingham, MA: OMG, November, 1994.

Orfali, R., D. Harkey, and J. Edwards. *The Essential Client/Server Survival Guide, Second Edition.* New York: John Wiley & Sons, 1996.

———. *The Essential Distributed Objects Survival Guide.* New York: John Wiley & Sons, 1996.

Otte, R., Patrick, D. and Mark Roy. *Understanding CORBA.* Upper Saddle River, NJ: Prentice Hall, 1995.

Pree, Wolfgang. *Design Patterns for Object-Oriented Software Development.* Reading, MA: Addison-Wesley, 1995.

Roetzheim, W.H. *Developing Software to Government Standards.* Englewood Cliffs, NJ: Prentice Hall, 1991.

Rumbaugh, J., M. Blaha, W. Premerlani, and F. Eddy. *Object-Oriented Modeling and Design.* Englewood Cliffs, NJ: Prentice Hall, 1991.

Saley, R. (ed.). *The Object Management Architecture Guide.* Framingham, MA: Object Management Group, 1995.

Schmidt, Douglas. "Using Design Patterns to Develop Reusable Object-Oriented Communication Software." *Communications of the ACM.* ACM, October 1995: 65-74.

Seigel, Jon. *CORBA Fundamentals and Programming.* New York: John Wiley & Sons, 1996.

Shaw, M. "Software Architecture for Shared Information Systems." *Technical Report No. CMU/SEI-93-TR-3, ESC-TR-93-180.* Carnegie Mellon University, March 1993.

————— and David Garlan. *Software Architecture: Perspectives on an Emerging Discipline.* Englewood Cliffs, NJ: Prentice Hall, 1996.

Shlaer, S. and S.J. Mellor. *Object-Oriented System Analysis.* Englewood Cliffs, NJ: Prentice Hall, 1988.

Stallings, William. *The Open Systems Interconnection (OSI) Model and OSI Related Standards.* MacMillan, 1987.

Stevens, Richard W. *UNIX Network Programming.* Englewood Cliffs, NJ: Prentice Hall, 1990.

Stroustrup, B. *The C++ Programming Language,* Second Edition. Reading, MA: Addison-Wesley, 1991.

Taylor, D.A. *Object-Oriented Information Systems.* New York: John Wiley & Sons, 1992.

Walden, Kim, and Jean-Marc Nerson. *Seamless Object-Oriented Software Architecture.* Englewood Cliffs, NJ: Prentice Hall, 1995.

Yourdon, Edward. "Software Reusability." *The Decline and Fall of the American Programmer.* Englewood Cliffs, NJ: Prentice Hall, 1993.

PLOP1= Proceedings of the First Conference on Pattern Languages of Programs. Robert Allerton Park. Monticello, Illinois. August 1994.

PLOP2= Proceedings of the Second Conference on Pattern Languages of Programs. Robert Allerton Park. Monticello, Illinois. September 1995.

[Buschmann and Meunier 1994] Buschmann, Frank and Regine Meunier. "A System of Patterns." PLOP1.

[Coplien 1994] Coplien, James O. "A Development Process Generative Pattern Language." PLOP1.

[Doble 1995] Doble, Jim. "Shopping List and Bag." PLOP2.

[Hopley 1995] Hopley, Allen. "Levels of Abstraction Pattern." PLOP2.

[Knopp 1995] Knopp, Jurgen. "Coordinators: Using Access Patterns for Parallel Programming." PLOP2.

[McKenney 1995] McKenney, Paul E. "Parallel Patterns for Synchronization on Shared-Memory Multiprocessors." PLOP2.

[Mularz 1994] Mularz, Diane E. "Pattern-Based Integration Architectures." PLOP1.

[Rubel 1994] Rubel, Barry. "A Pattern for Generating a Layered Architecture." PLOP1.

[Ruping 1995] Ruping, Andreas. "Framework Patterns." PLOP2.

[Sane and Campbell 1995] Sane, Aamod and Roy Campbell. "Resource Exchanger: A Behaviorial Pattern for Low Overhead Concurrent Resource Management." PLOP2.

Index

What's on the CD-ROM?

The CORBA Design Patterns CD-ROM contains the following directories:

\IDL—Contains OMG IDL for the CORBAservices.

naming.idl—Contains the OMG IDL specification for the Naming Service which associates a CORBA object with a name.

event.idl—Contains the OMG IDL specification for the Event Service which allows CORBA objects to send and receive notification of events.

persist.idl—Contains the OMG IDL specification for the Persistent Object Service (POS) which provide interfaces for controlling a CORBA object's persistence.

lifecycl.idl—Contains the OMG IDL specification for the Lifecycle Service which defines services for creating, destroying, copying, and moving CORBA objects.

concurr.idl—Contains the OMG IDL specification for the Concurrency Control Service which provides interfaces for creating, setting, and accessing locks.

extern.idl—Contains the OMG IDL specification for the Externalization Service which defines interfaces for storing and retrieving an object's state to a data stream.

relation.idl—Contains the OMG IDL specification for the Relationship service which defines interfaces for creating, describing, and traversing the relationships between CORBA objects.

transact.idl—Contains the OMG IDL specification for the Object Transaction Service which contains interfaces for allowing objects to perform a series of actions atomically.

query.idl—Contains the OMG IDL specification for the Object Query Service which contains interfaces for retrieving a collection of objects based on a specified search criteria.

license.idl—Contains the OMG IDL specification for the Licensing Service which provides interfaces to monitor the use of CORBA objects.

property.idl—Contains the OMG IDL specification for the Object Properties Service which associates one or more name-value pairs with a CORBA object.

\CORBA—Contains OMG IDL syntax definition and Object Request Broker (ORB) operation definitions needed to implement a CORBA-compliant ORB.

idl-bnf.grm—Contains the grammar of OMG IDL in Backus-Naur form (BNF).

corba.txt—Contains a listing and description of the CORBA operations necessary in developing a CORBA-compliant ORB.

\HTML—This directory contains an HTML version of the design pattern catalog presented in CORBA Design Patterns. The patterns are organized by design levels with hypertext links to Related Patterns.

Applic.htm—Contains the design pattern specified at the Application level of the CORBA Design Patterns framework.

System.htm—Contains the design pattern specified at the System level of the CORBA Design Patterns framework.

Enterp.htm—Contains the design pattern specified at the Enterprise level of the CORBA Design Patterns framework.

Global.htm—Contains the design pattern specified at the Global level of the CORBA Design Patterns framework.

\ANIMATNS—This directory contains a set of public domain animations which illustrate CORBA principles. They should run on most PCs with multimedia capabilities.

AppFrame.exe—Explains the data marshaling which occurs between two applications using an Object Request Broker to communicate.

Convert.exe—A detailed scenario of how an Object Request Broker may allow an application to utilize other distributed services.

Explan.exe—Illustrates the progressive simplicity of integration techniques ending with an ORB-based application framework.

Extend.exe—Highlights the advantages of incorporating Common Interface in an application vs. developing to custom interfaces which typically results in N x N integration.

\APP—This directory contains some source code for CORBA application illustrate some of the design patterns presented in the text. The Makefile programs are incomplete and will have to be modified slightly in order to compile the IDL and client and server source code. The source code are in the following directories.

AnyOps—Contains a rudimentary but highly extensible example source code for traversing and copying CORBA any data types in the C bindings.

Naming—Contains a partial implementation of the OMG COSS Naming Service specification. This pattern is discussed in the System Level Design Pattern catalog.

PartProc—Contains a toy video server implementation which contains features of the Partial Processing and the Distributed Callback Design patterns which are discussed in the Application Level Design pattern catalog.

WHAT IS FREEWARE/SHAREWARE?

Freeware is software that is distributed by disk, through BBS systems, and via the Internet free of charge. It can be freely distributed as long as the use it is put to follows the license agreement included with it.

Shareware (also known as user-supported software) is a revolutionary means of distributing software created by individuals or companies too small to make inroads into the more conventional retail distribution networks. The authors of Shareware retain all rights to the software under the copyright laws while still allowing free distribution. This gives the user the chance to freely obtain and try out software to see if it fits his or her needs. Shareware should not be confused with Public Domain software, even though they are often obtained from the same sources.

If you continue to use Shareware after trying it out, you are expected to register your use with the author and pay a registration fee. What you get in return depends on the author, but may include a printed manual, free updates, telephone support, etc.

USING THE SOFTWARE

Each of the directories on this volume contains a README which details the use of the directory contents. The animations require multimedia capabilities on a Windows 3.1 IBM-compatible computer with at least 4 MB of RAM. An HTML Viewer is required to view the documents in HTML format.

USER ASSISTANCE AND INFORMATION

The software accompanying this book is being provided as is without warranty or support of any kind. Should you require basic installation assistance, or if your media is defective, please call our product support number at (212) 850-6194 weekdays between 9 a.m. and 4 p.m. Eastern Standard Time. Or, we can be reached via e-mail at: **wprtusw@wiley.com**.

To place additional orders or to request information about other Wiley products, please call (800) 879-4539.

WILEY

Publishers Since 1807